Travels of Alexine

Travels of Alexine

ALEXINE TINNE
1835–1869

PENELOPE GLADSTONE

JOHN MURRAY

© Penelope Gladstone 1970

All rights reserved. No part of this publication may be reproduced, stored in a retrieval system, or transmitted, in any form or by any means, electronic, mechanical, photocopying, recording or otherwise, without the prior permission of John Murray (Publishers) Ltd., 50 Albemarle Street, London, WIX 4BD.

Printed in Great Britain for
John Murray, Albemarle Street, London
by Cox & Wyman Ltd., London,
Fakenham and Reading

0 7195 2044 4

To
*Alexine Tinne and Alexine Crawford
who made this book possible*

Contents

Introduction   xi

Part One – EUROPE
1. The Tinnes   3
2. Scandinavian Holiday   12
3. Grand European Tour   18

Part Two – EGYPT
4. Egypt   31
5. First Nile Voyage   37
6. Summer in the Holy Land   49
7. Second Nile Voyage   58
8. Long way home to The Hague   64

Part Three – THE SUDAN
9. Preparations for the Third Nile Voyage   73
10. Cairo to Khartoum in four months   81
11. Khartoum   92
12. The White Nile   101
13. First steamer to Gondokoro   111
14. Bahr-al-Ghazal Expedition   123
15. Journey into the Interior   132

16 The Slave Merchants	143
17 Survivors return to Khartoum	154
18 Tragic journey to Cairo	161

Part Four – NORTH AFRICA

19 Cruise of the Mediterranean	175
20 From Algiers into the Sahara	184
21 Final attempt to cross Africa	198
22 Delayed in Murzuch	205
23 Meeting the Tuareg	212
24 'La Croyante'	222
Appendices	227
Principal Sources and References	233
Bibliography	241
Index	243

Illustrations

Portrait of Alexine by J. A. Van der Hulst, 1839.
Reproduced by kind permission of Mrs. E. D. Strover facing page 4

Bust of Alexine. *Reproduced by kind permission of Mrs. E. D. Strover*   5

Portrait of Alexine painted in the Pyrenees, 1849. *Municipal Archives of The Hague*   20

Alexine, Harriet and Yetty photographed in Paris, December 1860*   21

Yetty and Alexine, Paris, December 1860*   21

Adriana Van Capellen*   21

View taken by Alexine from 32 Lange Voorhout, *c.* 1860 with the carriage darkened so that she could process her photographs on the spot. *Royal Archives*   68

Pen drawing of Sudanese tukuls by Alexine. *Reproduced by kind permission of C .E. Tinne*   69

Alexine in Cairo, 1865*   84

Alexine with one of her dogs*   84

John Tinne, Alexine's half-brother. *Reproduced by kind permission of Alex Tinne*   85

Vice-Admiral Jonkheer Jules Van Capellen. *Reproduced by kind permission of Baroness Constant de Rebecque*   180

The Dutch crew photographed as sailors by Alexine, Algiers, 1867, *Royal Archives*   181

The Dutch crew photographed as bedouin by Alexine, Algiers, 1867. *Royal Archives*   196

Alexine and the women servants she took on her yacht, Algiers, 1867. *Royal Archives*   197

Illustrations

MAPS

The Nile showing the voyage to Gondokoro and the
Bahr-al-Ghazal expedition   124/5

Algeria, Tunisia and Libya showing the journey from
Algiers and the final attempt to cross Africa   201

* *These photographs are now in the possession of the author who was given them by Barones
Constant de Rebecque*

Introduction

Dr. Livingstone, the famous explorer and missionary, recorded in his journal:

> The work of Speke and Grant is deserving of the highest commendation, inasmuch as they opened up an immense tract of previously unexplored country, in the firm belief they were bringing to light the head of the Nile. No one can appreciate the difficulties of their feat unless he has gone into the new country. Mr. Baker also showed courage and perseverance worthy of an Englishman in following out the hints given by Speke and Grant. But none rises higher in my estimation than the Dutch lady, Miss Tinne, who, after the severest domestic afflictions, nobly persevered in the teeth of every difficulty.

Alexine Tinne was born in The Hague in 1835 to be the richest heiress in the Netherlands. At the age of nineteen she first visited Egypt and from that time Africa was to become her passion. She died at the early age of thirty-three, the first European woman to attempt to cross the Sahara desert.

There is little to remember her by. Hitler's bombs destroyed many crates of her ethnological specimens stored in Liverpool, and a bomb completely flattened the English Church at The Hague, built in her memory. However, a little obelisk near Juba in the southern Sudan records her name. Alexine came as far as this on her voyage up the White Nile, and together with other early explorers her name is commemorated on the memorial at the Juba cross-roads. On the first and second sides are marked the names of five men who came up the White Nile on Mohammed Ali's expedition in 1840–41: also Bishop Knöblecher, the leader of the Austrian Roman Catholic missionaries who arrived in 1850. On the third side is marked Alexine Tinne, followed by the names of Samuel and Florence Baker, and John Petherick. The names of later pioneers, Gordon, Gessi, Junker, Emin, and Chaltin, complete the fourth side.

In 1861 Alexine, her mother Harriet Tinne, and her aunt Adriana Van Capellen, left The Hague to make their epic Nile

Introduction

voyage to reach this part of Africa. Many of Alexine's letters have been destroyed. Fortunately, her mother's diaries have been saved and upon these I have based much of the first half of the book. Harriet Tinne's diaries were evidently written for her personal use, and are often incomplete entries in sketchy English. Indeed, although Harriet and Alexine spoke to each other mainly in English neither excelled at the written word, and strange phrases and colloquialisms are sometimes to be found in the quotations.

Much of the material for this book had been investigated by hopeful biographers, but only through an extensive search was it possible to relate letters and papers, especially those stored in the Netherlands and Britain. Scarcely anything has been published on Alexine in England and many of the journals have not been published in England or the Netherlands, so that until now it has been difficult to get a complete picture of her. All quotations from diaries and letters have been edited and translated when necessary. These and other sources marked 'Tinne Family Papers' are owned privately by three descendants of Alexine's half-brother, J. A. Tinne. Sources marked Algemeen Rijksarchief come from family papers in the collection of Baron Constant de Rebecque deposited at the Royal Archives in The Hague in 1925. Alexine's cousin, Henrietta (Yetty) Siccama, married Baron Constant de Rebecque and it was their descendants who passed many of Alexine's letters to the Royal Archives of The Hague for safe keeping. It is from this collection that the photographs taken by Alexine have been reproduced. These photographs have caused widespread interest when exhibited in The Hague, as they are remarkably effective for such early photography.

I would like to thank Mr. Richard Hill for his help with the section on the Sudan. I would also like to thank Mr. Carel Gülcher and Baroness Constant de Rebecque of the Netherlands for reminiscences of those who had known Alexine and her mother, and information about the Van Capellen family and photographs of them; Mr. C. E. Tinne, Mrs. Dorothea Strover, Mrs. Alexine Crawford, and Miss Alexine Tinne. I am indebted to many Librarians, to the friends I met in Egypt and the Sudan, and to my family for their encouragement with the lengthy research. Finally, I should like to thank Mrs. Osyth Leeston of John Murray.

PART ONE

Europe

I
The Tinnes

The Tinne* family has been extinct in the Netherlands for many years, but there are still a number of descendants carrying the name in England. According to tradition an ancestor made his fame by climbing over the Saracen battlements at Rosetta at the time of the Crusades, and was thus named Tinne, the Dutch word for battlement. In remembrance of this hero, the Tinne coat of arms displays a section of battlement over which, on an azure background, are two gold stars.

It seems likely that the Tinne family were once Huguenots. Probably they originated from eastern Germany; certainly they can be traced as emigrating to Calais before settling in the Netherlands at the beginning of the seventeenth century. Here some members of the family soon found positions in the States General. So successful were they that by 1772, when Alexine's father, Philip Frederick was born, they were one of the best-known families in the Netherlands.

At the age of eighteen, having a gift for languages, Philip chose to join the foreign service, and was sent to London on his first post. Two years later he was recalled to The Hague to work in the Treasury, still earning a very low salary, of which he paid half to his father for his keep. Yet it was probably during these frugal years that he learnt the value of money; this ultimately led him to make a fortune for himself and for the family he left behind.

At the Treasury there was little to do, but his job had one fascinating side-line. It was his duty to visit the Post Office and to investigate suspicious mail with an eye to intercepting dispatches from Prussia, which country the Netherlands had good reason to suspect had plans for armed attack. These dispatches Philip skilfully unsealed, and re-sealed after making copies of the documents. (He later declared he had never opened any post except dispatches

* The 'e' in Tinne should be pronounced.

from Prussia.) But in fact the attack on the Netherlands, when it came, was from France. In 1795 Napoleon's army invaded the frontiers and set up a monarchy under the Emperor's brother, Louis Bonaparte. Philip lost his job at the Treasury and decided to seek his fortune abroad.

The Netherlands, however, retained the freedom of their vast colonial possessions, and at the age of twenty-three he sailed for Demerara, the Dutch colony in South America, now known as Surinam, to join a cousin. The voyage took two months, during which time the colony was captured and taken over by the British. Luck was with him, however, as many Dutch officials were left in office to run the country, and he found a post as a government interpreter. Later, thanks to his initiative and hard work, he was appointed Secretary to the Governor with a salary of £3,000 a year. He met and married Anna, the ninth child of William and Mary Rose, Scottish people who also had interests in the sugar trade.

At the age of twenty-nine, Philip decided to return to the Netherlands, but found it was not permissible to re-establish himself in his native land as he had been employed under the British Government. He therefore chose to seek his fortune in England. Already he owned enough plantations in the West Indies to bring him a regular income, and through friends of Anna's family he arranged to go into partnership with William Sandbach. In 1812 the business of Sandbach, Tinne, and Company was founded in Liverpool, and within a few years it brought immense wealth to both families.

Several times Philip made journeys back to the West Indies and Demerara to return to his sugar and coffee plantations, and spend some of the company's profits on buying more land and exploiting new ground. Indifferent to his own safety, he undertook this perilous voyage twice in time of war, and when he set sail in 1813 he was indeed lucky to arrive alive.

On setting up in Liverpool Philip had been faced with a problem: the question of his nationality. As a merchant trader he desired to own ships privately, but this he was not allowed to do as a Dutch national: although the Netherlands had been allianced to England at the end of the Napoleonic wars this rule still held. Not to be deterred, however, Philip paid in 1823 for a Private Act

Portrait of Alexine by J. A. van der Hulst, 1839

Bust of Alexine

of Parliament to be passed allowing him to take on British nationality. The years that followed were a period when the West Indian merchants made huge profits in cane sugar, and the family became very prosperous. Only one great sadness marred Philip's happiness when, in 1827, Anna died, leaving two sons in their teens.

Three years later Philip married Harriet Van Capellen. He was fifty-seven, and already thinking of retirement. His elder son, John, had been taken into his father's firm, and his second son, William, had gone into the army. On the occasion of his second marriage, Philip passed on part of his fortune to his sons. John and William both received generous benefits, and it was arranged that Harriet would have an allowance of £1,000 annually for her personal needs.

Harriet Van Capellen was the daughter of an eminent Dutch Vice Admiral. He had been born in 1761 of a family that originated in Friesland, and was one of the leaders who initiated the restoration of the House of Orange after the fall of Napoleon. Once during his early years in Demerara Philip had heard that a Mr. Van Capellen, as the Admiral was then, had been taken ill, and had 'assisted him back to health'. The Admiral never forgot this kindness and suggested that Philip should call on his family. When Philip did so, he met a formidable brood of nine children: the youngest, a boy of ten, destined to a greater naval career than his father, the eldest a young woman in her early thirties.

Vice-Admiral Van Capellen was famous for the part he had played in the Battle of Algiers in 1816, when the port was bombarded by an English squadron assisted by Dutch men-of-war commanded by him. In 1815 he was incorporated in the nobility of the new Kingdom of the Netherlands as Jonkheer. He became Grand-Marshall of the Court of the Prince of Orange, later King William II, in 1822. Subsequently several of his children held appointments at Court. Sara, the fifth child, was Lady-in-Waiting to Queen Sophia wife of King William III, Adriana, the sixth child, was Lady-in-Waiting to the Dowager Queen Anna Paulowna of Russia, widow of King William II.

In 1830 Philip married Harriet. Both preferred to make their home in The Hague, Philip feeling that if he retired he could live more easily on his income there. This he thought might be insufficient to allow Harriet to live in England in the style she was accustomed to before her marriage. At the same time Harriet was able to continue her close connections with the Court through her family and by 1834 her brother Theodore was a page there. The Netherlands were in a state of change especially when ten years later, following the abdication of William I, William II found himself ruling under a revised constitution.

Besides, life was a great deal brighter in The Hague than Philip and Harriet would have found it in Liverpool. They bought a house in Heerengraat, where they lived during the first few years of marriage. The Hague was a charming small city of canals and spacious streets, often bordered with avenues of trees and surrounded by parks and woodland. It had many splendid and gracious buildings, for Dutch architecture had been at its peak during the eighteenth century.

How did the Court set pass their time in those long-off days? They lived lavishly and considered no expense excessive for their pleasure. There was, indeed, plenty of amusement for the rich, including a never-ending round of balls, theatres, concerts, dinners, and evening receptions; and, as if there was not time for chatter at such formal gatherings, there always remained the custom of paying calls, when visitors would be received and visits would be returned.

When Princess Sophia of Würtemberg married the future William III in 1839 she did not care for this superficial life of entertainment, but she took a great interest in the arts and science. When she became Queen, Sara Van Capellen was a favourite Lady-in-Waiting, but Queen Sophia was very fond of Harriet, who could always be relied upon for her cheerfulness and practical disposition.

On 17th October 1835, Alexine was born. The little girl came as a prayer fulfilled, for Philip at sixty-three and Harriet at thirty-seven had feared they might be childless. At the end of November she was christened in The Hague by the Chaplain attached to the British Embassy, and was given the names Alexandrina Petronella Francina. Alexandrina was then a popular name, and Princess Victoria, heir to the British throne, had been given it as her first name. Petronella was, no doubt, chosen after Harriet's mother, who had died in the spring.

No special events are recorded during the first years of Alexine's life, but it is known that the family resided mainly in The Hague, and went away most winters. In those days, travelling was a very lengthy business. Trunks of luggage were carefully packed, inquiries made into methods of transport, and details planned in advance; but there still remained a feeling of adventure in every long journey, and a state of satisfaction on reaching the ultimate destination.

In 1842 the family all went to Nice, which they revisited in 1843, travelling on to Naples where they stayed a month before returning by Rome and Florence. They enjoyed Naples, full of poverty and sunshine then as it is today, and they passed Christmas there. Although Philip was a taciturn, modest man, he was proud of having married a Jonkyrouwe, but it was not until some months after their wedding that he realized, especially when they travelled, just how many connections she had. The following year Philip and Harriet returned again to Rome without Alexine.

Philip had been poorly in Italy and, never completely recovering, died in 1845. He had often stayed away by himself, and after his death rumours abounded that he had been employed as a spy and had been poisoned. This seems an unlikely story, despite the fact that as a young man he had intercepted dispatches.

Philip left between £80,000 and £100,000. In addition to provision for his two sons he gave generous financial help to both English and Dutch relations. In his will Philip bequeathed £33,000 to Alexine – then nine years old – to receive when she was twenty-one. He added a clause that until she came of age the interest on this money was to provide £600 a year for bringing her up. When, finally, in 1856, Alexine reached the age of twenty-one this bequest was worth no less than £69,000 – thanks to clever investment and, no doubt, an element of luck. In the last clause of his will Philip laid down that, should she marry, a marriage settlement must be made to secure her fortune.

Philip's eldest son, John, had married Margaret Sandbach, daughter of his business partner, and the family company was still going from strength to strength. William, the younger son, who had always been prone to epileptic fits, had left the army for the life of an invalid. His was a tragic life, and his ill-health was a constant source of worry to his loyal father and elder brother, both unfailingly affectionate.

To help pass the first months after Philip had died, Harriet and Alexine spent the summer of 1845 with John and Margaret Tinne near Liverpool, and visited friends near London, before returning to their beautiful home in The Hague. Some years previously Philip had bought this house in the most fashionable and central part of the city. It stood in Lange Voorhout, a few minutes' walk from the Binnenhof, the meeting-place of the States General.

As the family had spoken English together when Philip was alive, so Harriet continued to speak English with Alexine, though more French was spoken in society at The Hague. Alexine spoke French with her French governess. In addition, from her early schooldays she had spoken and learnt to write in Dutch. It seems that she had several tutors for different subjects, but it was her aptitude to grasp facts herself that was to make her truly professional in so many paths of learning. She was always happy reading, and there is a story that Hora Siccama, who had married Harriet's younger sister, Petronella, discovered Alexine sprawled on the floor over a book in the Royal Library. She was about ten years old at the time, and he noted that the large book that so engrossed her was on one of her favourite subjects – geography.

A letter preserved from an English governess, who was with Alexine during holidays, brings to light some of her scholastic aspirations:

Do you remember how we used to dream over our future studies and what we were to undertake together when we should meet again? Astronomy, geology, mineralogy, etc., etc., etc., in the way of Science. And then the literary subjects: logic, rhetoric, Greek, Hebrew, Arabic, and all the other things with hard names to them that we were to try and learn.[1]

Alexine was so much younger than her half-brothers that she was like an only child, but fortunately she did not lack companions of her own age. She had always been a lively child, and as a little girl was full of plans and new ideas. There were secrets to be shared with her cousin, Yetty, and letters, poems, knowing glances, and giggles passed between them in a language grown-ups accept but cannot understand. Hora and Petronella Siccama had two children: Yetty and Harco, both of whom became life-long friends of Alexine. Hora Siccama, a robust and jubilant Dutch lawyer, was full of fun and remained smiling even when his photograph was taken, the only grin recorded amongst a family album of straight faces. Alexine loved him for his jokes and called him Uncle Siccama. He was a frequent visitor to their home, and became more so when left a widower. Throughout her life she had no closer friend than Yetty, whom later she used as a precious link for news from The Hague when she could not face returning home after the tragedy of her mother's death. (Yetty married Baron Constant de Rebecque and it was their descendants who passed many of Alexine's letters to the Royal Archives at The Hague* for safe keeping.)

Only on one occasion was Alexine parted from her mother, and this was when Petronella Siccama died of consumption in 1848. When Petronella was ill, Harriet wrote to Alexine:

> She says she longs so much to die and she seems so easy in her mind, nothing to worry her. Oh God grant that when my turn comes I may be equally resigned to leave you. This time her children have their father, but you will be alone so I must not die yet.[2]

Petronella died in a spa in the Pyrenees, and Harriet meanwhile had left Alexine at Pau. During the next two winters they returned to Pau for long visits. The district offered lovely walks and rides which Alexine had adored from childhood. She had been portrayed in oils there when she was fourteen – riding a splendid Arab horse, dressed in an elegant riding habit and ostrich-feather hat, and with the mountains of the Pyrenees forming the background.

In the following year, 1851, the Great Exhibition was held in the Crystal Palace in Hyde Park, then still on the outskirts of London. Harriet and Alexine were amongst the visitors. It was probably during this stay in England that it was arranged for Anna, the eldest child of John and Margaret Tinne, to spend the next year with Alexine and her mother.

Anna joined Harriet and Alexine in Paris where they spent the winter; for the spring and summer they were in The Hague. It was in Paris that Alexine went to her first dance. She was still considered much too young, but on this occasion Harriet was pressed to bring her, and finally agreed on the assurance that the

* Algemeen Rijksarchief te 's-Gravenhage.

company would be very select. Alexine was thrilled. Mother and daughter dashed to a dressmaker who worked like fury, and a white muslin dress was delivered five hours after it had been ordered. Alexine, with two camelias in her hair, was ready just in time for the carriage.

The evening went off pleasantly enough, but the outcome was best described by Harriet:

> Alexine did not dance as she did not feel she could, but she looked so sweet and young that everybody was anxious to ask her to dance, and the next day I had a visit from Mademoiselle Treve, who came from the mother of a young Duke who had been smitten to ask if I would allow them to make my acquaintance: if I will marry my daughter in France and what fortune she had. I said she was too young to think of marrying yet and therefore I refused, etc., etc. They offered to wait, but there again I said I would never enter into an engagement so long beforehand. From what I heard it was the Duke of Fitzjames.
>
> Well, next day Robert Boull was sent for by a lady who had our name quite pat. She, too, asked for a young friend about Alexine. Boull said she was sweet, pretty, and rich and, therefore, much too good to be allowed to marry out of Holland. He said he was determined to do all he could to prevent her marrying any but a Dutchman.
>
> Only think of little Alexine! The best of all is that Alexine heard it all and only said, 'I suppose I am not obliged to marry.' I said, 'Oh dear, no.' Well then, let them ask!³

Before Anna returned to England, she and Alexine were confirmed together at the English Church at The Hague, a converted building modestly standing within sight of Alexine's magnificent home. The following winter Harriet and Alexine spent several months in England. In 1853 they returned to Pau, and then went on to Spain for the rest of the winter, where Alexine quickly mastered the Spanish language. Back at The Hague studies and pleasures mingled together. Although she had finished with regular schoolwork she still took lessons. Many of her hours were spent reading at the Royal Library, situated next door to their house in Lange Voorhout. She took up painting, and read poetry, studied geography, archaeology, botany and other scientific subjects, which always fascinated her; and she became a very competent pianist.

During the next few years Alexine found herself living amidst a flurry of parties and dances. Not strictly a pretty girl, she had a sympathetic face and lively eyes which readily turned her expression to a smile, and lovely hair. She was very self-assured for her age, always cheerful and friendly, and, one of her most charming assets, she had a great sense of humour.

As her mother was a personal friend of the Queen, Alexine was often invited to balls and receptions at the royal palace. At every summons a new dress was required, and Alexine, who was not very interested in clothes, would frequently forget to order hers until just before it was required. The dressmakers, who must have cursed her, somehow contrived to finish her dresses in the nick of time. At the palace the guests would arrive and assemble, anxiously standing round and waiting for the King and Queen to make their appearance. Alexine soon achieved a name for arriving with only a few minutes to spare, but how her friends looked forward to her coming! With a shy smile she would make her entrance. Her dress had only just been delivered. No matter, for her animated conversation soon put the people she met at ease, and, enchanted by her amusing stories, they forgot their nervousness by the time the King and Queen arrived.

2
Scandinavian Holiday

After a gay summer of social activities, Harriet and Alexine set off for Scandinavia. They were particularly excited about their holiday for, although they usually journeyed abroad in the autumn, a visit to the wild and beautiful country of Norway was a new adventure. Well known for excellent fishing and shooting for gentlemen tourists, Norway was considered unsuitable for ladies; the roads were so narrow and rough that it was impossible to go by carriage, and the inns were few and far between. But Harriet and Alexine were not the sort to worry. They had made inquiries as far as possible before setting out, and had planned a tour with Murray's handbook on Scandinavia.

On a fine morning in July 1854, they drove in their black and yellow carriage towards Utrecht, followed by another carriage carrying their two servants Jan and Flora, two dogs, and the luggage. The countryside was divided into large fields and scattered with windmills. Every breath of wind was utilized by these vast structures, the sails of which sometimes measured forty yards across. The farthest a single windmill could raise water was three feet at a time and often three or four mills would be placed in a row, each one pumping up the water a further stage.

Harriet and Alexine left their own carriage at Utrecht, and went on by hired carriage. By the evening of the first day they had covered eighty miles by road. Spending a night at Arnhem they continued by carriage the next day, caught the overnight train from Oberhausen for Hamburg, crossing the Elbe by steamer. Two days were spent there, and they then went on to Copenhagen by rail and steamer. 'A capital passage,' Harriet noted in her diary, 'we have a very nice cabin with two beds and a sofa.' On arriving at Copenhagen her first occupation was to send off several parcels and letters she had been given to post in Denmark. A pleasant week was passed in paying visits and making excursions.

Scandinavian Holiday

At Copenhagen the ladies boarded a steamer called the *North Cape*, which had been built as a British man-of-war and converted to a Norwegian coastal steamer. It was a sunny day and as the *North Cape* left the pier many people they had met waved them off. They landed first at Göteborg in Sweden, and the next day sailed on to Oslo, or Christiana, as the capital of Norway was then called. From here they planned to reach Bergen overland.

First, a guide, Olans Nielsen, was engaged to accompany them. Then to carry them across this hilly country of narrow and doubtful roads Harriet bought five ponies and five carrioles, one each for Alexine, Jan, Flora, Nielsen, and herself:

We almost feared to begin our journey in our open carts, but everything was ready so we set off. The funniest carriages I ever saw; each with one horse. There is room for one person in each, like a lid with a sort of chair, and behind a box on which the driver can sit if you do not drive yourself. We had to store our clothes and took only one change, but all our provisions as we were told we could get neither meat, bread nor wine, so we had some hams and cold tongues, etc., besides English biscuits and some sherry and brandy.[1]

Accordingly they set off, one behind the other, on a rainy afternoon in mid-August. The roads were rough, but the ponies trotted freely and briskly along, while the travellers concentrated on balancing on their seats, as the wheels jolted over ruts and stones, bouncing the box-like conveyances in uneven rhythm to the ponies' hooves. The curving roads ascended through pine-woods and grassy valleys coloured with wild flowers. As evening fell, they all left their carrioles to climb still higher on foot to gain a magnificent view over the wild and rugged countryside, watching the sunset die behind the distant mountains.

The journey to Bergen took ten days, the nights being spent at post stages or simple lodging houses. The people they met were extremely hospitable. They lived in log houses, and nearly every farmer had a spare building he would loan. Visitors were welcomed, and generally invited to share food as well as shelter. Although the national costume was not worn as widely as in the Netherlands, the ladies saw many of the peasants in it: the men in short jackets, breeches, gaiters and long red caps; the women with full long skirts over blue petticoats, dark bodices buttoned to the throat with striped sleeves and cloaks.

As they continued towards Bergen the roads became steeper and the valleys more narrow. The carrioles jogged along, the passengers casting care aside as the noble little ponies, plump and well kept, steady and swift, galloped down one hill at such a pace as to carry them well up the next. Soon the romantic forests, full of myths and legends which the guide tried vainly to explain, were left behind, and the vegetation became scarce, with only birch trees bordering the rushing streams and waterfalls.

Part of the way was so steep that Harriet could only compare it to the Simplon Pass. At times the route became a one-track mountain path and the carrioles had to be taken to pieces and carried on the ponies, their shafts sticking strangely into the air. At other times the luggage and ponies were taken on boats, and the carrioles towed behind through the fjords.

Eventually they drove into Bergen late on a wet, dark night, the ponies and carrioles muddy, themselves very ready for bed; but all the hotels were full. Moreover, the boat they had planned to take was to leave in two hours. Never daunted, Harriet and Alexine would have been prepared to catch it, but were prevented from doing so when they found it necessary to visit a bank before they departed. At two o'clock in the morning they eventually found rooms. Here they stayed, awaiting the next boat, for two weeks. Heavy rain persisted, and Alexine took the opportunity to learn Norwegian from the Dutch Consul, and evidently knew enough later to carry on a conversation, though brief, with the King of Sweden.

On 7th September they left Bergen on the *Christiana*, and cruised north to Trondheim. Arriving here they set off for Stockholm in carrioles once more. The journey took them eighteen days. The route was very rough and precipitous, but at least there was a road, which had been constructed in 1847. When it rained they got a soaking, yet Harriet and Alexine were in high spirits. They were curious about all they saw, the plants, especially those that grew near the snowline, and the various types of rock. They ate local food, often reindeer and feathered game, and everywhere they stopped they made friends and were pressed to stay. Describing one place Harriet wrote in her diary: 'The people were

Scandinavian Holiday 15

furious we would not stay there, but we intend going on!' At last the carrioles were packed up, and they were rowed over a lake before the last lap of the journey made by the new railway. They felt exultant to have come so far safely, and Harriet wrote in her diary:

And now we may boast of our good luck, having been about 632 English miles at this time of year in five open carrioles, besides our voyages, and have had no disasters or disappointments. Capital![2]

On reaching Stockholm the carrioles were sold, and Harriet and Alexine immediately set off with their letters of introduction. Harriet already knew the Princess Royal, and invitations to the palace followed. New dresses were ordered for the dinner-party, and afterwards Harriet recorded the evening:

The Princess Royal was in pink with ivy in her hair, and her two ladies had grey silk dresses with white scarves and red roses. She was so kind and affectionate. Shortly afterwards came the Queen in grey and Princess Eugene in a twin dress to the Princess Royal. Likewise the King then came to me, bid me welcome and talked for a long time. Then he went to Ali and inquired all about our trip into Norway, and spoke Norse to her.

There were no strangers at dinner but us and our Ministers. We were twenty-four at table, a plain but very good dinner and capital fruit. We went into another room to take coffee where we had another long talk with the King, and then Her Majesty, the two princesses and I went to sit round a table and talk, while Alexine with the two princes, four maids of honour and some young men formed a very merry group and seemed to have lots of fun. About 6½ the royal family went away, the King most amiably hoping we would return to see Sweden as he considered we had given all our time to Norway.[3]

During the fortnight spent in Stockholm they were busy visiting museums, seeing plays, and making excursions. On the last day, after a dinner-party and theatre, they slept on a boat in which they were to go by canal to Göteborg. Thence they caught a steamer to Copenhagen for a ball at the royal palace, of which Harriet wrote:

The ball was like most others. . . . Alexine had plenty of dances and amused herself very much, so did I for I had a great many friends and there was supper so that the time did not seem very long though we did not get home till three o'clock.[4]

From Copenhagen they sailed south across the Baltic to Szczecin (Stettin), and thence to Berlin by train. Harriet noticed that in Germany royalty used the train service so much that a special carriage had to be set aside for them, in addition to the usual first-class ones. From Berlin they caught the train to Potsdam, and the next day a royal coach took them to the palace of the King and Queen of Prussia. Knowing that the court procedures of the Prussian Royal Family were exacting and rigorous, they expected every formality. However, their visit led to an unexpected encounter, which was long afterwards talked about when they got back to The Hague.

At the entrance of the palace they were met by Princess Frederick. She excused herself as she had been summoned by the Queen, but arranged that they should be shown round the grounds by Princess Marie, a Lady-in-Waiting, and the Dutch Ambassador. It was a brilliant, sunny November day as the party walked through the gardens.

A broad carriage drive led up to the immense New Palace, which had been built in 1769 and resembled Versailles. It was lavishly decorated and furnished within. A long and exhaustive tour was carried out, and afterwards, seeing there was still some daylight, Princess Marie suggested that they should look at Sans Souci. This was the palace built by Frederick the Great in 1745, and was approached by an enormous flight of terraces. Sans Souci was fronted in glass and filled with vines, olive, and orange trees. The party filed through the central apartments to be shown the clock that had stopped at Frederick's death-hour, and the bedroom where the King had died. When they arrived it was found that the door was locked, but after trying to open it the visitors heard a faint scuffle inside.

'Open the door directly, it is me!' commanded the Princess in a loud voice.

The door was immediately unlocked and slowly pulled ajar, and peering from behind stood an upright figure wearing an old dressing-gown. The party were face to face with the reigning monarch! Excusing his attire, he at once explained to the intruders that he had settled down hoping for a quiet day to deal with his State papers, having given instructions to his equerry that nobody was to know where he was, not even the Queen. Harriet and Alexine were astonished at this chance meeting, the poor Princess looked fit to die of shame, and King Frederick William IV apologized profusely. None the less, he welcomed the visitors and talked with them for a quarter of an hour before asking to be excused to continue with his work.

Two days later Harriet and Alexine were invited to dine at Sans Souci. A royal carriage with a lackey called to take them to the palace. The King made fun of having been caught by them in his dressing-gown, the news of which had been round the court. Harriet noted:

The King was extremely kind. He was full of our visit, asked what we had been recommended, things still to be seen and invited us to stay for the approaching evening which he promised would be worth while. The Queen was more quiet but quite as friendly. The Princess Frederick, and indeed everybody, did all they could to amuse us so that we missed the train which the dinner guests go by.[5]

Leaving Potsdam the ladies travelled to Hanover, and then to Cologne where they visited the cathedral, still unfinished. They went on to Brussels, and finally spent two weeks in Paris. By the time they returned home to The Hague at the beginning of December they had been away four months.

3

Grand European Tour

The houses in Lange Voorhout were attached to each other but, apart from their universally simple and handsome design, each differed in detail from the next one. Large windows and a heavy front door, which was often surrounded by a porch, were generally in evidence, whilst upstairs sòme had balconies and others, perhaps set a little back from the street, were bordered by iron palings. There were four rows of limes planted down the wide avenue, making a shady place in which to stroll or sit, for park benches were placed under the large trees. The charm of the houses lay not only in their setting, but in their slight variation, and there was no doubt that Harriet's was one of the finest. The outside was extremely imposing, and the inside was nothing short of exquisite. A majestic front door was approached by six stone steps from the pavement, and to either side of this were reception rooms. Passers-by, when walking along the street, would often pause to take a quick look into these large rooms, for the windows were low enough to allow them a glimpse at the beautiful murals. Painted in soft and muted colours, these mystical hunting and woodland scenes formed a lavish background for the beautiful furniture Harriet had collected.

The house was fully big enough for entertaining on a large scale, though comfortable enough not to appear empty or lonely when only Harriet and Alexine were at home. Not that they were ever actually alone, for there were always several servants. There was Harriet's lady's maid, Flora. Efficient in her work and always kindly, she was a consistent grumbler, as was Jan, the manservant. He was for ever on the alert to see that all was tidy and in place should there be callers, and the silver that was displayed, gleaming on the dining-room table, was his pride.

About the house or in the garden, trotted, jumped, and yapped the canine family. Alexine's dogs were never shut away. Every day she would play with them in the garden behind the house and take them out for walks, often selecting her favourite one to call on friends, and even had a visiting card printed with a dog's name, as if to explain: 'I would have waited to see you, but my dog would not wait for me!'

Thirty-two, Lange Voorhout, drew an endless stream of visitors, for Harriet had been brought up to be hospitable, and she was a gifted and clever hostess. The society was very cosmopolitan, there being many representatives at the embassies and consulates, though as often as not little business for them to deal with. Harriet and Alexine considered it a duty to attend every social function to which they were invited, and to enjoy the numberless parties that came their way. In spite of this, there are social divisions in every society, and to be a member of the diplomatic set was not necessarily a pass to every family's front door in The Hague. But Harriet's party-giving did not run on the conventional lines of most of the other hostesses. In the first place, being exceedingly rich, she never had to worry over the cost of entertaining, and could afford to hold parties on as extravagant a scale as she wished. Secondly, unlike some, she was not fussy about the backgrounds of those she invited: so long as they proved lively or amusing they were acceptable to her and likewise welcomed to her house. In short, Harriet was a warm-hearted and generous hostess and she possessed a certain gusto that made her parties both pleasant and gay.

Each year the number of parties had increased since Alexine was fifteen, when Anna, John Tinne's daughter, had stayed with them. In those days the two girls had been on very friendly terms and Alexine had teased Anna about an admirer she had had, Prince Jean Caradja of the Turkish Embassy.

Now, although a Prince, he was so poor, that he only owned one shirt. Mischievous Alexine had painted a picture of a scene of Prince Caradja and Anna in married life. It showed the Prince in bed, covered up to the chin with blankets, whilst Anna was depicted standing over the washtub washing the one precious shirt, and Alexine, who had just made her entrance without knocking, was standing at the door, gasping, 'Oh, Anna!!'

Nothing ever came of this affair, which was perhaps as well. Anna soon married an Englishman and became Mrs. Berthon, and the Prince, it is said, eventually married a very wealthy woman – which doubtless ended his shirt difficulties. But as Alexine mocked Anna, she herself had fallen in love. Her fancy was a handsome young man, Count Adolf Franz Joseph von Königsmark, whose family lived in the Grand Duchy of Saxony. His uncle, Hans Königsmark, was Prussian Consul to the Dutch Court, and obtained a position for Adolf, who was a Lieutenant in the Prussian Army, as military-attaché.[1] Anna hated Adolf. She appears to have held a prejudice against Germans, and told Alexine he was a 'regular blond beast!'[2] However, as Harriet saw the affair blossoming she was pleased, for it seemed he would make a suitable husband for her daughter: twenty-five years old, considerate and well-mannered, he came from a wealthy family, held a good position and title, and was of the same religion. In addition Saxony was not too far distant from the Netherlands.

Two of Alexine's valentines are treasured by a family descendant today, both exquisitely decorated. The first has a lace edge, a centre of lilies-of-the-valley, and surrounding this some tiny stuck-on flowers. Whilst beneath each flower, is a word of minute writing:

> By love I hope to conquer
> Through every danger and constraint.[3]

On the second valentine, as much of a gem as the first, is written: 'You talk of love and constancy', and hidden under the four wings of a butterfly: 'At you, Fluttering Butterfly'. Moreover, by a clever device the little paper butterfly does flutter!

Unfortunately (for the curious), not very much is known of Adolf Königsmark, and even less of his friendship with Alexine. Speculation arose then, as speculation has arisen since, as to what went wrong with this happy friendship for it was certainly happy. The two young people always seemed to be in the very best of spirits in each other's company, and they, and everybody else who knew them, presumed that an engagement would soon be announced. At the time it appeared that such a marriage would be accompanied by every prospect of good fortune, for Alexine had fallen in love with Adolf, and he with her. His family approved

Portrait of Alexine painted in the Pyrenees, 1849

Adriana Van Capellen

Yetty and Alexine, Paris
December 1860

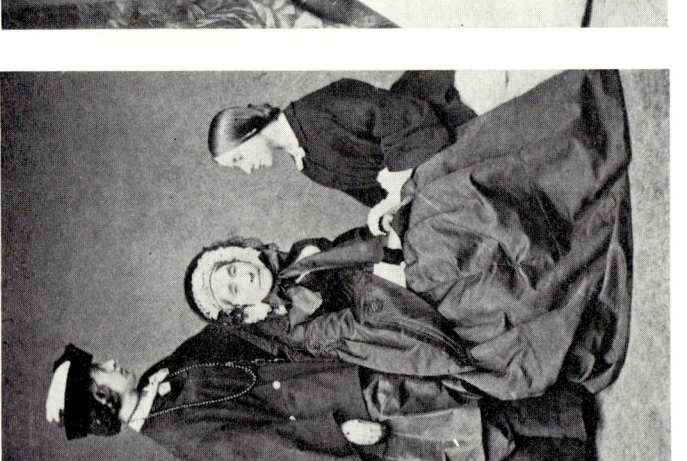

Alexine Harriet and
Yetty photographed in
Paris, December 1860.
(Note Alexine's spectacles)

openly of the match, and so did Harriet, at first. But the engagement was never announced. Suddenly it was as if a deep ravine had opened up between the couple. It was all off. The affair that had promised so well and had lasted so many happy months was crushed.

Harriet took Alexine to a ball at the home of the Königsmarks in Dresden in May 1855, and it was at about this date that the trouble began. Alexine was then nineteen and a half. She said she did not want to see Adolf again, but he was insistent and pleaded with her. Only two months after the ball Alexine and her mother set off on their grand tour of Europe knowing that they wanted to leave The Hague for a long time.

How did Adolf blacken his name? Who, except those directly concerned, knows which way human thoughts will turn and how people will react? What was his unforgivable and unforgettable offence? Was he caught cheating at cards? Was he intending to marry Alexine for her money? Or was he already married?

A little later Harriet wrote to Margaret, wife of John Tinne, describing the broken affair and how it stood:

'I think Alexine has been again dreadfully agitated about Königsmark as she has now decidedly and finally refused him, and I have likewise written to the Countess Mother begging her not to make any more attempts to change the resolution of Alexine to give him up. It has been a sad story, dear Margaret, and though God knows I do not envy you the happiness you must feel to see your two daughters respectably and happily married, yet I cannot help comparing what we have felt since a year! And yet it *seemed* all I could wish for Alexine. Name, rank, fortune, consideration, the wish of his family, the same religion, near neighbours, and as Anna can tell you, every appearance of sincere love on his part. Oh, it has been a cruel disappointment and I fear it will take long before Alexine will get over it.[4]

It was heart-rending for Harriet who could only advise Alexine strongly against the marriage. Surprisingly, the friendship that had seemed so wonderful had fallen to pieces. The romantic dream of the past now appeared to be a nightmare of the present. The two young people, wounded and pained beyond comprehension, felt that life ahead would never be quite the same again.

So it was that after the Königsmarks' ball Harriet decided to take Alexine on a grand European tour, with Vienna in view as the farthest point. They had been enchanted by their holiday in Scandinavia the previous year, and they spent much time discussing where they would go next. To reflect on this urge for adventure within its proper context, we should remember that it was considered unusual for ladies to make long journeys a century ago. Moreover, it was customary to travel accompanied by a gentleman, and, no doubt, in many a Hague drawing-room eyebrows were raised at the news that Harriet and Alexine were going by themselves; and the whispers and comments amongst their friends, and those who were not their friends, can well be imagined.

In 1855 when this grand tour began, from which they did not return for two years, Harriet was fifty-seven. She was an energetic and lively woman, but, though game for her years, she was aware that middle-age was creeping on. A few days after they started, at the end of a grilling-hot day in Düsseldorf, she wrote in her diary: 'I am really too old to travel. The boat makes me suffer, the getting-up deranges me, and the intolerable bad food makes me sick.' Yet ahead lay twelve weeks of travelling in Europe before they crossed the Mediterranean to Egypt.

With the customary luggage and after the usual bustle of last-minute preparation, Harriet and Alexine set off on 19th September 1855. There was still no station at The Hague, though the network of railways was fast spreading; and it was, therefore, necessary for them to go to Rotterdam before they could get a train to Germany. Their first stop was at Utrecht, from where they went twelve miles by carriage to visit Queen Anna Paulowna, the Queen Mother.

Harriet and Alexine were accompanied by the same two servants, Jan and Flora. This time no dogs were taken, possibly because they knew they were going far; but there was much luggage. Many and varied articles filled up the trunks including books, painting and photographic equipment, besides masses of clothes; and shoes and bonnets were packed in special boxes. As for passports, although these had not been necessary for Scandinavia, strict frontier regulations were in force in the Confederation of Germany, especially in Prussia.

Harriet preferred to go by train whenever possible because it was quicker than road, though this was not the only form of public transport. There were also diligences, drawn by four or more horses, that covered routes between the large towns, dropping and collecting post and passengers, and for that matter a good deal of local news too. Inside these large carriages there was accommodation for six people, and cheaper seats could be had on top. The passengers, generally unknown to each other, would sit for hours packed together, whilst those on the top benches would almost freeze to death in the winter. Not that the trains were much better: there were no corridors in them, no lavatories or restaurant cars and, of course, no heating. The German railways were famous for their efficiency, and the ladies, after being received by the Queen Mother, proceeded through Prussia and Saxony by train.

After visiting Düsseldorf, they went to Kassel, where they chanced to see a military parade of four regiments commanded by the Elector of Hesse-Kassel himself. The soldiers' uniforms and drill impressed them very much, for this was their first encounter with Prussia's military force about which they had heard so often.

Crossing Prussia into Saxony the four travellers continued their journey through the beautiful wooded country of Thuringia to reach Eisenach, where they had been invited to stay with the Grand Duke and Duchess of Saxe-Weimar. Harriet wrote in her diary:

The most beautiful palace I ever saw, with a fine lake and woods, and nothing could equal the reception of the Grand Duchess! The palace consists of several pavilions – ours was apart. Our rooms were very formal, and we had a suite of seven rooms with every convenience, a lackey to wait on us, and Jan was sent to a hotel as there was no room in the palace. After lunch, at which there were only the two ladies of the Grand Duchess and ourselves, we were received by H.R.H., and at about two she took us a long walk. We dined at five, before which we were presented to the Grand Duke who had been *à la chasse*. Alexine practised her various languages with the Grand Duke much to their amusement, and our dinner was very gay, after which we returned to our rooms to meet again at half past eight. We had tea, looked at prints, and had supper presented on trays, and at eleven to bed.

After seeing Weimar and Dresden, the party toured Saxony, accompanied by an equerry of the Duke of Saxe-Weimar. There were no roads other than tracks, and the equerry and Alexine rode horses, whilst Harriet was carried in a chair by two men. Tourism in the east of Germany was criticized by her for being somewhat artificial:

> We went first through a fine forest to a great height commanding a view of great extent and beauty, but spoilt by chairs and tables and rails as a place in itself. The next day we crossed the river by steamboat. Here we found a carriage ready to take us on as far as the road is good to a rather ridiculous waterfall produced by drawing a string and opening a sluice like a shower bath!!!

Harriet and Alexine then took a train to Leipzig where the annual fair was in progress, and 'bought lots of useless things', not for the first or last time, for shopping was always a temptation. Afterwards, they had short stays at Nuremberg, Augsberg and Ulm. The railway went no farther, and they went by diligence to Stuttgart. Then followed a visit to the King and Queen of Württemberg, parents of Queen Sophia of the Netherlands, who already knew them both well.

Afterwards they went to Munich and hired a private carriage to take them to Salzburg, a journey lasting two days. Even a century ago the Tyrol was a favourite area for tourists, and Harriet and Alexine were not disappointed. Up some of the steeper hills; it was necessary to have an extra horse to pull the carriage and Alexine was quite prepared to walk, in her buttoned leather boots, and a dress and coat reaching her ankles, her shining face bordered by a bonnet tied on with flowing ribbons. It was whilst staying in Salzburg that news of the cholera epidemic that was sweeping Vienna obliged them radically to change their plans. Because of this they decided to go instead to Italy.

Their minds made up, they set off in the same carriage that had brought them all the way from Munich, back through Austria. They stopped in Innsbruck, and for dinner ate chamois and partridge; and afterwards listened to their waiter playing the zither. Continuing along the road which follows the River Inn to Landeck, they found rocks being blasted to make way for the new railway which was being built to Vienna, and the carriage could scarcely get along the road.

The party had now to cross the Alps to reach Italy. It was November and there had been unusually heavy falls of snow. Harriet consulted the local postmaster, who said they could go by the Stelvio Pass, but as the snow lay three feet deep in places he recommended them to take a man to clear the road. Unfortunately, the weather became worse and they had to take the longer route by the valley of the River Adige to Bolzen. Hearing church bells ringing out from one of the villages they thought it was All Saints Day, but they had lost count of the date, and later discovered that this was a day of thanksgiving for the valley having escaped the cholera. Harriet, observing how devout these villagers were, pitied them living such a hard life. She noticed that all the people stopped whatever they were doing at noon and again at six to kneel for a few minutes in prayer. She asked herself: 'What would these poor people do without religion, which seems their only pleasure?'

The carriage jolted on through Bolzen and several villages; and though the road struck across pleasant valleys of vineyards and mulberry trees, it was always rough. Frequently they were kept waiting by wagons and carts coming from the opposite direction, as it was mainly single-track. After several days they caught sight of Lake Garda and arrived in Verona, where they said good-bye to the coachman on whom they had relied so long.

They were soon in Milan and saw the cathedral, but Alexine was most enthusiastic over the shops, until she exhausted her mother:

We took a pretty little open carriage, and Ali and I went to see all the palaces and promenades till I was half dead with cold and the other half with fatigue.

They returned to Verona by diligence, and for this journey Harriet booked all the seats inside the carriage, whilst Jan travelled on top. All had seemed new in Italy, but when they returned to the same hotel in Verona they were given a welcome warm enough for Alexine to remark that it was like coming home. 'Home to Verona?' reproached her mother, though she agreed it had been a marvellous day with magnificent views of the mountains.

The next day they left by train for Venice. No doubt they had read descriptions of the city, but the reality came as a delightful surprise, and after the first day Harriet wrote vividly of her impressions:

> Fine but cold. I really could not go out with Alexine but Flora did. The more one sees, the funnier it appears. This water, water, large boats, little boats, ladies and gentlemen, dustmen, beggars, omnibuses, private carriages, postmen and merchants, all gliding about in these long narrow black snakes.[5]

They enjoyed the holiday in Venice, but more exciting plans were astir; Harriet and Alexine had made inquiries about a voyage to Egypt. They were told the time estimated for a ship to cross from Trieste to Alexandria was 120 hours, and the cost of a first-class ticket was £18 each. This being considered reasonable, only the date remained to be fixed; but before this could be arranged Alexine fell ill with what nowadays would probably come under the category of flu. Alexine had never been ill in her life before, and her mother fretted for her only child as if she thought she would never recover. The malady, which started from catching cold in Venice, appears, however, not to have worried Alexine in the very least. As soon as she felt slightly better, she wanted to continue to explore Venice, including an expedition of the canals by moonlight.

The weather having improved, the ladies and their two servants left Venice for Trieste on 22nd November. Rising at four in the morning to catch a boat which left at six, they arrived in Trieste at noon. A cabin on a ship which was sailing to Egypt in five days' time had already been reserved, but, alas, Alexine's illness returned.

For three weeks they waited in Trieste hoping she would recover sufficiently to be fit for the voyage. Poor Harriet was in a dilemma. The decision to go or not was in the balance. First the doctor told Alexine she could, then he told Harriet she could not. Finally, however:

> I had the doctor again this morning and asked him, as an honourable man, to tell the mother of an only child if it could hurt her to go. He said, 'No. It would not.' He had said five days ago he would not

let her go unless she was quite strong and now saw nothing to prevent her. So we shall go. Now I shall not write until I am on the other side. God help us across! Everything was quickly arranged and the Consul brought me some money, and, after eating a cold chicken *à nous deux*, we set off in a little boat for the ship which lay a short way off.[6]

PART TWO
Egypt

4
Egypt

It was wonderful to be on board at last; and now that Harriet and Alexine were finally on their way, the excitement of being on the ship seemed positively exhilarating after the tedious days of waiting. The voyage started uneventfully; the sea was calm and the steamer was gently but powerfully carried along by her sails above and her vibrating, smoking engines below. The ship was a Lloyd's steamer, and must have been one of the earliest Mediterranean-crossing steamboats. As always, Harriet and Alexine went first-class. They shared a cabin, Alexine sleeping on the sofa and her mother occupying the only bed, until she discovered that the sofa was both narrow and hard, and, with a typical gesture of self-denial, let Alexine have the bed and took over the uncomfortable sofa for herself.

On board they soon made the acquaintance of two Dutchmen, Mr. Van Vheil and Mr. Van de Velde. These ex-naval officers were going to Egypt to sell the Viceroy a steamer. No doubt they were hopeful of making a stout profit on the deal and enjoying a holiday at the same time. Mr. Van Vheil, who had been there the previous year, talked with enthusiasm, and Harriet was interested to get information as to what costs were likely to be. Harriet and Alexine had been away from home for three months, and it must have been a pleasant coincidence to come across two fellow countrymen who, though they were dull in conversation and stolid in appearance, were eager to discuss Egypt and the Nile.

After a couple of days on board Harriet and Alexine found the steamer cramping and their little cabin restricting. They could not find fault with the meals, however, which were excellent and plentiful. At seven in the morning coffee or tea was served, at ten a breakfast or lunch with meat, vegetables, and fruit. The main meal was at four in the afternoon, and finally there was tea at eight o'clock.

The first stopping-place came two days after leaving Trieste when the steamer docked at Corfu for an afternoon and refuelled with coal. Next day the weather changed: the wind suddenly rose, the sea became choppy, and soon the little ship was tossing in a violent storm. As she began to pitch, everything in the cabin became disarranged. The porthole flew open and the sea sprayed the walls and floor, as Harriet rushed to close it. Alexine stayed on deck. The tossing sea fascinated her as she stood watching the giant waves, though scarcely another passenger ventured out the whole day. Harriet, lying in her cabin, was feeling weak and frightened as, in vain, she tried to relax. A dreadful night followed, and she recorded:

> The wind arose again, a horrid noise and the sails were put by for the boat began to heave and roll from side to side and the water splashed each time over the deck. I felt so ill and frightened I cannot describe, but Ali not a bit. She ate her supper – a woodcock, drank her bottle of beer and slept all night. I had my cup of tea and a biscuit.[1]

As Harriet lay awake through the night she got into such a state of anxiety that she began to wonder if they would ever arrive alive. She felt terrified that the storm might intensify to batter the boat to bits, and they would all perish. The weird, plaintive noises of the wind, and the resounding splash of the waves increased her fears.

The port of Alexandria was difficult to enter in the dark during rough weather, and it was necessary to wait overnight before docking:

> At last, however, a pilot did come and we got into port! Alexine went up immediately. I dressed and took a cup of broth so I did not see all, but I cannot describe what I did see. Fancy, fifty little boats full of all sorts of black creatures in every possible dress and undress, some with capes and mantles of fine cloth, some with turbans, some with caps, some in white shirts, some blue, red, or black coats. Oh, such a variety, all screaming and overturning each other to get the passengers from our steamer into their boats. Two dark gentlemen took charge of us, and a commissionaire from a hotel went with Flora and Jan, and the trunks in another boat.[2]

Before they had time to discuss the extraordinary scene Harriet and Alexine had arrived at the quay where they were pushed along by the colourful and excitable crowd. They then were escorted and packed into a crowded horse-bus on the way to the hotel. As it jolted spasmodically along the dusty streets, it passed between groups of people, street vendors, camels, donkeys, and various carriages and carts. The shops were all open and the town evidently wide awake as the driver urged his horses forward, weaving to right and to left wherever he saw an opening.

They were soon installed in a hotel overlooking a pleasant square, and the next morning a guide arrived and offered his services. He was not what they had expected, for he was a janissary, and after taking one look at his magnificent dress Harriet immediately said she would engage him. He wore a dark-blue jacket and white breeches, very ample and much embroidered with braid, a fez with a scarf tied round it on the head, a wide silk sash over his shoulder, and a long, curved sabre hung by his side.

The janissary suggested they should hire a carriage, but to this Harriet and Alexine immediately replied that they would prefer to go on foot. They always walked when possible, they explained, because they could see and observe much better that way. The ladies being insistent, the janissary deemed it not courteous to press his suggestion, and thus Alexine and her mother set off with him to see Alexandria on foot, a very unorthodox way for Europeans to behave on tour. Stepping between the groups that filled the roadsides, the visitors noticed the strange variety of people – from those dressed in rich materials of bright colours, to beggars clothed in rags. Along the mud street went fashionable carriages with boys running in front, rumbling carts, men on horses, mules, donkeys and camels. As they proceeded the crowds seemed to thicken, all the streets being a mass of lively, noisy folk, calling to each other in strange-sounding Arabic. Eventually, the effect of the noise and the fast-moving traffic, the dirt and smells, the animals and children, and constant molestation by street vendors and paupers, proved too much for them. They turned back, and afterwards, for any but the shortest distances, engaged a carriage.

They planned to travel to Cairo shortly as they had decided to make a Nile voyage, and this could not be made after March. Before they could leave Alexandria, however, they were delayed by some news that came in a letter from Adolf Königsmark. In this Adolf implied that Jemima Van Capellen, Harriet's fifth sister, was gravely ill, so that Harriet and Alexine felt they must remain and wait for further letters from The Hague before leaving Alexandria. A few days later they received news that Jemima had been poorly, but never seriously ill. The purpose of Adolf's letter giving the false alarm was not very far to seek. But he was not the only person who wanted them home. Their relations, both in The Hague and Liverpool, were concerned over the news that they were in Egypt. Even Queen Sophia of the Netherlands wrote to Harriet urging them to return; she felt they had gone far enough on their travels and 'she begged and warned us not to go away'.

The delay of waiting another week led to an invitation from the Princess, wife of Said Pasha, the Viceroy of Egypt. This came through Mrs. Russenaers, wife of Mr. S. W. Russenaers, Consul-General of the Low Countries in Egypt. Harriet and Alexine, ready in good time for two o'clock and dressed immaculately, were collected by Mrs. Russenaers and taken to the palace in her carriage. They drove through several heavily-guarded courtyards, each gated, and finally walked across a terrace bordered with orange trees. At the doorway they were escorted by Negro servants dressed in magnificent livery up a vast flight of steps to reach a large hall, and there at the end was the Princess sitting on a divan surrounded by her maids of honour arrayed around her on the floor. Mrs. Russenaers, who spoke fluent Arabic, introduced Harriet and Alexine, and during the audience acted as interpreter. The visitors were each presented with a pipe, exquisitely made with amber mouthpieces and jewelled stems. The Princess was interested to hear of their journey through Europe and their future plans. She was dressed in pantaloons of finely-striped silk with a jacket of cashmere wool edged with sable, and on her feet shone richly jewelled slippers. Over her black hair she wore a silk cap fastened with a magnificent diamond-spray brooch, and on her fingers many rings. Presently coffee arrived and the Princess poured the sweet and potent brew into tiny golden cups studded round the rims with diamonds. After a while they went on a tour of the palace. Many of the floors were of beautiful inlay, one done entirely in ivory and ebony; but the furniture was scanty and consisted of a few chairs and mats.

Egypt

During the next few days in Alexandria, Alexine decided to learn Arabic herself. She had plenty of opportunity to practise when she and her mother made visits to the bazaars to buy presents for friends at home. They went to see the steamer Mr. Van Vheil and Mr. Van de Velde wished to sell the Viceroy. A hundred men, as well as the crew, had been employed to clean and shine the steamer, and the interior was handsomely furnished and decorated with flowers. When the Viceroy came he soon agreed to the purchase, but at once gave orders that everything be removed from inside, for he wanted only the ship, masts, and sails, and to redecorate it throughout to his own taste.

Harriet and Alexine took the train for Cairo early one morning in January 1856, noticing the remarkable violet lights from the salt marshes which spread inland from the coast. For the last part of the journey they changed to a steamer; and as the pyramids came into view the sun was setting. Cairo presented an ethereal scene: against the pink sky rose the domes, turrets, and minarets from its many mosques.

On leaving the steamer they took a carriage to Shepheard's Hotel. By 1856 Shepheard's was a fashionable meeting-place, and most of the guests would assemble in the large dining-room where two or three hundred people of all nationalities were to be seen. They flocked to Egypt as tourists, sportsmen, artists, botanists, and archaeologists; for since the time of Napoleon's defeat in Egypt, an interest in her history had become fashionable. Shepheard's Hotel then stood in Ezbekiya Square in the centre of the city, overlooking the vast expanse of the old Ezbekiya, a plain planted with gigantic trees and bushes. It was a grim building with thick stone walls, but, as if to relieve the prison-like exterior, outside lay the magic of the East where rich and poor mingled. Rows of camels stood about, and Arab horses wearing colourful harness waited as their owners stopped to exchange gossip under the trees. There was always a motley collection of people, but amongst them women were seldom seen.

Whilst in Cairo they led an extremely social life, and amongst the large numbers of Europeans made friends with the family of Mr. Linant de Bellefonds, a Breton engineer and colleague of Mr. Ferdinand de Lesseps. They were pleased to be invited to the palace of the Princess, sister of the Viceroy. The days were full and busy. They went to the ancient Nilometre, and another day drove out to see the railway which was being built between Cairo and Suez. They visited the Citadel and the mosque of Mohammed Ali, where they admired the view from the terrace looking over the flat-roofed houses to the Nile winding away into the distance, and the sails of boats barely visible through the warm haze. Naturally, their extensive sight-seeing included a visit to the Pyramids of Giza. The surface smoothness has been worn away so that each stone forms a vast stair, about four feet high; and how Alexine managed to reach the top wearing a dress and coat to her ankles defies the imagination. Nevertheless, she did. The descent would probably have been even more awkward.

During their stay in Cairo, Harriet arranged to share a dahabiah for a Nile voyage with the two Dutchmen she and Alexine had met on the Mediterranean crossing. Later Mr. Van Vheil decided not to come, but Mr. Van de Velde accompanied them. There being a scarcity of vessels, the owners were asking as high prices as they dared. Harriet, however, was only concerned with quality, and after extensive inquiries engaged one of the most expensive, with a crew, to take them to Aswan.

5

First Nile Voyage

The best time to make a Nile voyage is at the beginning of the year. The season, from December to March, is a short one, but only during these months are both the river conditions suitable for sailing and the climate comfortable for Europeans. Harriet and Alexine were anxious to start in time to get to Aswan and back before the river became too shallow and the sun too hot.

There was no limit to their excitement as they installed themselves and arranged their belongings in the cabin. They looked out to see a stranger coming on board, and then laughed as they recognized Mr. Van de Velde who had shaved off his beard for the voyage. He carried guns and a fishing-rod, and a knapsack over his shoulder. Behind him trudged his black servant, Morgan, who carried stout leather cases, and then followed two porters, one laden with the Dutchman's trunk and the other with his boxes of ammunition.

Enjoying their first dinner on board in the little dining-room, Harriet and Alexine became aware of the lack of space, in spite of the dahabiah appearing so large. However, since the food was good and champagne had been uncorked, all were in good spirits. Every preparation had been thought out and they were ready to start but, unfortunately, could not move off until the wind got up. Below on the open deck the sailors sat cross-legged and sang to the beat of a drum. Late that evening, as they settled down for their first night on board, it was raining in the moonlight. The river seemed even more beautiful and serene as the light of the moon cast silver shadows on the waterside. The passengers went to bed happy with such a romantic start to their voyage.

Next morning they woke early to find they were still moored along the quay. An anticlimax, but it did not last long, for soon after breakfast the sailors began to tow the great boat from the bank. Yard by yard the vessel edged its way upstream passing the green fields and palm trees silhouetted against the cloudless sky. A breeze from the north suddenly arose at noon. The sails were quickly hoisted and the dahabiah began to make brisker progress. Along the waterside they saw villages of mud cottages, and there were several large houses, their gardens reaching down to the river. The ladies sat on deck-chairs on the top deck, Harriet doing her needlework and Alexine making some quick sketches. They both wore large straw hats to shade their faces from the sun. Alas, soon the wind changed and it was necessary for the crew to tow the dahabiah again. As they hauled, waist-deep in the water, they kept rhythm with the singing of songs which the passengers enjoyed.

After leaving Cairo the river winds ceaselessly, making it difficult to judge north from south after the first few bends. At some places the sailors had to wade across the river to pull from the opposite side to avoid the contrary wind. At one such crossing the breeze was so strong it whipped the dahabiah twice round in circles and the sailors had to swim to straighten its position before continuing their laborious task of towing.

The dahabiah measured about ninety feet in length and eighteen feet in beam, and carried two masts, the bigger one near the prow and a smaller one behind it. The cabins were built on the first deck and occupied only the after-half of the boat, and their roof formed a sun deck. This raised part caused the dahabiah to appear top-heavy, though it was stabilized by the weight in the hold which lay under the main deck. In the lower deck the servants and crew had their quarters, but as there were too many to sleep there, some spent the night on the open deck. The kitchen was situated forward in the boat, screened from winds by permanent partitions and, occasionally, a temporarily erected awning as well.

The crew on this dahabiah, hired for the duration of the voyage, consisted of the captain, known as the *reis*, one or two pilots, six to eight sailors, a cook and a waiter. There were also the Egyptian guide (always referred to as the dragoman), and Jan and Flora to be housed, and Mr. Van de Velde's servant, Morgan. They formed quite a boatload, for servants, crew, and passengers numbered about eighteen. In addition there were livestock: chickens, two or three goats for milk, and usually some sheep as well.

They had been on voyage for two days when the dahabiah

First Nile Voyage

struck a sandbank. As it was not yet dark, Mr. Van de Velde took the opportunity to go off pigeon-shooting, and Harriet and Alexine strolled along the river accompanied by the dragoman and another member of the crew, who were armed with big sticks for protection, lest the ladies should be attacked and robbed.

The next morning all the sailors pulled the dahabiah, and on board Mr. Van de Velde, the dragoman and Jan pushed with puntpoles. Pausing for a moment in despair at their lack of success, they heard the sound of a steamer approaching: the Viceroy's steamer pulling his dahabiah. On the suggestion of Harriet, Mr. Van de Velde rowed with all speed to ask if the steamer would give them a tow, but he returned having been informed that the Viceroy was asleep and could not be awakened – a negative response in view of their sad plight. Soon, however, Harriet had another bright idea; she would give the sailors a glass of brandy each. Whether or not this was the deciding factor, the dahabiah presently became free and was able to continue. Coming to the Viceroy's palace, where his steamer and dahabiah were anchored, they also chose this as a suitable place to moor for the night.

That evening a servant of the Viceroy called with a letter. Would the ladies like to stay at his palace? Harriet felt they should not consent, and wrote back explaining that they wished soon to be on their way. Meanwhile, the servant sat down and smoked a pipe. He was very perturbed when he heard the ladies were not accepting, for an invitation from Said Pasha was never refused. Perhaps he had a few words aside with one of the crew whilst he was waiting. In any case, a little later Harriet and Alexine went for a walk accompanied by two of their men; these escorted them to the entrance of the palace, reaching it so suddenly there was no chance to turn back. They were quickly ushered through the door and upstairs to a large empty room. Here, still overcome with embarrassment and understanding scarcely a word that was being said to them, they were seated by a window and offered coffee. The dragoman was fetched and, interpreting, explained that the Viceroy wished them to stay: the house was all theirs, and the next day they could see the garden. They smiled at the way they had been trapped but would not remain for the night, saying by way of excuse that they would like to call on their way downstream. On reaching their cabin Alexine kept laughing as she imagined them spending a night in the vast rooms of the palace, furnished with only a divan before the window, and a mat, lamp, and spittoon on the floor.

The first town to be reached was Beni Suef. Here the passengers wished to disembark to post some letters. With several of the crew they went to the Governor's house, but on arriving were told by the guard that the Governor was asleep and could not see them, the usual form of excuse. However, they left their letters for the post which were casually weighed and put into a leather bag to be taken to Cairo by messenger on foot. They took a brief walk through the town and on their way back a fantastic sight met their eyes: for there were fifty soldiers dressed in white and red, the Governor's guard of cavalry, watering their richly harnessed Arab steeds.

The dahabiah continued up the river passing by the monastery of La Pontie. The dragoman had warned them that the monks were in the habit of swimming after boats to beg for money:

We had been prepared so we were not surprised at hearing the well-known sound of 'baksheesh' from the water and to see four heads following our boat, till we gave the poor monks some money, which they put in their mouths as they swam back. We were rather astonished to see the crew calling out to one of these heads, who held on longer than the others, with joy and fun shouting at him, 'Christian'. Of course we gave him three piastres like the others, and then we found out it was only one of our own men who had done it for the amusement and, of course, the profit of the rest.[1]

The rich cultivation of young corn and the outline of the trees were mirrored in the still water as the great boat glided on. Now and then the scenery would become desert-like, and the river would reflect the colours of the golden sand, and shades of the dunes and hillocks. Here again are great bends in the Nile, so that the town of Asyut comes into view first on one side of the river and then on the other. Amongst the pink mountains in the distance the town is at once recognized and remembered by its many cupulas and minarets which pierce the opalescent sky.

Progress was disappointing, but contrary winds that lasted

First Nile Voyage   41

through the whole day would suddenly turn to a favourable direction by the evening. After much persuasion the reis agreed to sail by night, but scarcely was the last light out when he gave orders to anchor. If there was too much wind, he complained, the sails would be torn to shreds. However, the changing scenery compensated for much. They passed many mud villages and buffaloes up to their shoulders in water, standing motionless and cooling themselves from the hot sun. Along the bank yellow mimosa, the feathery tamarisk, the dom and date palms, and the spreading sycamore trees made the tow-path resemble a garden walk.

Luxor was a day's distance away when the dahabiah ran into a sandstorm. The wind started to blow violently, and immediately the air became a mass of fine dust. Alexine was fascinated as she watched the clouds of sand coming from the desert in strange formations. Whilst everyone else took shelter she stood on deck wrapping her coat round her in the hope that it would provide protection. Over the river the wind whipped up the water till it became like a choppy sea. After three or four hours the storm ceased, and all hands were busy trying to clean away the dust which had penetrated to every part of the boat.

For some time the dragoman had been to Harriet with various complaints, and now he said that the crew were working too hard and deserved to stop for a lengthy rest, to which she retaliated:

> Quite furious when the dragoman and reis said we should stop to take breath for the sailors. We stoutly refused. Then we agreed to give the reis fifty piastres towards the expenses if he would go on, so we went on all night, now and then getting on a sandbank, as our pilot is not so great.[2]

One evening the cook ran away saying he had not been given enough to eat. Naturally, Harriet and Alexine were horrified, as being Dutch they were always careful to see that there was plentiful food; but soon he came back saying he was not getting enough praise for his cooking! Another dramatic incident was when Mr. Van de Velde's gold ring was stolen. He had taken a swim and left the ring with his clothes, but it was duly returned by the reis the next morning, who complacently took the reward in exchange.

The passengers were within sight of Luxor when they were held up again, and no bribe nor strong words were of any use to keep the sailors at work. As they waited they saw with envy other vessels gliding down the river on their way back to Cairo. All the dahabiahs looked much the same, but could be differentiated by their flags. With the wind behind their sails and the heavy current in their favour these large boats moved at a great speed. Hardly had they appeared in the distance than they would swish past the marooned latecomers.

During the voyage the crew had been preparing a play and asked Harriet if they might have permission to perform it. The passengers were flabbergasted to discover most of the jokes were aimed at themselves. Here was a so-called Christian, the sailor who had begged for money with the swimming monks, out again to make baksheesh. Then Harriet, Alexine, and Mr. Van de Velde all saw themselves impersonated. Alexine laughed loud and long, and Harriet could not contain herself: even Mr. Van de Velde took the jokes well, and after it was over all were in good humour again. The Nile at Luxor is ethereal, and the setting sun's golden rays on the blush-tinted hills made a glorious finish to the day. As the moon emerged, the colours of the evening turned to silver lights and grey shadows, and the crew and passengers went to bed feeling united, at any rate for a short time.

The next day the dahabiah was heaved up to Luxor yard by yard and finally drew up at the landing stage. Here, three thousand years ago, situated on the west side of the Nile, was the city of Thebes, ancient capital of the Pharaohs. Two miles away from Luxor on the east side of the river lies Karnak, the biggest collection of temples in the world, and even the quay of Luxor has a beautiful temple dominating the little village. Much has been discovered during the last hundred years, and it is interesting to note that Harriet and Alexine did not mention the temple of Luxor, which is as large as an English country mansion, but was then half hidden. Every year the ruins had collected more sand; and, surrounded by the busy village and quay, had become embedded in litter and filth until it resembled a mass of small hillocks.

Harriet had a letter of introduction to the English Consul, and on arriving she and Alexine went by moonlight to call on him. He was a small but very pompous Egyptian, called Mustapha Alpha, who had enough self-importance to make them laugh. They asked him to make arrangements for them to go sightseeing, and the next morning two horses and five donkeys were waiting to take them to Karnak. Karnak consists of a group of temples, the size and quantity of which it is difficult to describe. The visitor feels dwarfed by the immense pillars, the avenues of stone rams, the magnificent entrances of huge pylons, and overawed by the number of ruins and the way they seem to spread as far as the eye can see. They also made excursions to the Valley of the Kings, and temples the other side of the river; but as they planned to stop again on their way back from Aswan, they decided to stay only three days. But this had to be prolonged:

Although we had wished to leave this evening the dragoman came with a petition from the reis to stay, as he had married and wanted to see his wife, so we consented to stay.[3]

Harriet said she would wait for the evening if the reis would sail through the night. This extra time gave Alexine a chance to see Karnak a third time, on this occasion by moonlight, a favourite excursion for tourists. Later that evening the dahabiah left Luxor, the passengers contented with all they had experienced, hoping the boat would make good progress through the night. However, the reis anchored at one o'clock when he thought everybody was safely asleep. Harriet, for one, was not, but she was too kind-hearted to complain.

On 16th February the dahabiah reached Aswan; and as she did so one of the crew put up a cry, for he had seen the first crocodile, and Mr. Van de Velde had offered a reward of two piastres. There were already two boats along the quayside, one of which shot off a cannon in welcome. No sooner had the vessel touched land than it was rushed at by guides offering their services, vendors with numerous wares, and a mass of donkey boys and dancing girls, all pressing and jostling in their anxiety to extract some money from the visitors. Indeed, some of the crowd jumped on deck, but their enthusiasm was not well received. The passengers at once ordered their dahabiah to land on the opposite side. They were left in peace as they crossed the river, but as they docked further crowds appeared. To avoid being molested they went in the felucca, or small rowing boat, to see the ancient Nilometre, a graduated pillar, by which the annual flood was measured.

The next day Alexine and her mother took a felucca upriver to see the first cataract and the temple of Philae. To the tourist who had come up from Cairo much of the fascination of the cataract which lay beyond Aswan was due to the complete change of scenery. For so far the river had been running over sand, and the cataract presented a profusion of harmonious colour of reddish rocks, leafy shrubs and grasses growing near the water. The water rushed in two or three narrow gorges through and over the rocks; so there was great difficulty in taking a dahabiah upstream. The temple of Philae, which lies south of Aswan and was beyond the rigours of the cataract, stood on a verdant island which might have been created for it, so perfect was its situation. Though the temples at Karnak and Thebes excel in grandeur, Philae surpasses them in its supreme grace and proportion to the island it stands on. The buildings consist of a principal temple and several subordinate chapels. Their beauty was acknowledged to be paramount for they boasted a unique setting. When the Aswan Dam was opened in 1902 public outcry demanded that Philae should not be totally submerged. But the Dam was later heightened until the temple was visible only at low Nile. Although it lies downstream of the High Dam, this favourite spot of Alexine, as indeed of all Nile tourists, is in danger of permanent submersion at the hands of the engineers.

After a few days at Aswan the dahabiah started on her return journey. A north wind went on blowing, so that it was necessary for the sailors to row, and planks on the lower deck were taken up to allow them to sit. The mast and sails were laid along the upper deck, leaving nowhere for the ladies to go except their cabin. They stopped several times, and saw the temples of Kom Ombo, Edfu, and Esna: the last they considered 'much too cleaned out'.

Harriet and Alexine went again on shore to see the garden of Said Pasha. Since their previous experience they were particularly anxious not to go near the palace. For once the dragoman was not with them, and Harriet explained to a sailor that she did not want to see the palace – or so she thought. Alexine realized at once that, speaking Arabic, her mother had muddled her negatives, and that the sailor had understood her to have said: 'There is no house.' He wished to show her that the Viceroy had a house, and a very fine one too, and no sooner were the words uttered than Harriet

First Nile Voyage

was taken by each arm and briskly marched towards the house she had so earnestly hoped to avoid. Alexine laughed as she followed the comic trio, but the afternoon finished well for they went up to the roof, strewn with carpets, and had a magnificent view over the river and the surrounding mountains. They were pressed to see the setting sun, and on leaving were presented with posies on behalf of the Viceroy. As they made their way back through the garden, the scent of the orange and lemon trees was luxuriant.

On returning to the dahabiah they found the dragoman and complained of his absence, but he shrugged off his guilt. That evening the crew indulged in drug-taking. They even persuaded Harriet to try some of the mixture, but she was cautious enough to refrain from swallowing more than a minute quantity, though she felt it would not be polite to refuse. As a result, most of the sailors were in a stupor; and, with the persistent north wind, progress was almost nil. The indefatigable travellers, not to be done down, then made inquiries about going by camel to Luxor. None were available, but the delay gave Alexine an idea, and as soon as they arrived she wanted to make a desert crossing to the Red Sea.

Complications arose shortly after they got to Luxor. Mr. Van de Velde went ashore to collect mail and contact the Consul, but returned saying there had been a revolution. Harriet was not sorry over the failure of their plans, 'but oh, to see the despair of Alexine!' she commented in her diary; but the next day:

> Before breakfast the English Consul and the chief of the rebels came to our boat. The latter had been to Keneh and complained to the Governor of the Province of the hardship of making his men soldiers. His complaint had been attended to and the Viceroy had promised that this tribe should be respected. He had come back to Luxor last night and made a feast of dates and dancing, and there had been guns fired to congratulate the Arabians who are good friends with all the inhabitants of this place. It is with the chief himself we are to make an arrangement to go to Quseir and we are then to return here to Luxor.[4]

The ladies, after spending the day at Thebes, went to sleep to a background of argument between the men, but they were too tired to care, and turned a deaf ear to the men's disagreements. When they awoke next morning to a continuation of the same voices, they felt irritated and annoyed. As usual, Mr. Van de Velde kept calm, and decided to fetch the Consul to sort out the dispute. Harriet had ordered the dragoman to get camels and tents, and it was soon discovered that the price of the camels was excessively high because he wanted to make a vast profit for himself. Eventually, after arguments culminating in shouts and screams, a new contract was drawn up.

They arranged to leave the following morning and meanwhile spent the day exploring the beautifully painted tombs in the Valley of the Kings. Finally:

> After a late dinner Alexine and Mr. Van de Velde rowed home some people whom we had employed, to the great glee of our men who admired us from the dark.[5]

Alexine, Mr. Van de Velde, and Flora boldly mounted their camels and triumphantly set off. The gait of their steeds was very uncomfortable, but to begin with none of them would admit this. Harriet, who was riding on a special saddle, could not stand the torture. Her saddle was like a sofa; and although roomy to lie on when the camel was stationary, it tipped her about like a tossing ship as soon as the beast began to move. To make matters worse, before long the latter was giving disapproving grunts and snorts and his movement became more and more spasmodic. Afterwards Harriet rode a donkey, which seemed so small she felt she was on a hare.

The party took five days to reach Quseir. Each day they packed early and were ready to leave at nine, and continued moving all day, except for brief stops, until four or five when they set up their tents for the night. By that time the tourists felt almost too tired to eat any dinner, but fortunately the cool evenings revived them for the next day. At first the route lay across a sandy plain, only broken by occasional hillocks. The party would camp at a dreary village where they could take on fresh supplies of water. Later on, the way became more interesting, as they came to strange-shaped rocks, and the landscape became more undulating. They saw some gazelles. Over one area the path was spread with round pebbles of every colour: white, orange, magenta, dark blue, lilac, olive and yellow, which lit up in a profusion of richness. Alexine, whenever she had the chance, took her weary camel up a near-by hill to get a better view of the country through which the little caravan was passing.

After ten days the party caught a glimpse of the Red Sea. It was a thrill for all and a mercy for Harriet, who had been almost shaken to death by the pitter-patter of her donkey's steps. They approached the sea and continued along the coast for the last six miles to reach their destination, Quseir. Here they had arranged to hire a villa for two days before starting their journey back. The message had been sent ahead to the Austrian Consul by dromedary, a form of camel express.

Near Quseir they were met by a party of Egyptians, who introduced themselves as a deputation from the Austrian Consul. As they rode into the town the Consul's family were waiting, and Harriet found herself surrounded by a sea of chattering faces as she sat on her donkey, relieved that they had arrived. After the Consul, an Egyptian, had made a speech of welcome she saw fit to reply, although she had not understood a word he had said. Likewise the entourage did not understand her English; but they showed their appreciation by lining up to kiss her hand, with warm smiles and gestures of admiration.

The villa reserved for them was a whitewashed house and above the entrance hung the Dutch flag. Naturally, the tired tourists were very pleased to see it, but on entering were taken aback to find it had no furniture of any sort and no glass in the windows. Fortunately, about twenty men stood near the front door awaiting instructions, and they soon set to work bringing in carpets and beds and making at any rate some of the rooms habitable. In the evening the Austrian Consul arrived with English newspapers, and the ladies unpacked some of the books they had brought with them to show him. Evidently, Europeans were something of a novelty in Quseir, for the next day they were followed by what appeared to them to be the entire population, and the little boys were so curious that:

> The Governor said the first boy to follow us was to have 500 lashes. It is impossible to tell what admiration they had at the sight of our gloves, our watches, and the sight of our skin, which was not burnt.[6]

By now Alexine had become proficient in speaking Arabic, to the surprise of all. 'She speaks like a book,' commented her proud mother, who recorded how, at the Governor's house, 'we brought our books and they were all enchanted with Ali's learning.'

The journey back to the Nile at Keneh was as painful to Harriet as before, but she bravely held out, tortured by headaches and the discomfort of her donkey. She, more than anyone, appreciated the cool comfort of the dahabiah. 'I could not get up, I was so dished,' she wrote in her diary, but she only spent an extra hour in bed the next morning.

A fortnight later the dahabiah reached Cairo, and Harriet and Alexine went to Shepheard's Hotel. It was the end of March, they had been away for ten weeks, and Alexine had already resolved to make another Nile voyage the following winter. Until then she and her mother decided to spend the summer in the Holy Land. For a few days they were busy shopping. Harriet was disappointed not to find guide-books or maps on Syria, but Alexine added to her luggage by buying a hat, two veils, and an Egyptian costume.

6
Summer in the Holy Land

On 20th April 1856, Harriet and Alexine, with Mr. Van de Velde, left Alexandria to spend six months in the Holy Land, before returning to Egypt to make a second Nile voyage the following year.

The shops in Cairo and Alexandria had produced little in the way of books and maps, but Harriet and Alexine were fortunate, for in a sense they took a guide with them. Mr. Van de Velde had travelled there extensively a few years before and they were able to rely on him for most of their information. Indeed, one wonders why, having written a two-volume narrative of his travels, he chose to return. Perhaps he was accompanying them more as a duty, for no doubt he felt they might run into difficulties without him, and Alexine's ideas of where she wanted to go can only have aggravated his sense of responsibility. Unfortunately, his fears were amply justified, for on arriving at Jaffa Harriet recorded:

> This is Asia, we are a little frightened. There is a revolution in some parts close to here which may prevent our journey or render it very dangerous, not to Jerusalem, but afterwards to Damascus. However, we have some time before us and precaution may be taken by the time we are to start. Our tents are placed on a field of flowers and between fig trees, pomegranates, and large cactuses. There are many rocks before the town, and the sea dashes between them – such a new scene. Continual running in and out of our Consuls: French, Dutch, and Belgian. At last at five all went off except us, and then we took a quiet walk in the most beautiful orange garden I ever saw.[1]

After seeing Jaffa with the Dutch Consul 'a very handsome young Turk', the party of twelve people, including a janissary Harriet had engaged called Osman Aga, set off towards Jerusalem. They all rode horses, except Flora and another servant who went on donkeys, and Harriet on a chair carried by two mules. Four camels carried the luggage. It was a journey not easily to be forgotten, and as they moved off they rode in silence. Behind them lay the azure sea, along their path were avenues and gardens glittering with blossoms of orange, pomegranate, and fig trees. Along the wayside and in the fields was a mass of wild flowers: scabious, vetch, marigolds, daisies, sage, and thyme. The olive groves made a shady pathway for the cavalcade, and the tourists found the fresh atmosphere particularly welcome after the dry climate of Egypt.

The night was spent at a convent, and at seven the party set off again in the cool of the day, first going across a plain and then taking the mountain pass to Judaea. Although this was the usual route, there was no road, and the track often resembled the bed of a mountain stream; but between the stones grew a profusion of black lily, orchid, and iris. As the road gained height it became rougher, and at one stage Alexine's horse slipped and disappeared down a rocky gully, but luckily she was not hurt and the horse soon got up. The party did not reach Jersualem till later than planned, and it was necessary for them to pay to have the gate opened. That evening a declaration of peace was being celebrated following some local disturbance, and as they rode through the entrance they found the city lit up and crowded:

There were illuminations and fireworks in honour of the peace. We met the Governor with a procession of soldiers. It was like the time of the Crusades. Really and truly we are in the Holy City: the streets lit up with glass chandeliers looked old and wonderful. All the houses are built across the streets. We rode in this order: first a horseman, then my chair with two mules, the other horses, our two janissaries with silver sticks, then Mr. Van de Velde with his friend, Alexine with Mohammed, and Jan with Michael, and so we went to Max's Private Hotel.[2]

The next day was Good Friday, and Harriet and Alexine spent the morning exploring within the walled city. The city was full of pilgrims who had gathered for Easter, and Harriet and Alexine went on a tour of all the famous places accompanied by Osman Aga who preceded them everywhere they went carrying his silver stick which he frequently tapped to draw attention to his well-dressed charges. This merely annoyed Harriet, but with her limited

Summer in the Holy Land

vocabulary of Arabic she could not make him understand her disapproval.

On the afternoon of Good Friday they went to the Church of the Holy Sepulchre, built over the rock where Christ was crucified, to see the annual ceremony of the miracle of the Holy Fire. They were taken to the gallery, and saw the church become packed with people: on the right side were the Greeks, on the left the Armenians, and at the back the Copts. As the ladies waited and watched, the unruly mass became more and more excitable and impatient, until they eventually stampeded. Thus the ceremony of the so-called miracle, which really consisted of the Pasha's men placing flaming torches under the iron grating, proved to be a frightening experience:

The noise of all the men crying for the fire and stamping to make it come from the ground was like the yelling of so many fiends: it lasted for two hours. When the procession attempted to go three times round the Sepulchre, at the second turn of the Greeks the Armenians wanted to begin and a battle ensued. The Pasha then gave the signal, and to get first at the flames, which now issued forth from a hole in the floor, the people overturned each other and their screams were hideous.

Then the battle stopped for a moment only to begin again with double fury. Sticks and stones were hurled in a frightful and disgraceful way: soldiers were brought into the church to separate the combatants. The Pasha was hurt, pictures of Christ were torn, lamps broken, and the church presented a scene of horror.

All the fire was later put out but it was past three before the church was cleared enough for us to leave. Our tribune and our janissary behaved very well, and when there was an idea of our being stoned they placed themselves in front of us with their silver sticks. We brought home many relics. Another ceremony in the Church of the Holy Sepulchre tonight but we won't go.[3]

An expedition to Jericho and the Dead Sea took them three days. Harriet sat in a chair carried by two men, and the rest of the party went by horse or donkey. The road was very rough, and after some miles the chair came apart, and was left with one of the men to repair it, whilst Harriet continued by horse. The party had four lancers, who had been provided by the French Consul in Jersualem, though they evidently gave the Dutch party a feeling of aggression rather than protection. Fortunately, Harriet was quite unperturbed, and Alexine seemed to revel in the way these strange men dashed about on their excitable horses doing their lancers' fantasia, or, as she described it, 'leaping over ditches and firing pistols'. The cavalcade passed through Jericho where they found a few Arab huts on the site of the once-glorious city, and then arrived to find their three tents had been erected in the middle of a bedouin camp. In the evening they were entertained by dancers yelling and springing round with drawn sabres, whom they patiently applauded though they looked on in horror.

Next day they passed over a barren plain to reach the Dead Sea, and in the evening made their camp with mountains in the background, orange at the summit deepening to lilac near the water. Still headed by the four lancers, the cavalcade rode to the River Jordan, where they paused to rest:

> We remained till our friends warned us to go back. There was a tribe on the other side with whom they are at war. Apparently, our tribe had stolen and killed two men, so we left.[4]

'Friends', Harriet had written, and friends the lancers had become by the time they returned to Jerusalem, for they were the first visitors to call at their hotel with a present of camel's milk. They had never been inside a house before and much admired the furniture.

Though Harriet and Alexine had been in Jerusalem only seven days, when they went to the English Church they became aware how many people they had met. One afternoon they were invited by the English Consul to climb the Mount of Olives, and the party did not arrive back until after the city gate was closed, and they only had it opened for them on the assurance that they were the Harem Frangi, as they had become known in local parlance.

Within a few days they set off on a journey to Damascus, though there were setbacks on the eve of departure:

> The Master of the Mules came to say it was impossible to give us animals for our journey as Mr. Rothschild was crossing the desert to Damascus, and that the Pasha had recommended that Mr. R. should have the best. I was glad, but Mr. V. de V. did not take it so calmly. He went to the French Consul and complained.

Summer in the Holy Land 53

Alexine met two Dominican friars whilst at the French Consulate, and arranged for them to come in the same party. However, later in the day the Dominicans said they could not come for risk of not being back by Thursday, for that was Ascension Day, when every portable altar was to be taken to give services for the many pilgrims who would be assembling on the Mount of Olives.[5]

Harriet rode on a chair held between two mules, and since the animals never moved in unison she was terribly uncomfortable, besides enduring the fear that the chair – constantly racked – might fall apart again. They found little rest at night, for the guides always installed their tents in a bedouin camp where the noise of dogs barking, camels roaring, and children screaming, never seemed to stop. This was known to be a very dangerous route, and to dampen their morale, the weather became showery. As they rode through the drizzle along grassy plains and huge cornfields, they were held up by some farmers going to market who warned them of the dangers of assault by local bedouin. The best they could do was to continue, although the little cavalcade was too small to put up an effective defence should they be attacked. The party trotted on and, mounting a stony ascent near Nazareth, they saw four horsemen below, waiting by a fountain. Who were they? It was a sight to quicken the pulse as the horsemen were evidently looking out for them:

Half-way we were stopped by four fine-looking men who said they were the sons of the French Vice-Consul, and that Mr. de Lesseps* had written we were coming and they were to watch out for us. They led us to the home of their father, very Greek, their mother, and two of the sons' wives. We were given orange juice, pistachio nuts, and coffee. After this they took us to the place our tents had been pitched near the fountain from which the Virgin really did fetch water. It was here she and our Saviour lived for thirty years. Our dear friends were rather a bother as they came and sat quite late. They are to go with us everywhere they said![6]

They remained two nights and would have preferred to stay on, but chose to continue, as Harriet explained:

* Edmond Ferdinand de Lesseps, French Consul-General in Syria, son of Mathieu de Lesseps, and brother of Ferdinand de Lesseps, founder of the Suez Canal.

We left again by going up a hill and then down a plain. The last look at Nazareth was beautiful as it lay on the hill. I would like to have stayed a week if I had not had so many friends.

For the next part of the expedition to Damascus Alexine had got a bedouin sheikh to travel with them. The entire party were up at five, when a messenger came from the sheikh saying that he was delayed as his horse was being shod. However, they soon learnt that he would not start because it was a Friday, the Moslem day of rest. The remainder of the party started at sunset, and the sheikh and his men caught up with them just in time to avoid a disastrous encounter with some savage bedouin; but when he announced that Alexine was a French Princess, they were so surprised that they held back. Harriet described the incident in her diary:

On a bridge stood eight or ten armed bedouin to dispute our approach and I saw that in a moment we were to have a battle, but our Chief Ede said there was a French Princess and the French Consul's son, so after a little *pourparler* they went off. We had passed by two camps of black tents belonging to some men who came to offer their assistance in case of attack. We gave them coffee and thanks. There was great talk amongst our people. Some wanted to return for more guards but I preferred to trust to them we have. We spent the evening in the most beautiful spot, a romantic bridge with ruins and the river forming a natural cascade. The noise of the running water made me sleep beautifully.[7]

At the end of May the cavalcade entered Damascus, and Harriet and Alexine were pleased to get some post. However, news that Adolf Königsmark was waiting for them in Smyrna supposing they would be on their way back to the Netherlands, agitated them, and Harriet did not know how to reply to a letter from his mother.

During their stay they watched the annual caravan leave for Mecca. The whole town turned out at five in the morning to see some ten thousand men form up in a procession, headed by two troops of soldiers who led the Pasha, surrounded by his bodyguard. Many more soldiers followed, dressed in brightly-coloured uniforms. In contrast to the procession the women, watching from windows, balconies and roof-tops, all wore white.

They went to a fashionable Jewish wedding; and Harriet, who was familiar with luxurious entertaining, was quite overwhelmed:

Summer in the Holy Land

It seemed like a complete fairyland. There was a square with a beautiful marble pavement, and fountains playing shaded by large orange, lemon, and pomegranate trees. In the square more than a hundred men in the rich dresses of the oriental were walking about or sitting on divans of marble and mosaic. We passed through this and were shown into a salon full of the most splendidly dressed ladies I ever saw, their heads covered with jewels and flowers and their dresses of the gayest silks. The salon was finer than I know how to express and in each of the courts was a fountain surrounded by flowers. We were seated on a sofa, the seat of honour, next to the bridegroom. We had sherbert, coffee, and confections. After that there was dancing. Each time a new lady danced she took the hand of the Consul and mine and bowed to us when it was over.[8]

Alexine loved Damascus and was soon tempted to dress in local costume, and was amused when Harriet did not recognize her under a veil. While there was a full moon Harriet suggested leaving for Beirut, but confessed: 'Alexine seems rooted to this place and as I do not know what filthy hole awaits me I don't like to force her to go.' Poor Harriet often pondered over the unorthodox routine into which she had fallen. What was the relationship between mother and daughter so far away from their homeland and how did each view the other? Alexine was capricious, self-opinionated, and dominating, and her mother recognized character traits she herself had shown, but had been disciplined against as the eldest child of a large family. Alexine had known what she wanted since she was old enough to talk, and Harriet, enchanted by her child's pleading eyes, had always succumbed. Now Alexine was a young woman, and Harriet saw her behaving on occasions like a spoilt child, but she felt defenceless. Harriet felt defenceless? The people who knew Harriet would have doubted such an explanation, yet it was true; for Alexine had an even stronger will than her mother.

After four weeks, at the end of June, the ladies and their entourage left Damascus. It was only possible to travel in the early morning before the heat of the day became intolerable. Harriet had already anticipated the difficulties they would encounter and after travelling non-stop for two days experienced a night when:

The wind was so high we were obliged to place large stones on our tents to prevent them blowing away and slept in our clothes. I certainly do not admire Syria, and shall never wish to come again if and when I leave it![9]

Of course she never would have encountered such trials and tribulations but for Alexine's fanaticism for seeing strange places; and where Alexine chose to go she knew she must follow. Yet there were many compensations:

> One evening the sunset was superb and shone like an orange on the rich heaps of corn which covered this part of the plain. A large pool of clear water with hundreds of sheep, cows, donkeys, and camels drinking. High mountains covered with snow on every side as we are between the Lebanon and the Antelebanon, and soon a full moon increased the beauty of the scene.[10]

On their way back to Beirut they visited Baalbek, and were fortunate in meeting an energetic young Englishman who showed them around. Baalbek is a magnificent conglomeration of fallen temples, their massiveness second only to Karnak in Egypt. The fallen stone work blends into an impressive picture dominated by the clear blue sky and snow-capped mountains on the horizon, but in describing Baalbek one is invariably lost for words, and Harriet excused herself the trouble because 'all books on Syria mention it'.

Afterwards the party took a detour to reach the Cedars of Lebanon, climbing to a great height to reach snow, although it was mid-July:

> We mounted about 8,400 feet and then descended to a nook to see the cedars, a beautiful grove of three aisles containing 325 fine trees. People say there are 500 but several are very small and there are only twelve very large, old ones. They are wonderful. Some four feet in circumference. Most looking healthy and their spreading branches green against their rough trunks Many names are cut but I would not put ours. There are lots of people here and I think this place and Jerusalem are the best of all we have seen in Syria.[11]

The journey back to Beirut was arduous with more than the usual difficulties of rough roads and restless nights, but the exquisite scenery spurred them to keep going, and it was a

Summer in the Holy Land 57

thrilling moment when the sea burst into view. Owing to the heat of July they did not stay in Beirut but at a monastery called Sainte Roc on the outskirts of the city. Only four monks remained to greet the party, who arrived after dark and found the building illuminated, its white walls throwing mauve shadows in the lantern-light. Immediately the church bells began to ring out loudly, and a monk begged them first to enter the church in thanksgiving for their safe arrival.

Mr. Edmond de Lesseps, the French Consul-General in Beirut, of whom they had already heard so much, sent up 'a cargo of things to amuse us: maps, books, photographs, Chinese puzzles, blow pipes, pearls, and what not. Also a quantity of old *Times* but new to us as we have not seen a paper since Damascus.' New curtains and covers were bought in Beirut, but they did not need to hire much furniture as:

We still have our beds, stools and other articles of furniture belonging to our tents. Can't get nice stockings in Beirut, yet stockings I must have as all our trunks have not come. The town is really very handsome and one can find almost everything except baths, and we had great difficulty in getting a piano A. wishes to have.[12]

Yet somehow a piano was obtained and brought up to Sainte Roc carried by ten men, and a piano tuner followed. The days passed pleasantly, and Alexine enjoyed riding while her mother went for long walks. However, they were unable to forget they were living in a monastery, and on saints' days the bells rang out so loudly that they were nearly deafened by the noise. 'We were stunned,' commented Harriet, and one of the servants told her he would not mind becoming a Christian like her but for the bells!

Sainte Roc was an enchanting place to stay. On the one side it overlooked the sparkling Mediterranean, and behind stood the fine hills of the Lebanon. As autumn drew on into winter the mist cleared to show that the highest parts were covered with snow. In November they spent four weeks in Beirut. Here two large trunks were sent to their hotel. They had so much luggage already they could not remember where they had mislaid them, but decided it was probably Alexandria.

7
Second Nile Voyage

'How strange Egypt seemed even after Syria, so gay, so noisy, such a variety of people and things,' wrote Harriet in her diary. In Egypt, it seems, she and Alexine were happier than anywhere else, but in letters she explained that the need for a second Nile voyage was due to Alexine's health. Health of mind or body, one wonders, when one reflects that Alexine had set her heart on a second Nile voyage during the first.

Alexine had been impatient to leave Beirut, and they had almost started a week earlier on a boat which they knew had very poor accommodation. 'There is only a ladder of ropes to get into this ship. I cannot do this but Alexine is so unhappy that I will try,' wrote Harriet; but Mr. Edmond de Lesseps firmly put a stop to her endeavours, and forbade them to make reservations until a better ship came in.

Finally, they sailed to Alexandria in the middle of December. Christmas found them enjoying turkey, roast beef, plum pudding and mince pies at Shepheard's Hotel in Cairo. The typical pattern of life returned. One day Alexine would be suffering from some malady and Harriet would call the doctor to see her, and the next was spent trekking across the desert on donkeys not to return till dark. Various visits to friends were made; they were invited on to a Dutch frigate one starry evening, and, of course, did quantities of shopping. Alexine found a Hungarian tailor to make her two dresses, whilst Harriet found equipping the dahabiah, which she did in detail, took up all her shopping time. It seems that wherever they stayed they drew attention to themselves, so that the more ordinary run of society inquired of each other who the dashing ladies were, from where they had come, and where, where on earth were they going?

Before they left Cairo Harriet had written in her diary, 'Alexine's *beau rêve* is now to go to Khartoum', but they were to be

Second Nile Voyage

disappointed. They had been told that there was no chance of getting so far without a steamer, and none were available. Harriet had asked Mr. Ruyssenaers, the Dutch Consul-General in Alexandria, to hire a steamer on her behalf, which he said he was quite unable to do, although she was told there were about two hundred on the Nile. Mr. Ruyssenaers then recommended they should call on Linant Pasha, whom they already knew well, who might 'perhaps think of some other feasible tour'.

Mr. Linant de Bellefonds, who became Linant Pasha, was a Breton engineer who had been engaged as Minister of Public Works by Mohammed Ali to improve the irrigation of crops. He also played a vital part in negotiations over the Suez Canal, and had explored in the Sudan. As Mr. Ruyssenaers had perhaps predicted, Linant Pasha advised them against going to Khartoum as he evidently felt it was unsuitable. As an alternative, Alexine planned to go up the Nile to Asyut, and make a desert tour to the west.

The start of the second Nile voyage much resembled the excitement and activity of the first, but naturally they made good use of their experience. They decided they would like more space and therefore hire a bigger dahabiah. This meant that a larger crew was needed, and this time Harriet was determined to have control. Before sailing she told the dragoman to let the reis know she herself would give orders to the crew.

It was a particularly fine evening as the dahabiah cast anchor, and one which Alexine was to remember with nostalgia many years later; the gaiety of their first dinner on board attended by many friends, the atmosphere of peace on the river as the sun silently disappeared, the trees and houses thrown into purple shadows, and the last lingering lights playing on the distant pyramids. However, all was not ready. Invariably, the Egyptians left their final duties until the morrow, and they could not set sail until the provisions for the voyage were rowed out the next morning. They then set off, soon to discover to their intense pleasure that this dahabiah, which had an unusually large sail, passed every other craft except the steamers. Each day the wind changed; bitter cold and a north wind ballooning the sails alternated with bright sunshine and calm when the vessel came to a halt; days of despair, followed by days when 'we went like fun leaving all behind us!'

Arriving at Asyut, Harriet and Alexine sent for the Governor to help arrange an expedition on camels, but this was impossible owing to the danger of attack by one tribe of bedouin against another. They decided to wait until their return voyage, or make a desert tour from Aswan or Wadi Halfa, and continued hopefully upstream.

The river winds so wonderfully one sees the sun rise on the same side of the boat as we see him set, though of course we are going due south. Our boat is the best sailer on the Nile. We passed Lord Sligo which is considered a very good one and Lord Lennox, and as both Lords like fast sailing it was a triumph for us, and we had a bell put on top of the sail.[1]

At Keneh they received a call from Lord Sligo and Lord Lennox, who arranged a visit to the temple of Dendera, a massive ruin of astonishing size and beauty. The sunshine and gaiety of the local people enchanted everybody.

Next they stopped at Luxor where they were recognized by the donkey boys who reminded them of Alexine's first attempts to speak Arabic. They could not fail to be touched with such a warm welcome and to find so many friendly faces round them. In the evening the crew were given a whole roast sheep, there was music and dancing, and the reading of Arabic poems by the dragoman from a book of Alexine's. Once again they made inquiries about a desert tour but found it impossible to gain the co-operation of the local bedouin.

Five days later the dahabiah reached Aswan. On the far side of the river seven magnificent steamers were moored, the property of the Viceroy, their white and gold paintwork glimmering in the water's reflection. They were told that no camels were available 'for love or money', as they had all been taken over by the Viceroy. Alexine was very disappointed, but amused herself by taking the two felucca boys into the town to buy them white coats with coloured turbans and sashes.

To continue, it was necessary to pass the first cataract by the shore, and then change to another smaller boat for the next part of the voyage. Therefore, the day after arriving Harriet and Alexine made an early start to the village above the cataract, where they had been told there were dahabiahs for hire. They found one which looked ramshackle and dirty, but the owner assured them it would be clean and ready in two days, and a deal was made for £17. Meanwhile, there were expeditions in the felucca through the cataract to the glorious temple of Philae.

Before leaving Aswan they posted many letters, knowing there would be no reliable postal stations where they were going, and partly because they did not know where that would be. Changing boat was to prove a major exercise. From early morning there was a flurry of activity as five camels, ten donkeys, and a collection of small boys waited ashore to transport the luggage. This included furniture, bedding, pots and pans, and foodstuffs from live chickens to jam, and drinking water.

On arriving that evening the boat was found to be dirty. Harriet ordered everything to be scrubbed out and the crew to clean themselves up. All set to work, and presently the camels' loads were carried on deck, the furniture was put into place, clothes put into cupboards, books put on to shelves, and pictures hung on the walls. Harriet and Alexine worked together cutting out and sewing new curtains and cushion covers. All the crew slept in the open, Harriet and Flora had divans in the sitting-room, and Alexine slept on a divan at the end of the deck. It was not until a few days later that the reis showed Harriet the reference he had been given:

> Our reis showed me what he thought was a recommendation from an English family he had served before us, but the paper said the boat was dirty and dangerous, the reis stupid and everything so badly arranged that he warned others not to be taken in! The poor man was so angry he tore up the paper. I gave him one saying the boat, though old, was safe, the reis very pleasant and the crew ready and anxious to please, which is the truth.[2]

It took the party only a week to reach Wadi Halfa as they were favoured by a brisk northerly wind. The ladies found this part of the river much as they had expected, for in Cairo they had purchased two large volumes on the voyage of Maxime du Camp, with photographs taken during 1850 when he had sailed up to Wadi Halfa. They stopped to look over several temples, but were most excited to reach Abu Simbel, the massive temple dedicated to Rameses II, which overlooked the river and was cut out of solid rock. At this time, 1857, sand had silted some twenty-five feet high, covering part of the legs of the four vast statues of Rameses II; but it was still possible to get through the central entrance by crawling into the top of the doorway. Harriet, who was suffering badly from insect bites, decided she would not attempt the climb, but Alexine took Flora with her to explore the inside of the temple. They scrambled up the steep hill of sand and entered the doorway on all-fours to reach the lofty interior, and by lamplight saw the marvellous wall carvings which depict scenes of the successes in war and the prosperity in peace of Rameses II, who lived in the twelfth century B.C.

A day's more sailing and the boat arrived at Wadi Halfa. Again Alexine made widespread inquiries about hiring camels, but was told there were none to be had. They could go no farther by river owing to the second cataract, and reluctantly realized they had come to the turning point of the second Nile voyage. Before starting back they made an expedition to see the second cataract, riding along the riverside by donkey. Like the first cataract, this is caused by bars of hard rock crossing the path of the river, but the second cataract is utterly different. The rocks are grey and black, and the sand copper or brilliant orange according to the time of the day, making for dramatic colour. Yet the river seems melancholy.

Sadly, Harriet and Alexine turned back. The voyage from Cairo to Wadi Halfa had taken seven and a half weeks, including many stops; and they now took two weeks returning. They sailed to Aswan and changed into the large dahabiah which had been waiting; but before the next part of the voyage Alexine was tempted to spend another day at Philae where, her mother reports, 'she took some views'. It seems that Alexine had her camera amongst her luggage but did not often unpack it owing to the complications involved in processing photographs.

When they reached Luxor there was a heavy mist that made them feel quite nostalgic for their own country. Three pleasant days were spent sightseeing, and they saw Karnak again by moonlight. Following a long day out sketching they returned to be reminded it was Sunday:

Second Nile Voyage

On our return we saw on a height beside the town a tent pitched and all the English had been to church, each bringing his stool or chair, the service being performed by an American clergyman.[3]

The voyage back was very slow, and Alexine became listless and her mother unhappy to see her dissatisfied. There was a prevailing north wind and, to make matters worse the reis pointed out a gravestone:

Saw the grave of a poor man who had been detained here eleven days by the contrary wind and died here. I fear they will have to bury us here too![4]

They had planned to leave Alexandria for Beirut by a boat on 27th March, but were so delayed that they only arrived back in Cairo on that date.

8
Long way home to The Hague

In Cairo Harriet and Alexine found a great welcome. No doubt they had worried their friends with talk of going to Khartoum, or of making an expedition across the desert. Now they were back again amongst familiar faces but still feeling disappointed they had got no farther up the Nile. On returning to Shepheard's Hotel they were pleased to find letters awaiting them, as Harriet expressed it, 'from every part of the world'. Evidently many of their relations and friends were anxious and felt it was an opportune moment to press them to return home. This they now proceeded to do, but not directly or without event.

In mid-April they left Alexandria for Beirut. Seven months later they sailed on to Turkey via Cyprus and the Greek islands, then up the Adriatic to Italy, and made a final detour to Vienna. Besides taking back quantities of souvenirs they had collected, they had with them Halib the Egyptian cook, and Matruka, Alexine's tall, long-haired dog.

In Beirut they bought extensive equipment for camping, including tents, a china service, and a canteen of silver. They installed their camp outside Beirut before setting off to see Palmyra, for planning took six weeks of patience and determination.

The journey by horse, with camels for the baggage, took five days, and as there was no road, they had to navigate by the position of the sun. The weather did not remain fine for long and soon Harriet and Alexine were glad to find shelter from heavy rain under the vast umbrellas they had with them. They passed through several woods, where they were amused to see wild boars scuttle away. In her diary Harriet described their arrival:

> At four the ruin of Palmyra! The first sight was not satisfactory: it seemed like the chimneys of steam engines, so high. Then we saw a whole long street of towers, and farther on a mass of pillars, columns

and walks. The Sheikh came to welcome us and I gave him two cloaks, one of cloth and the other of silk. He invited us to his harem and went with us to the town which is all inside of what was the temple of the sun. Altogether we were very interested, but it was not to be compared with Baalbek or the least of the Egyptian temples. On the top is a fort and on it a sentinel stays day and night to warn the people to bring inside the wall any animals that may be in the fields in case of danger. We were walking under the colonnades when we were told in haste to go to our camp as there was a cavalcade in sight. All the animals were put away, but it was a false alarm! Some merchants going to Baghdad and wanting to buy camels. We did not go out of our garden after our fright but sat enjoying the trees.[1]

The party spent only twenty-four hours at Palmyra, but had time to explore the temples, tombs, and salt pits. There were frequent alarms which seemed to worry the bedouin more than the tourists:

We should like to stay here but our bedouin are so afraid they have begged us to go. It is unheard of to remain here more than twenty-four hours and all the neighbouring tribes are enemies. We had a good deal to pay but I don't regret it. We have seen what so few have seen, and have remained longer than any Europeans.[2]

On their way back there were further clashes with tribes of bedouin. Once, as the guides careered off towards some unknown horsemen, they shouted at Harriet to remain quiet and not to follow them. 'It would have been difficult!' was all she could comment.

For all the false alarms, one evening the cavalcade really *was* attacked when they passed by the camp of a tribe that had sworn vengeance against their camel driver, whom they accused of having stolen a little girl. A skirmish followed, swords were drawn as the horsemen dashed to save the camel driver, whilst women and children grabbed at the horses to deter them. Harriet and Alexine could take no part, only watch; but they were relieved nobody was killed before their cavalcade got away. Later that evening, a man arrived in the dusk and was caught spying on the ladies, but they discovered he had been sent by Mr. de Lesseps, who was worried because the party had been away so long.

It was the end of May by the time they returned to camp outside Beirut again, to find violets and roses flowering in profusion. After such an exhausting expedition it was hardly surprising that Alexine and Flora felt ill. Even Harriet became depressed and poorly. To make matters worse letters from Adolf and from his mother, Countess Königsmark, arrived. Harriet had again heard rumours that Adolf was awaiting them at Smyrna, and she asked Mr. Edmond de Lesseps's assistant to write and make inquiries. At all costs she and Alexine felt they must avoid him whatever the inconvenience to themselves. As if to fill in time they made many excursions, and during August went to Tripoli. They finally left Beirut in September. It was a sad farewell, and scores of friends came to see them off, many of whom they realized they would never see again. It happened to be a feast day and, as the little ship sailed away into the inky calm of the sea, many bonfires illuminated the hillsides.

A night's sailing brought them to Cyprus where they stopped to unload cargo, and in another two days they reached the island of Rhodes. After being pestered by mosquitoes and gnats in their cabin they were thankful to arrive at Smyrna. It took two boats to bring the party and their luggage ashore, and mother and daughter were met by some friends they had made in Alexandria, and lavishly entertained during the next week. They went to a banquet to celebrate the new railway; this was attended by the Pasha and followed by fireworks. Looking at the wonderful variety of costumes they felt that they were dreaming; and referring to the people they had met Harriet commented: 'It is not possible to be kinder than these ladies were to us.'

Harriet and Alexine then took a boat to Istanbul, sailing through the Aegean Sea by way of the Dardanelles and Gallipoli, into the Sea of Marmara. Harriet told the captain how disappointed she was they would not be arriving by day to see the famous view of Istanbul, but he assured her he was in no hurry and offered to delay their arrival. They had some Dutch friends in Istanbul and soon they all set off to watch the Sultan arrive at his mosque:

At twelve he arrived on horseback, riding very slowly, attended by his Ministers and General and many men on foot. A great many horses finely harnessed, wearing saddles and bridles covered with pearls and diamonds, were led before him. He noticed us immediately and fixed his eyes on us, but did not bow or take any notice. The gentlemen of our party took off their hats.

They explored the town enthusiastically and were invited to many parties and receptions, and on Sunday went to church in the British Embassy. They were very impressed by the magnificent carriages of ladies attended by black slaves, but noted the women did not veil their faces as heavily as those they had seen in Egypt and Syria. By the time they were due to leave they had seen the Sultan several times, and 'he seems to recognize us', commented Harriet in her diary.

From Istanbul they took a steamer to Athens. Arriving early in the morning they at once hired a carriage and had seen much by breakfast time, and at the end of the day Harriet was to record: 'I think we have seen all Athens. Drunk of tiredness!' They then returned to Smyrna by boat, and decided to sleep on board until another steamer arrived to take them to Trieste. Did they purposely not go to a hotel to avoid meeting Adolf, who they had heard had come out to Smyrna to meet them? As if to make sure they would not see him, they only took a brief walk into the town. Returning, however, they were met by the captain who said a gentleman had called and left his name. They were both horrified, but the captain told them Adolf had come armed with a circular signed by the head of Lloyd's shipping in Smyrna, allowing him access to every boat in the service. He dared not offend such an honoured person, it was more than his name was worth. In sheer desperation Harriet explained who Adolf was and why they must avoid him at all costs, but it was of no avail:

Having talked out every means of escape in vain we locked ourselves up, but Adolf contrived to find us and burst into our cabin. I need not repeat the scene he made, all his tears and his words. I told him I did not wish to travel with him and would leave him to choose where he would go and we would do the reverse. That was no use. Whatever we did *he* would do: wherever we went he would go, so as our plans were made we followed them.

When the steamer for Trieste came in the ladies hastily moved into it, and locked themselves in again. Alexine resolutely refused to leave the cabin, and Harriet soon discovered that Adolf was pacing the deck in his efforts to corner Alexine. Two days later the ship stopped at Corfu, but for once they did not go ashore. Adolf managed to get into conversation with Halib and poured out his story, but with no success. After a very tedious voyage the steamer arrived at Trieste. She had rolled all the way up the Adriatic and docked in a thunderstorm. As Harriet unlatched the door, Adolf broke in:

I had a long talk with K begging him to leave us, which he at last promised to do if we would allow him to see us again in Vienna which, as I could not prevent, I condescended to do to get rid of him!

Having arrived by train in Vienna, Adolf followed them to their hotel and again begged Harriet to let him see Alexine, but without success. They spent four days in Vienna, saw the royal stables and royal jewels, visited the palaces of Schönbrun and Belvedere, and enjoyed the company of a young Englishman they met. In an effort to evade Adolf they got up at five to catch the train to Prague, but on their arrival they found him at the station ready with a carriage. After the twelve-hour journey they had no energy to escape him:

He had ordered rooms and a nice dinner at the Blue Star Hotel. What could we do but what he pleased!

Three days were spent seeing Prague, and they then left for Dresden by the beautiful route along the Elbe. At Dresden, Adolf's home town, with Teutonic persistency he again approached them, and begged to go in the same carriage for the rest of the journey to The Hague. Harriet refused, but allowed him to dine with them on the last evening. For all his faults, and though he had been so tiresome, she and Alexine felt distraught, for 'the parting was horrid, he seemed heart-broken'.*

After Dresden, they only wanted to get home, spending two quiet nights at hotels on the way, and once staying in bed until eleven, an unprecedented occasion. They arrived in Amsterdam too late to get a connection to The Hague, and spent the last

* On 1st March 1863 Adolf Königsmark married Elizabeth von Kleist, by whom he had four children.

View taken by Alexine from 32 Lange Voorhout, c. 1860 with the carriage darkened so that she could process her photographs on the spot

Pen drawing of Sudanese tukuls by Alexine

night of their journey there. When Harriet completed the final page of her diary they were installed again at 32 Lange Voorhout:

> Sent for Mr. Van de Velde who was enchanted to see us again. After that I went to pay Christine Gülcher a visit. It is not possible to express the sensation Halib and Matruka made. There was such a crowd the police were obliged to come and keep order.
>
> For dinner we were at home in The Hague. I never saw my nice house with so much pleasure. Alexine and I enjoyed everything, so comfortable, so clean, so our own. We only grieve we must go to England before the winter to settle with John. Oh, our dear, sweet house. There is truth in the old song, 'There's no place like home.' I hope never to leave it again, not an unreasonable wish at my time of life.[4]

The day Harriet and Alexine got home was 6th November 1857. In the summer of 1861 they set out for their third Nile voyage, but before that they visited Liverpool and Paris more than once, and went to Germany and Poland in 1858, and Baden-Baden in 1859 and 1860.

PART THREE
The Sudan

9
Preparations for the Third Nile Voyage

In July 1860 Harriet and Alexine again started preparations for leaving their comfortable home in The Hague for another journey to Egypt. This time, however, Alexine had decided to get further than they had been before, and gradually Harriet had been persuaded to submit to a journey that appeared to lie eternally before her, to leave her relations, her friends, and her home for the thrills of exploring unknown lands.

So now they were going. Assuring her many brothers and sisters that all would be straightforward if it were planned, Harriet generously invited her sister, Adriana, to join herself and Alexine. Somewhat surprisingly, Addy accepted, for she was going through a difficult period. She was now forty-eight and was still love-sick from an affair she had had some time before in Russia, and the haunting memory of happy times which now seemed so far away, as indeed they were, was still intense. Addy had been beautiful in her youth and was elegant and serene now, only overshadowed by a melancholia that embarrassed her relations in the presence of friends, for it was a sadness she could not cast off, a profound grief that never left her even when others around were cheerful.

Addy was tall and slim and, like the other Van Capellens, she had a large face with a somewhat heavy chin. Her features were good, her eyes, skin and hair were beautiful, and because she was so tall she stood out amongst the other ladies of The Hague, though she held herself aloof and confided in few. Love-affairs never can be traced exactly, but it is certain that Addy's was a fascinating one, and the history of this hidden romance would be more interesting, even today, if it were possible to verify it.

She was born in 1812, the sixth child of Vice-Admiral Jonkheer Van Capellen and his wife. She was fourteen years younger than her eldest sister, Harriet, and though Sara, the third sister of the family, was chosen as Lady-in-Waiting to Queen Sophia, the reigning Queen of the Netherlands, the younger sister Addy was chosen to be Lady-in-Waiting to the Queen Mother, Queen Anna Paulowna. Queen Anna Paulowna was a sister of Tsar Alexander I of Russia. She married King William II of the Netherlands, but returned to her native Russia more than once after her marriage. With her she once took Addy, the attractive Jonkhouwe Van Capellen, a quiet, reliable person, as her Lady-in-Waiting. Addy took an immediate liking to life in Russia for she had been brought up to formality, and her striking height and pleasant smile led her to be popular amongst the Court set. She often met the reigning Tsar, Alexander II, nephew of Queen Anna Paulowna. There is little doubt that he, who had been educated for leadership with a rigorous upbringing, and she, reserved but intelligent, soon found they liked to share each other's company. Alexander, tired of the German princess he had married and who had loyally borne him seven children, wanted an intimate association. But the friendship was terminated by Addy.

Later Alexander focused his affection on another young woman, whom after many years he married. Addy returned to Europe with certain presents she had received from the Tsar and memories of Russia that were to haunt her for the rest of her life. About this time she gave up her position as Lady-in-Waiting. The reasons for her resignation were open to doubt, but in 1864, shortly before she died, she wrote a note to Alexine mentioning this decision which had weighed so heavily on her mind:

> When I threw up my position I had the approval of *all* those who heard my *reasons*, and they admitted that I could not sacrifice so much to my dignity, and they thought as well as I did that I was doing right.[1]

Harriet, realizing that Addy was unhappy, offered to take her to Egypt in the genuine hope that she would enjoy the change but, from the beginning, it was not a success. Addy was used to high-class living and, unlike Harriet, she could not adapt herself to the discomforts of travel.

Although Harriet was sixty-three (though she liked to keep her age secret) she was still as excited as ever with the anticipation of travelling somewhere new and unknown, and this time Alexine

Preparations for the Third Nile Voyage

was indulging in an expedition to Khartoum and up the Blue Nile to the little-known interior of Ethiopia. Already she had studied the account of the travels of James Bruce, the Scottish explorer *Travels to Discover the Source of the Nile in the Years 1768–73* which although widely read was seldom believed. Years later it was proved that many of his experiences which read like fiction were, in fact, absolutely true. Some doubts have been raised about the exploits of our bravest explorers, and Alexine, who is worthy of being placed in this category, has had her full share written by those who speculate without checking the facts.

The Tinnes' friends in the Netherlands, and many outside that circle, were full of chatter about the new expedition. They did not seem to trouble about the real problems that silently worried Harriet and Alexine, such as the heat of the tropics, their provisions, equipment, and safety amongst unknown people. Rather, society talked because the ladies were going off completely unescorted. It was shocking to hear they were again going to Egypt alone, and as for travelling to the Sudan and Ethiopia! Bothered by such tiresome comments, and aware that more was said behind their backs than was actually addressed to them, they were thankful when the departure date was finally fixed.

Alexine had decided to go by ship from Amsterdam to Marseilles where she would meet her mother and Addy who were to travel by train. On 20th July 1861 Harriet saw her daughter off at Amsterdam. After certain negotiations the entire first-class section of a small ship had been engaged solely for her party, which included three Dutch servants, Halib the Egyptian cook, three dogs, and the party's thirty-six pieces of luggage. It was a sad parting on a beautiful evening, for the yacht club fête was on and the water full of illuminated boats and reflecting their coloured lights. The scene was very gay and music could be heard in the distance. After seeing Alexine on deck Harriet sat alone in the big carriage that had conveyed the party from The Hague, and as the ship pulled away she had the carriage moved to get a better view. As she lost sight of the vessel she was seized with loneliness at the prospect that lay before her. She hated leaving Alexine; and though she would be meeting her at Marseilles in a fortnight, the fact that they were off on another long escapade preyed on her mind, for now there could be no turning back.

Returning to The Hague the house seemed deserted and desolate, but fortunately the next days were fully occupied when friends finally came to make their farewells. Amongst them the Queen called and invited Harriet to join the royal party for dinner on her last evening. It was held at the 'House in the Wood', the residence the Queen preferred for unofficial entertaining.

On the way to Marseilles Harriet met her stepson and his wife, John and Margaret Tinne, in Paris, where they spent a few enjoyable days sight-seeing and dining at the best restaurants. She and Addy then took the night train to Lyons and, passing through the beautiful Rhône country, reached Marseilles in the afternoon.

Harriet was relieved to see Alexine again. The party had had a good voyage, and it was soon decided to again reserve the entire first-class section of a merchant ship sailing for Alexandria via Malta. They left Marseilles on 10th August; the sea was calm and their first stop was Leghorn. Here, Alexine took the opportunity of an afternoon trip to Pisa. Sailing on they reached Malta the following day. The blazing heat did not keep the ladies idle, and they took a little boat round the island ('it seemed all rock') and a walk in the town where:

> The houses and streets all seemed to be of the same white stone, and the people were of all nations and in their national dresses. Soldiers of the English garrison in their white uniforms stood out in the crowds.[2]

A further voyage of two days brought them to Alexandria, where they noticed the city had been tidied up and improved since they were last there. Two days later they left for Cairo by train. Here they had reserved rooms at Shepheard's, but since they would not be starting their voyage until January, they proposed to rent a house in the meanwhile. They employed a dragoman to help them select one and after seeing several were delighted to find their ideal, situated just outside Cairo. Before moving in they had to wait for their beds and bedding and canteens of silver and china to arrive from Alexandria. Alexine had brought her music with her and now arranged for a piano to be installed.

The visitors lived lavishly and expensively. They hired twelve camels to move their luggage, a horse for Alexine to ride, and three donkeys so that the servants could do commissions and bring back the provisions. They already had Halib, and now engaged an under-cook, a boy to clean, another to attend the donkeys, and a sice or groom for Alexine's horse. In addition there were two gardeners and a guard to keep off marauders. As well as Flora, Alexine had a lady's maid called Anna, and there were two men servants, Sacker and Hendrik. 'I think we shall be pretty comfortable,' Harriet wrote back after mustering this small army of servants.

Alexine rode most afternoons, except on Sundays when she gave her sice, Mustafa, a day off and she and her mother would take a walk. When she rode, Mustafa ran alongside her dressed in a yellow and red striped satin shirt, white trousers, an embroidered waistcoat, and a loose blue and white cotton coat fastened at the shoulders with silver buttons and girdled by a black cord with silver tassels. Yellow shoes and a yellow tarboosh with matching silk turban completed his outfit. Alexine herself had a taste for the dramatic when it came to dressing up. Apparently, she wore a large feather in her hat, a flowing black skirt, and a shirt of stiff white cotton. One can imagine her trotting briskly on her Arab horse with the elderly sice chasing after her in an effort both to keep up and maintain his personal dignity. Harriet discovered, to her amusement, that her daughter was referred to as 'La Reine de Naples'.

The first greeting visitors got on reaching the house was from the dogs, and the canine family of three which had come from The Hague was soon enlarged by a couple of puppies found abandoned. When Hendrik, who had been brought to look after the dogs, complained in dismay of increased work, Harriet tactfully solved the problem by offering to pay him an extra £1 a month if he would care for the puppies.

Wherever they went the ladies found themselves amongst friends. Delightful hostesses, always ready with lively conversation, full of tremendous *joie de vivre* and good humour, Alexine and her mother were immensely popular whatever the occasion. They had almost no inhibitions and no barriers to friendship, an ideal seldom met a hundred years ago, for they mixed naturally with people of all nations and races. 'We thought we should be here quite alone, quite unknown,' wrote Harriet in her diary, as the callers seemed to appear from nowhere. For the Dutch ladies to remain unknown anywhere, when Alexine was for ever dashing around and making inquiries about all the curious new things she came across, and Harriet was famed for her charm and hospitality, was impossible.

Indeed, during their stay, they came across most of the eminent people living in Cairo. They met Mr. Ferdinand de Lesseps,* to whom they had previously been introduced, and who now suggested they should take a train to Suez to see the canal being built under his administration.

As usual, the most frequent visitors were the Linant de Bellefonds, the Beeton family of five sons and a daughter. Before the second Nile voyage Alexine had asked Linant Pasha whether it was possible to get to Khartoum and he had strongly advised her and her mother against such an idea. Now the same questions were asked, 'but he did not encourage us to go. He said the climate was very unhealthy and many such things, though this did not move Alexine'.

They hoped for better news from Mr. Gilbert, since he had just returned from serving as English Consul in Ethiopia, but he was no more encouraging:

He knew all the places we wanted to visit, but was quite of the opinion *we* could not go beyond Egypt.

Dr. Suquet, who also knew Ethiopia well, was equally disillusioning:

We received him and with pleasure, firstly as we had heard so much of this great Abyssinian traveller, and secondly as we expected him to clear away every difficulty. . . . He had been in Abyssinia for ten years but he strongly advised us not to attempt it. He said for women the country was unsafe, impossible. He even *tried* to frighten us about Khartoum. This made Ali angry without changing her intention. It was altogether a visit quite the reverse from what we had hoped.[3]

Dr. Krapf, a German Protestant missionary, gave the ladies kinder advice. He was the first European to record having seen both Kilimanjaro and Mount Kenya, the two vast snow-capped mountains that lay near the Equator, and from where many suspected the true source of the Nile to be. Since he was the sole

* Ferdinand de Lesseps, founder of the Suez Canal, son of Mathieu de Lesseps, and brother of Edmond de Lesseps, previously French Consul-General in Syria.

Preparations for the Third Nile Voyage 79

expert who had approved of Alexine and her mother going to Khartoum and beyond, his suggestions were enthusiastically taken up:

Dr. Krapf talked a deal with Alexine about a place to remain for the summer. He spoke of Gondar, the capital of Abyssinia, as a healthy place, the King Theodore as a friend of his to whom he would give us introductions, and afterwards we had quite arranged in our minds to go to Khartoum according to the journal he gave us.[4]

It appeared that if they set off promptly they could travel during the months of January, February, and March, and spend the rainy season between April and September at Gondar. It sounded quite satisfactory, but many problems still lay in their way. At last a decision was made to go to Khartoum and reside there for a little before making further plans.

Since leaving The Hague there had been many expenses, and now Harriet considered it necessary to write for a transfer of a second £1,000. In particular Alexine had been extravagant in buying a horse, and a white donkey which alone had cost £70. Harriet had arranged to have money transferred to the Bank of Egypt in Cairo. Now it was realized that money would be needed if they stayed in the Sudan, and finally arrangements were made, and Harriet noted in her diary:

They have given me £200 in gold, £90 in silver dollars, a banker's note for £200 for a house in Khartoum, and a credit for £500 more. These two last sums at 10%. I have written for a second £1,000 from Glyns and have besides transferred Fl. 10,000 to the Bank of Egypt from the bank in The Hague. I hope this will take me as far as Khartoum, but really money flies so fast there is no keeping account. Halib has spent between provisions for the boat and for the desert, tents, camels, saddles, and a hundred nameless articles more than £400.[5]

The day for departure was drawing near and Harriet had been advised to travel with a janissary to the Sudan. Linant Pasha pressed her to take one of his sons, but instead she re-engaged Osman Aga, who had been with her in the Holy Land, and now became *vakeel* and leader of her entourage of servants. She also obtained a Firman, a passport as it were, from Said Pasha through Mr. Ruyssenaers, the Dutch Consul-General in Alexandria.

Whilst Harriet and Alexine were busy making plans, Addy was beginning to wish she had never come. She could not decide whether to continue or not, and Harriet did not like to press her. In the end, however, rather to everyone's surprise, she chose to travel with her sister and niece. As their departure drew nearer the luggage was packed up and Harriet wrote in her diary of the last day in Cairo:

It is getting very uncomfortable. All our books are packed up, all the furniture we did not find in the house gone and planks we had placed turned into extra boxes. This is our last night and Alexine played some tunes we may perhaps never hear again. Everything is sad for the last, but it is a good time to leave the country without regret: so many lifeless trees, all the oranges picked, and the morning and evening really cold.

Cairo to Khartoum in four months

We are in three boats: us, the Europeans, Halib, and the two Arab domestics in one; the horse, the donkey, the canopy and part of the baggage in another, and the big baggage in the third with our guards. The first boat contains five dogs, two canteens and provisions for a year![1]

Thus Harriet briefly described the three boats in a letter home, never hinting at the endless confusion and complications which in reality took place. Whilst in Cairo she had tried to hire a steamer with the help of the Austrian Consul, but the few were in great demand and none were to be had at any price. The three boats were to sail under the Dutch flag and to proceed in line. The hour for starting was fixed for noon on 14th January.

This was the third time Harriet and Alexine had been up the Nile and it might be presupposed that the journey would be uneventful, but this was certainly not the case. They were delayed in leaving Cairo, because the decks were crammed with their friends and acquaintances who had come to wish them farewell, and then found difficulty in getting off the dahabiah owing to the crush. When the flotilla eventually set sail some of the servants were still shopping and had to be picked up at the first village, and it was then discovered that the dahabiah was leaking and a vast amount of provisions had already been spoilt. It was necessary to put all ashore, and a shipwright and the reis spent the night repairing the damage.

Several dahabiahs had left Cairo on the same day, and it was not long before they were on friendly, if internationally competitive, terms with these others which were constantly changing place. Although Harriet realized the prestige involved in keeping in front, and gave the reis a tip to stay ahead, she did not enjoy the unsteady motion; and an elderly lady on the German dahabiah whom she spoke to, agreed she felt likewise. She and her husband, she said, were travelling 'for health'. The English boat was also full of invalids sunning themselves. There were seven people on board who were cutting expenses by having no dragoman, but, commented Harriet: 'They seemed to make out pretty well, this sailing hospital!'

Evidently when sailing the Nile in a dahabiah, travellers were well aware of the craft near by, and it was easy to observe all that was going on on board, so that the very familiarity of seeing each other brought the passengers together. There were also the Scandinavian and the Sardinian boats, the Russian, and two Italian ones. The Russian dahabiah was the one that the Dutch saw most often, but they had little or no communication with it – even though, whenever it passed, it fired off a gun in warning reminding them of a traffic horn. All the dahabiahs except the Dutch and the smaller Italian one were only going as far as Aswan. Evidently the fact that the Dutch were going to the Sudan was big news to the others, and Harriet discovered that Alexine had been nicknamed 'La Reine de l'Equateur'. At Luxor, twenty days after leaving Cairo, the Russians' curiosity got the better of their aloofness and they introduced themselves.

After seeing Luxor and the surrounding area, for three days the Dutch flotilla continued upstream. When there was a wind they sailed, otherwise they were towed, occasionally experiencing the inevitable difficulties of being stranded on sandbanks and getting afloat again. Other delays were caused by stopping to bake bread (it seemed to Harriet that the more provisions she gave the crew, the more they ate), and by taking the dogs ashore several times each day. Once they lost sight of the luggage boat, but it caught up after two days.

By the time they reached Aswan the travellers, though of differing nationalities, had come to know each other. All the way along the crew on the Russian dahabiah had taken a dislike to the Dutch second boat which contained the animals. At Aswan tempers reached boiling-point because the Russian dahabiah moored between the Dutch boats, and Halib and Osman Aga went off to the Divan to demand formal apology from the Russian. This being unsuccessful, Alexine gathered all the men concerned together in the evening and, speaking in Arabic, told them to end their quarrels. They applauded her speech and caused no more troubles. Most of the tourists had been through difficulties with their crews, and the Sardinian boat had several of their sailors left behind and imprisoned, but this did not appear to worry the remainder. Passengers, servants, and crews had by now found friends, and for the smaller dahabiah of the Italians and the three Dutch boats that were continuing, it was a sad parting. However, they were soon preoccupied with their future plans.

The first cataract is now obliterated by the Aswan Dam built at the turn of the century. Before, about four miles of the river was scattered with rocks and boulders of all dimensions, and only with the greatest skill and with the strength of scores of men to tow them, could boats be pulled up the rapids. First, most of the luggage and the animals were taken out to lighten the boats. Then camels had to be obtained to transport the load to above the cataract. The hauling of the boats through the cataracts was a terrifying manœuvre which took two days and is best described by Harriet:

> I must say I have never seen anything so awful as this passing the cataract, not the Rhine at Schaffhausen nor the fiords in Norway are to be compared to the difficulties of pulling a ship between the rocks against a very strong current. The screams of the men hired to help and a violent north wind all seemed to increase the danger. We could only get over one rapid and then we were obliged to stop for the night below the village of the cataract, as it is called. All the men went home and we seemed deserted by the world though we are but a couple of miles from Aswan.[2]

The next three rapids were passed through the following day, but so powerful was the current of the river it was a near miracle that the boats were not smashed to pieces. The drama of the episode was again portrayed by Harriet:

> There was more wind than yesterday, and though the ship did pass without injury, still there was one moment, when going full sail she was nearly crashed to a rock and even Alexine *owned* she was afraid. The first day there were too few men but today I think there were too many, certainly more than two hundred. We all sat on the rocks unconscious

of the danger till near six o'clock, and I was burnt to a cinder. A French party who had come on dromedaries to Philae saw from a high point the operation of the ship passing and ran to see it in wonder. I was glad when we lay to at Philae though the wind was still a storm.³

Alexine, alone with the crew, had chosen to stay on the dahabiah whilst it was traversing the cataract, accompanied by her favourite dog, Matruka. Immediately on arriving at Philae she told her mother she wanted to see the famous dancing girls, and a messenger was sent to fetch them. As it was already late and there were many tourists, it seemed unlikely they would come, but at ten they arrived. The wind was still blowing so fiercely that they could not cross the river, and arranged to dance in the temple of Philae which is situated on an island and was nearer their shore. It was a clear, moonlight evening and probably not the first time the dancers had performed in the temple, for within a few minutes they had improvised a stage. Lanterns were placed on the walls, carpets on the floor, chairs for the spectators and a curtain erected. Then followed an unforgettable display of gaiety and laughter and the dancers performed until two o'clock, by which time the audience were tired out after their strenuous day. Following this entertainment Harriet wrote in her diary:

I must say Alexine's spree succeeded in a way few sprees do. Everybody seemed pleased. One of the sailors said he was sure we should go to Heaven because we amused the people so much!"⁴

The flotilla then sailed on for three days to reach Korosko. It was at this point that the expedition left the boats behind and cut across the great U-bend of the Nile to reach the river again at Abu Hamad. This desert crossing between Korosko and Abu Hamad was the route usually taken by travellers going to Khartoum, for it was about one-third of the distance of the river. Besides, the innumerable cataracts and rapids made navigation virtually impossible on this part of the Nile. The region of the Nubian desert traversed by the caravan routes came under the rule of the Ababdeh tribe, and all travellers were asked to pay certain fees for the privilege of crossing their land. Whilst in Cairo Harriet and Alexine had been given letters of introduction to the Sheikh of the Ababdeh tribe by Mr. Ferdinand de Lesseps

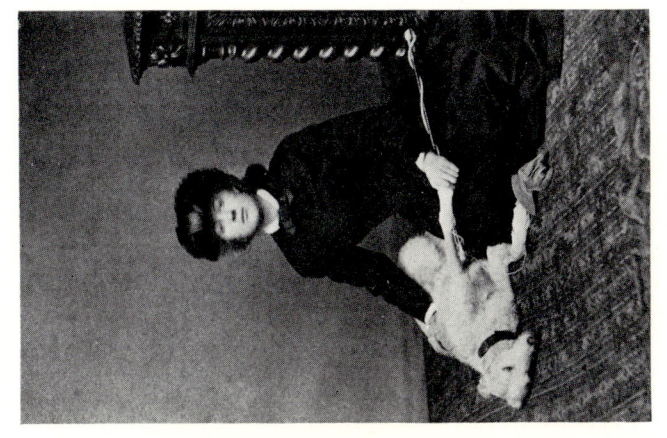
Alexine with one of her dogs

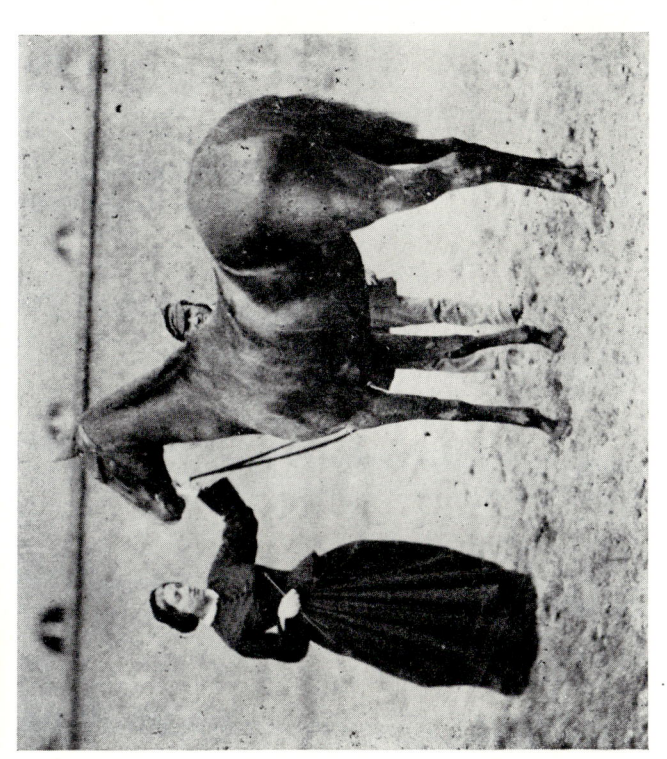
Alexine in Cairo

John Tinne, Alexine's half-brother

Cairo to Khartoum in four months

and Mr. Linant de Bellefonds, who had both travelled with the Viceroy to Khartoum in 1856.

Korosko was more than half the way from Cairo to Khartoum. The expedition so far had taken five weeks and was to take another seven weeks before arriving in Khartoum. Looking back they were reminded of the friendly tourists who would by now be on their way back to Cairo from Aswan, of the dahabiah and its comforts; and of the cooling breezes of the Nile. They were well aware that the severest part of the journey was about to begin. Meanwhile, Halib ordered the six tents they had brought from The Hague to be unpacked and erected, and transferred the smallest Dutch flag from the boats to the top of Harriet's tent.

The immense quantity of provisions had to be taken off the boats and divided into individual camel-loads. In addition to the luggage there were the horse and donkeys and the five dogs. After much organization the expedition was at last ready on 25th February to set off across the desert and into the Sudan, but not before Alexine had recorded that the departure time seemed a simile of her death hour:

> There are so many things to do at the last moment and one is always taken by surprise when the last day comes![5]

Harriet, Addy, and Alexine breakfasted before daybreak, but it was two o'clock before the camels were packed up and everybody was prepared to set off. It seems that Alexine alone was complacent enough to observe the scene of the huge caravan, with her mother and Addy riding camels, and the vast quantity of belongings they were transporting to Khartoum. In a lively letter she described the departure to her cousin, Yetty:

> Vous pensez, vous imaginez que la scène et quel départ! L'horreur et les cries de Tante Addy. Mama et Hendrik perchés sur les dromadaires, l'étonnement et les cries, non moins violents, des cinq chiens chargés dans leur niches sur les chameaux.[6]

The five dogs they took were carried in panniers, as were six sheep, several cages of fowls and turkeys for consumption on the journey, many crates of eggs and vast quantities of bread, biscuits, and flour. In addition, one of the heaviest items was the drinking water which was carried in goatskins.

Considering that the caravan was so numerous, it was hardly surprising that the departure was noisy and disorderly. As for Harriet, she admitted she only 'saw what we had' on the second day of the journey, when she rightly commented 'we have a large family', though typically the size of the entourage she had collected did not worry her unduly. The caravan consisted of 102 camels, 6 guides, and 30 camelmen, though the number fluctuated as the journey progressed. Two of the camels had their young moving alongside them. The servants included the two lady's maids, Flora and Anna; the courier and valet, Sacker and Hendrik; the vakeel, Osman Aga; Alexine's sice, Mustafa; the head cook, Halib, and two assistant cooks; and at least three other Egyptian servants of lesser importance. In addition several sailors attached themselves to the cavalcade, and of these three travelled all the way to Khartoum. In charge of the entire caravan was the magnificent Sheikh Ahmad, a very distinguished young Nubian who, over the years, escorted many important people over the Korkosko to Abu Hamad crossing. By 1862, he had evidently already cultivated a diplomatic code of behaviour, for after meeting him Harriet commented:

He is black as coals, not the blue Negro black but a rich, glowing black with the most intelligent face possible, a fine nose, and a pretty mouth with a well-trimmed beard and moustache. He talked with all like a gentleman and his manners were above par.

The first day the expedition rode for only an hour. Although the caravan had not covered much ground the ride fulfilled a practical purpose: to see what was still needed whilst there was still time to go back! After this they started a routine of setting off at eight or nine and travelling without stopping until around four, when they would arrange the camp for the night. The route passed amongst jagged, black rocks with strange conical peaks rising steeply to great heights, and along valleys full of herbage. This was a newer road than the one more generally used, but pleasanter since the old road was littered every few yards with remains of dead camels.

The ladies were travelling with their bedding as well as beds and camping equipment, and now it came in useful during the day as well as the night, for Addy was packed on her camel between cushions and mattresses. When first tried, this unorthodox idea was such a success that Addy arrived 'almost fresh' and bravely proclaimed she preferred camel to horse; but after a few days she became pathetically weary, and only forced her frail body to continue the rigorous journey because she had to, for at this stage there could be no turning back. Indeed, after only three days on camel-back in the scorching sun several of the Europeans were becoming desperately tired:

> Everybody was very tired except Alexine. Poor Addy quite done up, Anna in a jelly, Sacker broken-backed, and the worst is so little sleep, but the cool evenings are a great pleasure. One knows that after the day's work one can feel refreshed.

Soon Harriet chose to ride the white donkey but the rest of the expedition continued to ride camels. To aid her little steed she would start off an hour before the main caravan, so she could give him a rest in the middle of the day. As she went ahead of the others she arrived at the baksheesh stages before them. Sheikh Ahmad had told her that there were five of these places where fees would be demanded, but forgot to warn her when she would be approaching the first. One morning she was making her way quietly on the donkey accompanied only by a sailor, when suddenly from behind rocks some bedouin rushed at her with drawn sabres demanding their fees. Harriet was momentarily taken aback, but characteristically coped with the situation confidently. Sheikh Ahmad had stated the amount would be ten florins, but here the bedouin put on an entertainment with a dance and a dervish, and charged her thirty-five florins because, they explained, there were so many in the caravan. Indeed, there were! She noted that the caravan that had set off from Korosko had grown to twice the original size, but she did not let such matters worry her and was pleased to pay what was asked.

A week later she was riding ahead of the caravan when:

> Half-way and in the boiling sun was the second baksheesh place. I asked to wait till we came to some shade, so the Arabs stuck spears in the ground, spread a scarf over them, and I sat under it to see them dance, and when the rest came up I gave them £2 which it seems satisfied them as they were very grateful.

At the same time as her mother was keeping in front of the

caravan for safety, Alexine was acquiring the dangerous habit of dropping behind. One day she and Halib did not catch up with the expedition until more than an hour after halting, and Sheikh Ahmad became agitated and remonstrated with her because he knew there were many hostile bedouin lurking near the route. But in spite of the Sheikh's frequent warnings she liked to explore alone if she felt curious, and would amuse herself wandering from the camps in search of hidden wells.

It is difficult for those who have not known the desert to imagine its many moods and variety of beauty, and there can be few routes which equal the way this caravan passed in March 1862. Harriet, in spite of the discomfort of living in a tent, made longer and longer entries in her diary as the days went by, for she could not resist writing lengthy descriptions of all she saw. The scenery proved to be different from what she had expected or experienced before. It is interesting to note, too, that the expression 'the living desert' is so frequently included in her diary entries:

It was beautiful country, wild but romantic and so green, almost like a grass road, winding up and down between the rocks. I never saw a less dismal desert. Besides our party there are the other inhabitants' marks: ostriches, gazelles, etc., though, of course, we frighten them.

Moreover, the scenery was constantly varying, and a day or two later she described the caravan passing beneath the shade of some trees in a valley which was like an English park. Then on they rode into some mountains, reminiscent of the French Alps but more splendid and majestic than any she had seen in France. The amazing colours are described again and again: the red and black rocks, the white sand with pieces of marble and granite, the coarse gravel abounding with pebbles of agate and jasper. She remarked on the fine trees and bright flowers, so strange and new to her, which she was able to examine when she went on ahead. Sometimes, after a day's journey, she would join Alexine for an evening stroll and they would together find interesting plants and flowers. More often than not the camp was situated in an attractive position, as Sheikh Ahmad, when he got to know the visitors better, realized how deeply such matters were appreciated. Nor was the desert seen only under the sunlight, but was also admired under the full moon; and Harriet recorded how she woke up one night and took a walk after the noisy wind had prevented her from sleeping:

> The moon was just setting behind the immense mountains we had passed and which formed a background to our tents. The moonlight made everything look like snow. Sacker was enchanted. He agreed with me that the wildest passes in the Alps and Pyrenees are not to be compared with what we went through today. In the evening the sky had cleared without rain, and such a sky! The last three or four days the deep blue softening down to grey, and at sunset and sunrise the horizon was completely orange. It is too beautiful to describe, and one gets spoilt and forgets to admire it every day.

After an exhausting desert crossing of eighteen days the expedition arrived at Abu Hamad, back on the Nile. The prolific vegetation bordering the river was like balm to the tired eyes of the travellers. During their stay they were hit by a very severe sandstorm. It was a mercy they were not still in the desert, but nevertheless it was a frightening experience with sand blowing so thickly it was impossible to tell when night became day. Nothing more could be seen but a murky outline of the camp whilst the wind whipped the river into foam. At the first warning of the storm the men darted round the tents fixing extra cords and stakes. Harriet, Addy, and Alexine quickly packed up all the luggage they had opened, laid themselves down on their beds fully dressed, and prepared for an uncomfortable night.

At Abu Hamad Alexine went off into the surrounding country with Sheikh Ahmad, Osman Aga, and some of the men, and they returned with two young ostriches and two young gazelles which she decided to keep. To add to these it was necessary to buy a goat to provide milk for the gazelles. The problem of how to carry the extra animals, and to care for Addy, who was too tired to continue by camel, during the next part of the journey, was solved by Halib, the ingenious head cook. He suggested they should hire a small boat and that this should meet up with the caravan every night. It was necessary to employ six sailors to pull the boat upstream, but Harriet felt it would at least afford a rest for Addy about whom she was becoming very worried.

Sometimes the ladies went by camel and sometimes by boat;

some days were hot and calm, and some so windy they could not keep their parasols up. They passed through many villages and were often entertained by the local inhabitants.

They saw the tomb of Andrew Melly who came from Liverpool and was one of the earliest Europeans to visit the Sudan. On his way back in 1851 he had died, and a monument had been erected to his memory by Latif Pasha. They read the epitaph: 'Love for science and natural history sent him to Khartoum with his wife and two sons.'

On 23rd March the caravan arrived at Barbar, the capital of the province of Barbar, and first place of any size they had reached since entering the Sudan a month earlier. The reception the caravan received was one of the most colourful occasions of the whole journey, for they were treated like royalty and welcomed by eleven sheikhs on camels, whilst Harriet jogged along on her faithful donkey much to her own amusement. They were then presented to the Governor who offered them his house and garden.

The expedition was delayed at Barbar for a few days to join in the great feast at the end of the fast of Ramadan. This coincided with Harriet's sixty-fourth birthday on 1st April:

> It is a great day for them. The Governor, commandant, and all the soldiers, foot and horse, were out gun-firing at sunrise prayers. One can never understand at what hour or what place for when we three went to see the fun, we met them coming back. It was then $7\frac{1}{2}$. The men, wherever we saw them, were all dressed in new dresses, all white and fresh and they saluted each other as they passed, like at the Prussian Easter.
>
> We were hardly home when they came to wish us a happy fête, the chief of the artillery, the drummers, the dancing women, the Saints, all our own servants and all those of the Governor!

They could think of no suitable gift for the Governor, so decided to buy a little girl of twelve for his wife, and to give her Alexine's yellow silk dress and scarf. They also provided presents for his nephews and money for the two soldiers, the servants, and the gardener who had looked after them.

On saying good-bye to the Governor they were introduced to his harem and met his family of some fifty or sixty children. Then

Cairo to Khartoum in four months

the expedition installed themselves in several boats and set sail for Khartoum. They hired two dahabiahs, the post boat, and two luggage boats. It was very warm, and the heat of the sun beating down on the decks was at times excessive, causing several of the Europeans to become ill; but the crews were a merry lot, and there were games, dancing, and music in the evenings. Hippopotami had been recorded in this part of the river, but they did not see any. There were, though, many crocodiles, and quantities of birds of prey, such as vultures and sea eagles. There were many rats on the boats, which Harriet treated as inevitable. She also made light of a nasty episode when Alexine returned late from her solitary evening walk having been frightened by a bull who would not allow her to pass back to the boats. She insisted on going off by herself, and her mother could not make her see that this was unreasonable. Harriet well knew that Alexine was fearless, and wherever she was her fellow-travellers reached the same conclusion.

11

Khartoum

The little convoy drew into Khartoum on 11th April 1862. It was late afternoon when they arrived, having passed by a large caravan of camels and horses laden with grain, which was setting off on some long journey across the desert scrub; for the capital was an important centre of merchandise. It stood, as it were, at one of the cross routes where North met South and West met East. One cannot exactly estimate how far the Dutch travellers had come. From Cairo to Khartoum is a thousand miles as the crow flies, but because of the curves of the river and the indirect route, they may well have covered two thousand miles. Since the previous July they had probably covered five thousand miles in travelling from their home in The Hague.

As the Nile leaves Khartoum it divides into two giant tributaries. From the south the White Nile flows from the true source, whilst the Blue Nile flows from Ethiopia in the east. At the junction the milky water of the White River can be seen mingling with the clear mountain water of the Blue River. Slowly, as if reluctant to do so, the two streams come together, relentlessly forced by the surging currents that eternally carry the vital water to Egypt. Khartoum means an 'elephant trunk' in Arabic, and the capital takes its name from the shape in which the river flows round it.

The four boats, sailing under the Dutch flag, passed by a few big houses with large gardens running down to the riverside, and several groups of shacks, and drew up alongside the quay. News of their arrival took little time to penetrate. A steady stream of curious onlookers soon appeared, staring and waiting to see what was happening. Alexine at once sent Osman Aga to make inquiries about renting a house, but he met with no success, for having reached Khartoum, most people bought or built their own houses. However, shortly afterwards, a brightly painted barge of red and green, rowed by ten sailors dressed in a uniform to match, drew alongside with a messenger sent by the Mudir, or Governor of the Province, offering to help the newcomers. They knew of no house to let, and so it was arranged to camp alongside the boats.

The first priority for Harriet was to post letters to her relations in The Hague and Liverpool with news of their arrival after four months' travelling without mishap, which was truly a great achievement. Wherever she was Harriet wrote a great many letters. Addy was prolific in her correspondence too, but hers did not have her eldest sister's sparkle and wit. Alexine did not often write to her relations. She was apt to rely on others sending off the news, and the truth was, as her mother once admitted: 'She is lazy. I am not.' Harriet sent Sacker with her letters, no doubt hoping he would return with some for her, to the French Consul, who, she had been told, was the renowned Mr. Thibaut.

Before the tents had been erected Mr. Thibaut had arrived to greet Harriet, Addy and Alexine, assuring them of every possible assistance, great or small, whilst they were in the Sudan, and generally overwhelming them with his enthusiastic geatures. From the beginning Alexine took a dislike to Mr. Thibaut as he offered his advice before it was asked for, and benevolently insisted that he should accompany them on any expedition they might choose to make. However, Mr. Thibaut was too well established in Khartoum to take any notice of Alexine's aloofness, and said he would arrive at nine the next morning to present the Mudir. Harriet did not relish the prospect of receiving such an important person in her tent, and was up in good time to arrange that a sofa and two carpets had been carried in to make it look a little more habitable.

The Mudir arrived in his red and green barge accompanied by Mr. Thibaut and two colleagues. One was a Greek merchant, Mr. Dimitri, and the other was the Head Pharmacist of the Sudan, Mr. Tirant. The visit did not go off too well and probably everybody was glad when it drew to a close:

> It was rather a stiff visit – quite official. The Mudir Mohammed Effendi I thought was not so nice as our friend at Barbar, but everything

that was proper was done for us and after the usual lemonade and coffee they all left. As he understood a little French the Mudir had not brought an interpreter, but Alexine did not speak a word.[1]

At three o'clock Mr. Thibaut was back again at the camp. This time he brought three dark-skinned ladies with him. Mr. Thibaut, who was nearing seventy, had been French Consul in Khartoum for thirty-three years, and had come out to the Sudan as a trader before. He was well-known for exporting the first live giraffes to the London Zoo, and had also sold animals to the Paris Zoo. He had married a Sudanese slave. Although he had lost none of his French affections, he wore Turkish dress and appeared as a flamboyant figure to the Dutch visitors who felt so new to Khartoum, and were quite undecided as to where they would go next.

Mr. Thibaut now introduced them to his daughter, Sophie, a rather carefree possessing black girl, and Mrs. and Miss Barthélemy, the Sudanese wife and daughter of a Belgian merchant. Mrs. and Miss Barthélemy were very gay and talkative, and told Harriet and Alexine how they went up the White Nile to their trading station every year. Until this time Alexine had thought of an expedition to explore the Blue Nile, following it to central Ethiopia; but now she at once became interested in the White Nile. Having come so far she looked forward to the next stage, and the Barthélemys made the White Nile sound fascinating and travel so simple. There can be little doubt that by the end of this day she had virtually made up her mind that she wanted to make a voyage up the White Nile, and that Harriet had agreed too, though she was not sure that such a voyage would be 'good for health', as she observed that Mrs. and Miss Barthélemy:

> Look like squeezed-out lemons, yet they say they have never been ill and enjoy the excitement of the boating and the savage life.[2]

As the visitors left, Harriet noticed that Mr. Thibaut had brought them in the Mudir's barge which he was obviously making as much use of as possible. She wittily commented that the Mudir's boat was used for transporting people in Khartoum in much the same manner as her black and yellow carriage in The Hague, which was always carrying her friends and her friends' friends, yet very seldom herself, to and fro like a public carriage.

Within a few days the Dutch ladies were invited to call on the Mudir. They spent the whole day preparing themselves, and at four-thirty the red and green barge called to pick them up. Again it was a very formal visit, and though both sides wanted to know the other, no very close contact resulted, particularly owing to Alexine's indifference at a time when her knowledge of Arabic would have been useful:

We were received with all military honour, the soldiers under arms. We were put in a pleasant large, cool room, but without other furniture than divans and slaves and soldiers. The poor Governor, who understood a little French, tried to say a few words, but Alexine did not speak and our conversation all passed through the Consul and Mr. Dimitri, the Greek gentleman, who came with the Governor to us. After trying to speak of the country, the heat, etc., the building of the house he lived in and the one he is building opposite for his harem who are still in Cairo, we went off. The Mudir doing the civil till the last moment stood till we were off.[3]

Exactly a week after their arrival in Khartoum an exciting event occurred. A steamer with two Italian tourists returned from a voyage on the White Nile, and their example was to make Alexine fully decide to do likewise. The two young men, called Count Cavour and the Marquis of Arconate, were cousins, and had to get back to Italy before Arconate's leave expired in July, allowing themselves three months for the return journey. In 1862 it seems that almost everybody living in Khartoum was discussing the White Nile's source. It was the talking-point of the moment, for a year previously Captain Speke and Captain Grant had been sent out to East Africa by the Geographical Society on an expedition to discover the source of the Nile. If all went well they were soon due to get to Khartoum by way of the White Nile, but already they had been delayed for several months in Uganda. Until the source could be established, until a reliable map was drawn up and proved to be acceptable, the White Nile was endlessly disputed by educated people all over the world. Although the Italians had not been very far, their return was greeted with great excitement and curiosity, especially by the Dutch visitors. Harriet wrote in her diary:

18 April. Good Friday. This morning's grand event: the steamer arrived from the White Nile and the two Italians who have been nineteen days absent. Sacker, Hendrik, and I had tears at hearing the sound of the paddles, and when the boat of the Italians passed, Sacker could not contain himself and flew off to town to see them. They (the Italians) gave a terrible account of their voyage and are all ill, but that only made Alexine cross without changing her plan.

I am so vexed with these Khartoum people who put the White Nile into our heads. All was arranged to go up the Blue Nile for the rainy season till we came here, and everybody we consulted then advised the White Nile and now they all draw back. At any rate we cannot and will not stay at Khartoum and we shall look for some village on the banks of the river which are not inundated.[4]

During their stay in Khartoum, Harriet, Addy and Alexine remained living in their tents, but managed to make themselves quite comfortable, though as the days wore on into May it became exceedingly hot. They were fully occupied making plans for their anticipated voyage up the White Nile when an unexpected disaster occurred. The two Italians were shortly returning to Europe with their servants, and one day Alexine came into Harriet's tent to tell her that Sacker and Hendrik wanted to go with the Italians' party. This came as such a blow that Harriet could not at first believe it, and the men were so ashamed to be leaving they did not have the courage to tell her themselves. She had engaged Sacker as courier to look after them, and now she had greater need of him than before: that he should ask to return to the Netherlands was incomprehensible. That the weak-willed Hendrik, who would have been some sort of substitute, wanted to go too, was a double shock. As she busied herself fixing their wages, and letter-writing, the men reconsidered their decision. But the temptation to go was too great, and to add to the bitterness of the parting several men, European and Arab-speaking, came and shouted, 'Shame!' at the doleful Dutch servants. Up to the last minute Sacker could not make up his mind. He was frightened by what he had heard of the White Nile, but felt much indebted to Mrs. Tinne. On the day of departure from daylight until the boat left at nine he could not decide which course to take until Harriet insisted he should go, and he, demonstrating his foolishness, added that he would return after three months with his family. To add to Harriet's consternation she had another shock when the Italians thanked her for a large box of tea. As she explained:

Sacker had hinted that these gentlemen had not tea enough for their journey and I had said: 'Oh, I can't spare any tea. It is all I drink and when it is done I can have no more, so don't mention it to the gentlemen that I have some still as the provisions are getting so low.' After I had said this, and at the last moment he ought to have felt more kindly for poor old me. It was a shame to rob me. I had given them meat, bread, six sorts of provisions, raisons, brandy, coffee, water, two beds complete with curtains and £80, so he ought to have been satisfied.[5]

At nine the dahabiah sailed away, well-loaded with an ostrich, hyena, cats, monkeys, parrots, and many other animals. Both parties fired a salute of farewell, and the ladies stood waving their handkerchiefs and hats until the dahabiah disappeared into the distance. A melancholy desolation overcame the camp, though they had been able to console themselves a little by sending a few presents back to Europe. Typically, Alexine was tempted to go shopping for more gifts after the dahabiah had left, and Osman Aga was sent to catch up the boat which he luckily succeeded in doing.

The ladies had been turning over in in their minds what presents they could give Sheikh Ahmad as a fitting reward for bringing them to Khartoum, as he was now due to return to Korosko. They decided on a revolver, two silk gowns, a cloth dress, and £30. He appeared grateful, but quickly passed the gifts to a friend waiting outside the tents, and himself remained to make conversation. He had evidently taken a great fancy to Alexine and was invariably in her company, although her feelings are not recorded and she seems quite ready to have seen the last of him. Harriet hoped they had thanked him sufficiently, but had her doubts. ('I think he ought to be pleased – as to content, these people never are.')

Yet, if three of the party had now left, their entourage was still very large. It had numbered eight when they had left Europe, and now consisted of thirty-eight people, all of whom they were responsible for feeding. As if that were not enough, Harriet and Alexine bought two little slave girls, Rosa and Tulba, to give them a good home. They came from the northern Sudan, and Rosa was to remain with Alexine all her life.

Osman Aga, the vakeel, now came into a more prominent position. Indeed, every time the ladies left the camp they were preceeded by Osman Aga and another guard of the Mudir. In addition to his silver stick, Osman Aga never went out without his sword, two pistols, and a gun. Harriet and Alexine were astonished how he managed to carry so much on him! They were soon familiar with Khartoum which was not very extensive, though Addy would not venture out. They found plenty of bazaars, and came across some well-built houses, including the mission buildings, but the streets were for the most part narrow and dirty. There were constant visits to the friends they had made, the Barthélemy family in their cottage in a wood of sweet-smelling shrubs just outside the capital, the Thibaut family in their ramshackle house with its beautiful garden, and the Tirants. Often Alexine and her mother went on donkeys, and when they were out late would return to the camp by the light of lanterns.

Several times they discussed their future plans until late, and on one occasion Alexine, who was becoming very restless, did not undress or go to bed all night. She realized that it would be a great asset to hire the steamer whatever the price. It was very small, but that was not surprising since it had been transported in sections along the usual route from Cairo. The owner, Halim Pasha, was Governor-General of the Sudan but lived in Egypt, and Mr. de Tanyon, a French trader, had been left in charge and hesitated to give Alexine an answer to her frequent demands. She knew that the steamer, being the only one in the Sudan, was worth securing at almost any cost if they were to follow up the White Nile during May and June. No doubt she used her persuasive powers on Mr. de Tanyon, and the outcome was that he made a compromise: if she hired a dahabiah then he promised to give a tow for part of the way up the White Nile. Beyond this further plans would be made later.

The ladies were able to hire a large dahabiah that had been used by the late Dr. Peney, a French physician, who had come out to the Sudan as Chief Medical Officer to the Egyptian troops. He had died a few months previously on an expedition with Andrea Debono, a Maltese trader, to discover the source of the Nile, and it seemed ironic that an esteemed doctor such as he had succumbed to tropical disease. Harriet and Alexine carefully calculated that they would be able to fit their servants, luggage, and provisions on the dahabiah if they took another boat with them. Eventually a plan for a voyage leaving Khartoum on 11th May was decided upon, exactly a month after their arrival. Because a great many preparations were necessary, they started to pack up well in advance. There was a vast collection of clothes, bonnets, and shoes which the ladies had brought with them. Also a small library of books, Alexine's painting equipment, her camera, and all that was required to process photographs. They had iron bedsteads, mattresses, blankets and sheets, and canteens of silver and cutlery besides a quantity of china. They also took the six tents and many articles for camping needs, though, at the same time, they made provision to build a house, should they feel inclined, on the banks of the White Nile. As if by magic, the most competent builder in the Sudan offered his services to Harriet, which she gratefully accepted. Pietro Agati, an Italian bricklayer had come out with the Austrian missionaries in 1853 to build their station in Khartoum, comprising a church, cloisters, and priests' cells. These buildings were the first to be made of brick-work since the ancient times of Ptolemy, all the other houses being of straw and mud. Pietro the Mason, as he was known, diligently consulted the ladies in detail as to materials he would need that would not be available up the White Nile.

In addition supplies of food for several months in advance were necessary, and Mr. Thibaut's assistance was valuable in regulating prices of the provisions and numerous articles they chose to buy from local merchants. Money became one of the chief worries, for although Harriet had made plans for an arrangement with the Bank of Egypt in Cairo, the banker in Khartoum insisted he should pay all her bills. To her this seemed a tall order and one that she told him she would not agree to. Finally, Mr. Thibaut helped her to obtain cash and pay for the provisions. Two days before they were due to set off the Mudir asked for nearly four months' pay in advance for the two boats, the crew, and the soldiers he had hired them. Costs were rapidly mounting up. People in Khartoum wondered how they would manage to meet them, but Harriet and Alexine had no reason to be anxious that they would be short of money, however much they were overcharged.

The White Nile

On 11th May 1862, Harriet, Alexine, and Addy Van Capellen left Khartoum for their voyage up the White Nile. Their dahabiah was very heavily laden, for they had been advised to be well supplied with servants, soldiers, and crew, and a vast quantity of provisions to feed them; so that when they finally departed there was little space for their own comfort. So crammed was the dahabiah, in fact, that after a few days it was necessary to moor in order to wash the dirty laundry ashore, for there was no place to spare on the boat. In any case the flotilla was frequently stopping. The ladies had their five dogs on board which had to be put ashore at least twice a day. Following the dahabiah sailed a nuggar carrying the soldiers, Alexine's horse and donkey, and more provisions.

The dahabiah had left Khartoum in the early afternoon and at six o'clock it reached the steamer which was to give them a tow for some miles up the river. On the steamer awaiting them were three friends, Mr. Thibaut, Mr. Tirant, and his son, who had missed them in Khartoum and were so keen to bid good-bye they had ridden donkeys along the bank. In a happy atmosphere they all enjoyed a good dinner together on the dahabiah before it finally set off.

Next day the boats were experimentally taken in tow by the little steamer, but after an oppressively hot morning a gusty shower broke, bringing so much water into the dahabiah that they were forced to a standstill. It soon appeared that the dahabiah had been leaking and it had to be bailed – a perplexing start for the passengers. Above them storks circled higher and higher preparing to migrate to Europe. The flat, grassy banks of the river reminded the Dutch tourists very much of their homeland and an overcast sky made the resemblance greater.

On coming up to the first village the steamer let loose the

dahabiah with a sudden jerk. The wind was very strong so that the reis quickly cast anchor in the centre of the river to avoid being carried downstream. Alexine was furious with Mr. de Tanyon, who was supposed to be in charge of the steamer, firstly for unhitching the tow rope so abruptly, and secondly for not sending his felucca to get the ladies ashore. However, when she pursued him to the bank she saw him chasing the reis of the dahabiah with a stout stick. Her temper quickly subsided as she watched the men disappear and heard them shouting insults at each other. Taken by surprise she forgot her complaint and left them to fight it out.

The first part of the voyage was doomed to disappointment, and in spite of being towed by the steamer progress was very slow. Neither Harriet nor Alexine felt that the country was interesting enough to warrant them stopping to camp, and whenever the steamer came to a halt the dahabiah had to be moored a considerable distance from the shore to guard against it running on to sandbanks and oyster-beds. The monotony for which the White Nile is famous was already beginning to tell. This was frustrating, since as far as Khartoum there had been many European travellers before them, but few had pioneered the White River; and the brave ladies were expecting more excitement as a reward for the initiative they had shown.

The first voyage of any distance to be made up the White Nile by a European is recorded to be that of Mr. Linant de Bellefonds, the famous engineer. As early as 1827 he had sailed about 150 miles up the river. Alexine had asked Linant Pasha, again and again for his advice, and he had always replied that such a voyage was entirely unsuitable for her and her mother. His counsel, like many others, though few could have been more valid, had at once been brushed aside by Alexine.

More extensive expeditions had been made under Mohammed Ali, the previous Viceroy of Egypt, in his quest for precious metals and stones which he felt sure lay hidden in unknown parts of the Sudan. After many months of preparation Mohammed Ali's first expedition set off from Khartoum in 1839. It turned back after several weeks, having got within a hundred miles of Gondokoro. A second expedition of the Viceroy set out in 1840, and a third in 1841 reached as far as Rejaf, a village beyond Gondokoro, where the rocks and rapids make it impossible for

The White Nile

any boat to navigate the river further. The ladies themselves were now to penetrate as far before returning to Khartoum. Records of Mohammed Ali's expeditions may well have been read by Alexine, for amongst those taking part in them were several Europeans who kept diaries, including Thibaut, two French engineers called d'Arnaud and Sabatier, and a German scientist called Werne. D'Arnaud published letters and a map of the newly-discovered regions in the journal of the Geographical Society of Paris shortly after the expeditions. Werne wrote a book, *Expedition to Discover the Sources of the White Nile*, in which he recorded that there were 250 soldiers and ten boats, and that they had taken a ten months' supply of provisions on board. Sheikh Ahmad had been one of the participants and probably proudly recalled its splendour and suspense to Alexine. Though Mohammed Ali's expedition had got so much farther up the Nile than any other, it returned with no information as to the source, but it was generally agreed that the great river rose from a point south of that which they had reached.

It was recognized that snow-capped mountains lay farther south, near the Equator, and it was therefore widely presumed that the source of the Nile emerged near these. Dr. Krapf, the German missionary, had seen these, now known as Mount Kilimanjaro and Mount Kenya, when he travelled towards the interior from Mombasa in 1850. It will be remembered that Harriet and Alexine had met Dr. Krapf in Cairo and that he, the only eminent person who had given them encouragement, had advised them to make their voyage from Khartoum up the Blue Nile.

Werne also found evidence that these high mountains existed somewhere south of Gondokoro, for he recorded how he was sitting sketching the scenery of some hills when a party of local people approached him and, seeing his drawing, gesticulated that some far greater mountain lay ahead. Placing their hands together the Africans held their thumbs vertically indicating the immense size of the mountain which stood so high. Werne suspected that the Nile originated from a source near the great mountain, and the waters flowing off it contributed to the annual flood.

Alexine was obsessed with the idea of hiring, for themselves, the steamer which she suspected would be at a premium just because it was the only one. It was particularly disheartening to her that the voyage had not so far been interesting, but she looked ahead. However, after a few more days the steamer halted because Mr. de Tanyon had been taken ill. Harriet sent him powders and pills from her medicine chest, but he did not emerge from his cabin. Three of the sailors on the dahabiah also fell sick and to them too Harriet prescribed liberally from her limited supply of medicaments. She opened a new bottle of castor-oil for one of the men; but to her distress he died the next day. His friends gave him a ceremonial funeral and it was evening before they returned. The day lost had added to the many delays that made Alexine and Harriet anxious to move on. They could not understand Mr. de Tanyon's behaviour and resolved to have it out with him, but the next morning when he called on the dahabiah they were horrified to see him looking deathly white:

All we said or intended to say stopped before his pitiful face and heaving breath. God help us in this awful climate. What a responsibility we have on our heads.[1]

However, the flotilla continued slowly until they reached the trading station Mr. de Tanyon had spoken of. This place was called Jebel Dinka, and was none other than a zeriba, or slavery station. Although Harriet and Alexine had no doubt heard that these existed, to arrive at one was to come face to face with all the horror and torture this ruthless trade involved. Here men and women, old and young, awaited their fate, many of them chained. In due course they would be sent to Khartoum and thence to Cairo or Sawakin, the port on the Red Sea, and many of them would, before shipment, die from fatigue or disease from the rigours of the long journey. Alexine had the courage to satisfy her curiosity at this zeriba. She walked off to see the slaves, returning the next day ready to do all she could to relieve their suffering. But for once she felt helpless.

That night there was a break-out from the zeriba when forty slaves escaped, of whom only four were retaken. The ladies were awakened by the cries of the men recaptured, and the beating by the overseers. As soon as it was light Alexine set off determined to buy the recaptured men, but soon saw that this was out of the question. She was shocked to see the men linked by chains to a huge pole, but felt still more sorry for the old, underfed people, who lay about pathetically on the ground. The best she could do was to help feed them, and she paid for two oxen to be killed.

During the evening she returned to the zeriba to ensure that the slaves were receiving the meat from these oxen. She was approached by a Dinka woman with a baby in her arms, begging her to buy her little son who, with his grandmother, had been seized by another slave-merchant. The tall, lean Dinkas are one of the largest tribes that inhabit the White Nile, and the gentlest of people. As the woman took her hand and pleaded with her, Alexine felt she must save the family of six from being divided, by paying for them and taking them with her. Unfortunately in her innocence she did not realize the consequences of her generous gesture, for afterwards the merchants could accuse her of buying slaves. A few weeks later whilst still camping at Jebel Dinka the entire family disappeared, or may have been retaken by force and hidden.

Alexine had chosen a site for the camp on a near-by hill, but Harriet felt uneasy about being near the zeriba, especially when an old man of the neighbourhood appeared to ask for Alexine's hand in marriage! It was therefore decided that an alternative place should be selected farther up the river, and Mr. de Tanyon agreed to Harriet having the steamer to return to Khartoum and collect more provisions and money. At the same time she would take the dahabiah back so that it could be repaired or replaced.

At the end of May Harriet left for Khartoum. Apart from the crew and Flora she took Halib, who was suffering from an abscess of the throat and needed medical care. He had been with the party since the second Nile voyage, and had been invaluable as interpreter. She much regretted his leaving and for the first time she missed Sacker. However, to compensate for these misfortunes, an Italian trader happened to arrive on the scene and asked to join the expedition. He was called Carlo Contarini and offered his services as interpreter and courier. This was agreed to and Harriet realized how useful he would be in the circumstances, for she wrote of him:

> He has been twenty-two years in the habit of *going* which for Alexine is a great point, and he is afraid of nothing.[2]

As Harriet waved from the steamer she felt unhappy about leaving Alexine and Addy, but her anxiety did not last long. In thirty-six hours she was back in Khartoum, though the steamer had taken a week going upstream with the tedious delays.

On arriving she stayed with the Barthélemy family, where she was able to enjoy home comforts again. Since Mrs. Barthélemy was Sudanese and Harriet did not care for the local dishes, Mr. Thibaut had meals sent for her and Flora each day. Gradually, she came to depend on him as he made arrangements for her to order further provisions and make payment in advance to hire the steamer for a year. At the time this seemed a sensible plan but he never imagined the unfortunate consequences into which it would lead him. He also settled for her to take more money and pay the crews' wages five months ahead. Though the price asked for the steamer was exorbitant she never doubted its value. Here was an innovation which Harriet felt would eliminate any dangers which might befall the expedition.

Whilst Harriet was in Khartoum a famous English couple arrived. Samuel and Florence Baker had been exploring in Ethiopia and travelled to the Sudan to join the search for the Nile source. Samuel Baker was a large, brazen, and vigorous man, highly ambitious, and a magnificent big-game hunter. His gun likewise was of formidable proportions for it was so heavy that any other man could scarcely lift it to his shoulder, let alone aim it. Harriet was amazed to hear that his wife had shot an elephant in Ethiopia. She would have enjoyed meeting the Bakers but, hearing they were going up the White Nile, felt they might expect a tow from the steamer which she was reluctant to offer since she already had the dahabiah to take with her.

Likewise Samuel and Florence Baker heard about Harriet and Alexine Tinne. Perhaps it was as well they never met. Although Samuel Baker travelled with his wife, and she like him wore loose trousers and gaiters with a blouse and belt, he criticized the ladies for their audacity. He expounded his views in a letter to his brother John:

> There are Dutch ladies travelling without any gentlemen . . . They are very rich and have hired the only steamer here for £1,000. They must be demented! A young lady alone with the Dinka tribe . . . they really must be mad. All the natives are as naked as the day they were born.[3]

The White Nile

On 28th May Harriet returned in the steamer to meet the rest of the expedition at Jebel Dinka. Behind it was attached the dahabiah and an additional nuggar to carry the vast quantity of extra supplies. It had been intolerably hot during May in Khartoum and the steamer was pleasantly cool in comparison, and she was thankful to relax after the departure which had not been without anxieties. Her money had arrived late and she had discovered the reis of the steamer drunk and only a few of the crew ready to leave at the arranged hour. She was obliged to allow the reis time to recover from his stupor, but on waking he ran off. By then most of the sailors had put in an appearance and were able to chase after him, and, with the help of several policemen, bring him back on board. As the three boats finally left the quay Harriet was seen off by a row of friends. They had taken her to their hearts and were sorry to see the brave traveller leave as the steamer paddles gathered pace and the boats disappeared round the first bend of the river. It was four days before Harriet was united with Alexine and Addy again.

Harriet continued to sleep on the steamer, and each day she and Alexine would go on donkeys to explore the country, or sometimes Alexine would go off alone. They enjoyed seeing the flowers and animals on the hill, including wart hogs, gazelles, and porcupines; also a musk cat and leopard which were caught by the men. It was during July that Alexine's favourite dog suddenly died. She had bought Matruka during the first Nile voyage and had taken her everywhere. The dog had been her closest companion, and now she was broken-hearted although she had four other dogs to amuse her. As her mother reflected, 'we have had Matruka so long and to her are attached so many souvenirs'.

The rainy season was by this time well under way and each day there were frequent storms often followed by sunsets of fire, so realistic that Alexine at first felt certain the colours came from the natives burning their *toich*, or grazing land. As usual the ladies were not without callers, and during their stay at Jebel Dinka the brother of Mohammed Kher, the most dreaded slave-dealer of the Sudan, came to ask if he could offer any help, and provided quantities of food to replenish the expedition at his own cost. Also two Belgians visited them. They were Mr. Barthélemy, whose wife Harriet had stayed with in Khartoum, and Mr. Pruyssenaere. Harriet and Alexine quietly observed how much these two men knew about the Sudan; but did not feel they were in good company. From Mr. Pruyssenaere they purchased further supplies of gunpowder and shot.

Amongst the merchants who traded in the Sudan, many had changed their trade gradually from ivory to slaves during the 1850s – causing accusations, just and unjust, frequently to be made against them. It seems that Harriet and Alexine had had little reason to be aware of this. They treated Mohammed Kher's brother at face value, and accepted the hospitality he lavished on them. Now, to their surprise, they learned that Barthélemy and Pruyssenaere designed to have him sent to Khartoum and imprisoned; and meanwhile held him captive in their dahabiah. Harriet was at a loss to comprehend the situation, and insisted that the Belgians free their prisoner, which they reluctantly agreed to do.

After seven weeks at Jebel Dinka the expedition packed up in their three boats (see Appendix 1) to continue their voyage. The rains were getting progressively heavier and the thunder and lightning were an everyday occurrence, but Harriet and Alexine were as always determined to enjoy themselves. Fortunately, they did not need to depend on a north wind now that they had the steamer, but were anxious lest she was struck by lightning, being made of metal. This imaginary catastrophe never happened, but they were taken by surprise when the steamer's engine boiled over. As the snorting vessel came to an unsteady halt, it started spitting hot water and clouds of steam erupted, until the engine had cooled. Luckily Contarini came to the rescue in time to save an explosion which would have been disastrous to the passengers on deck. Following this terrifying experience, the usual sequence of punishment took place as the negligent sailor was held down and flogged.

After a further five days on the river they arrived at Kaka, the zeriba of Mohammed Kheir, arch slave-merchant of the Sudan, and although the travellers were a little excited they were not unduly alarmed at the prospect of meeting such a character. It was half-past two in the morning when the boats approached and, to assure the inhabitants of Kaka they were friends, at once began firing guns. They were received with silence, until an hour later when suddenly:

> There was a dreadful return of salute!! And the whole population of Kaka came out to welcome us. There were several other boats lying before this village which consists only of straw huts built like beehives. There seem a great many of them and before we were well awake two cows were killed for us, and sheep sent, tomatoes and aubergines, beer, etc. Alexine came very early on our boat and Mohammed, who had asked to be received as soon as we were ready, was sent for. He came on horseback followed by men with lances.

But the guards on the dahabiah would not allow the slave-merchant on board before being announced, and the next thing the visitors knew was that he had turned away in a rage. However:

> After half an hour he came but the fun was over. Alexine had intended having a great feast and now she wanted to leave directly, but all our men were so beautifully dressed and it would have been such a disappointment that I asked her to stay one day at least so we might make some provisions as we shall get no more now until the mountain. He offered us his garden, invited us to his house but we refused all his civility. We took a walk and found the village is surrounded by a thorn hedge. All the people *quite* naked and not a tree nor a plant growing all round ever so far, a desolate place. At five Mohammed Kher came to pay us a visit, and proposed us to become his associates – that is to adjust him with money, to find arms and nourishment, and he would conquer all that remained of these poor devils and give us the title he now takes himself – Sultan of Sudan![4]

The slave-trader was evidently getting into difficulties financially, but he had no success in getting the Dutch ladies to join his partnership. Probably he had never met a boating party doing a pleasure cruise, and did not know whether to treat the strangers as friends or enemies.

The next day they were again entertained when all the people of the village came and danced before their boats. Alexine chose to sit under a near-by tree and was soon joined by Mohammed Kher, and Harriet and Addy watched from the dahabiah. The noisy music and dancing went on throughout the day and into the night without ceasing. Alexine, captivated with the animation and colour of the scene, asked to stay on; yet she could not sum up the situation. Harriet could never bring herself to accuse anybody of being evil, and explained the malice of Mohammed Kheir by forming the opinion he was out of his mind. In a sense she was correct in her assumption, for the slave-trader was tormented for want of the power that had so nearly come his way. He had conquered and devastated hundreds of the vast Shilluk tribe and longed to be proclaimed their king. The Shilluks pay great reverence to their true king and ruler, and had no respect for the slave-trader in spite of his bribes to the government to recognize his rule.

Mohammed Kher later fled to the mountains, but after several years was brought before the Divan in Khartoum and flogged by order of the Governor-General. Samuel Baker, whose accusations had brought the brigand to justice, ordered that the whipping should cease at one hundred and fifty lashes, after watching him howl for mercy.

After a week's stop Harriet, Addy and Alexine set sail, thankful to leave the dismal scene of Kaka. Neither Mohammed Kher nor his brother appeared to wish them good-bye, and Harriet recorded her opinion in her diary:

I suppose he is ashamed of himself. He is going to send a boat to Khartoum and send in it as slaves all the miserable Shilluks who have put themselves under his protection under pretence that they have stolen the best of his cattle and killed his cows. There was one tall powerful man who made resistance and he had him shot. I am so glad we are gone. That man is a bad coward. I pity him as in this country one can do all the harm one likes but no good, but I repeat I am glad we are gone without having been drawn into a scrape by him.[5]

13
First steamer to Gondokoro

The little steamer towing the dahabiah and the two nuggars chugged up the White Nile all through the night. The next day they stopped to collect wood. They were still in the heart of the Shilluk tribe; and the steamer and its passengers caused intense curiosity on the part of the local inhabitants. On halting at one station Harriet described how Alexine was presumed to be the Sultan's daughter.

It was here we had to take the greatest care for fear of being attacked. All the men went with guns: all the soldiers and Alexine went on land to encourage them of course. *She* was not afraid. All at once a tall Shilluk with a necklace for dress and a lance came peeping. Contarini saw him and spoke to him. He was a spy to see who we were for there was a report that a daughter of the Sultan was arrived: that she rode on horseback and she was come to help them. Alexine gave him a piece of cotton and he went away pleased to report that it was all true, and a chief of the King came to visit us, likewise a friendly old man. He sat down with Alexine and took coffee. She gave him some cotton, two brass bracelets, twenty onions, and some durra, after which he had the courage to come alone with Alexine and all our men with guns into the felucca to the steamer where he admired the engine.[1]

The next day they waited whilst the men cut wood, and again the Shilluk chief arrived surrounded by fifty tall, black comrades. A crowd of the naked men swarmed on to the decks of the steamer where they met the three white women and immediately remarked with looks of amazement at their long and ample dresses and were amused at the gloves they wore. They then turned in wonder to the furniture, especially the magnificent deal table, then to the chairs and cushions. The Shilluks had never seen such clothes or furniture before, but the engine of the steamer seemed nothing less than magic! Everybody smiled happily and nodded, and when they finally departed Harriet and Alexine remarked on their visitors' good manners. The Shilluks presently returned with the gift of a cow which was slaughtered and brought on to the steamer.

After a walk and with a fresh supply of wood on board the party were pleased to set sail again. The boats stopped at Malakal, the residence of the King of the Shilluks, but there was a storm raging and, since no one appeared, they set off again after an hour. The crew pronounced they could see Shilluks with spear in hand peeping from their *tukuls*, the beehive-shaped straw houses; but the ladies were preoccupied in their wish to reach the tributary of the Sobat. Here they had hopes of finding a site to install their camp over the next few weeks. This proved to be a very unsuccessful detour, since it was impossible to find enough wood to supply the steamer.

Above the entry of the Sobat the White Nile, still winding in large bends, travels due west to Lake No, a vast stretch of water. Lake No joins another important tributary which runs in from the west, the Bahr-al-Ghazal, which was to be the route of a future expedition. Beyond Lake No the White Nile turns south again. This part, called the Bahr-al-Jebel, is much narrower than before and only allowed five to ten yards to spare on each side of the steamer. But it is not the diminution of the river which causes travellers to puzzle, so much as the anomalous twisting of its course, which curves every fifty yards or so alternately to the right and left. Harriet vividly described the bends to be 'really almost like circles' and 'almost to north and south'. As on a merry-go-round at a fair the passenger trusts that these fantastic movements cannot last long; but he is wrong. The river winds its crazy ambit for 150 miles as the crow flies. This is the sudd region, where the blocks of vegetation always tend to obstruct the river. Nowadays, the White Nile is kept clear, but a hundred years ago the sudd would build up huge masses, firm enough for elephants to cross, until the river, pushing with the accumulation of its flow, would burst through at a different point.

The commencement of the sudd is a thrilling part of the Nile, yet it is one of the loneliest and remotest areas of the world. The flatness, vastness, and monotony of the swamp echoes a unique stillness, and the traveller senses a strange feeling of futility. The mass of waving rushes overruns the land and dips into the rivers, their incoming channels and lagoons. The papyrus, consisting of tall stalks topped with a huge, feathery, dandelion-like puff, often grows twelve to fifteen feet high. It is a symphony of different tones of green, and green is again reflected in the milky-coloured water. The land being so flat, magnificent white, frothy clouds scatter across the clear blue sky, and the sunrises and sunsets have to be seen to be believed. It is truly a mysterious part of the world, where beautiful flowers blossom abundantly for but a few hours. Every evening before sunset flocks of magnificent birds come sweeping along the water on their homeward flight. Exotic coloured ducks, spur-winged geese, pelicans, plumed cranes and egrets, flash past; but the glimpse seen from the boat is a brief one. With the noise of a gentle breeze the birds fly by, a splendid fantasy, but one no voyager can analyse in words. At the same time swallows circulate around the boat, quite unaware of its movement and only intent on finding their food by vigorously dipping and rising after the river flies.

Here herds of elephants march almost hidden by the vast height of the reeds of papyrus. Only their ivory tusks or a perching row of egrets make them visible to the onlooker on the boat. In the drier season Mrs. Gray's antelope and buffalo will come down to feed in these areas; but it is the beasts of the water who always thrive in the sudd. The hippo, huge and hideous, surfaces in the water as if to inflate his bloated body. His pink nostrils, bulbous eyes and square jaw, are seen for a moment by worried passengers on the boat, and then he plunges to the muddy depths of the river and comes up again, perhaps at once, perhaps not for several minutes, often to be joined by another hippo, then another, until a mass of vast, heaving brown bodies are rocking the water. Such sights did not worry Harriet and Alexine. They watched these repulsive animals with curiosity, and seemed to enjoy the friendly individual who followed their dahabiah and remained by it for the night, his form clearly seen in the lightning flashes. More dangerous and (although seldom seen these days) prolific a hundred years ago, were the swarms of crocodiles, often partly hidden. Apparently dozing in the mud or by the water's edge, they remained wide-awake, ready for the human intruder.

Food for the expedition was becoming short, especially meat, and although they saw giraffes, elephants, and hippos, no hunter could manage to get close enough to the animals before they moved off on hearing the steamer. It was dangerous, too, to wound the intrepid hippos, which might have attacked the boat if provoked.

Although the sudd region gets tediously monotonous, the ladies never suffered any lassitude. They were fully occupied with worries over their crew, who – haphazard and drunken at the best of times – could hardly steer the steamer herself, and still less so the dahabiah and nuggars that she towed along the bending river. The two ropes frequently snapped and sometimes the boats became muddled up, so that a great deal of the wood that had been assiduously collected was eaten up by the ever-hungry steamer before they were ready to start off again. In addition, the risks of grounding held up the flotilla's progress. More than once Harriet, Addy and Alexine woke during the night as the boats crashed with a thump against the shore, the tow rope having again broken.

The boats stopped from time to time when they arrived at zeribas or trading stations, but these were all found to be completely deserted in the Bahr-al-Jebel. The scarcity of elephants had sent the merchants farther south to new regions, though it was clear they had been around recently. During the waits the dogs would be allowed to run; Harriet, Addy, and Alexine would take long walks; and sometimes Alexine would ride her horse. Throughout the voyage the hunt for wood had to go on, and since virtually no trees grew in the sudd the men took to collecting timber from the abandoned zeribas. The furious rate at which the little steamer consumed all the wood the three boats could carry never failed to astonish them.

One day a dismal halt was imminent because of lack of wood, but Contarini arranged for a party to go off upstream in the felucca to search for trees. Meanwhile, Harriet and Addy had the idea of having a tent erected on the steamer's deck, so that they could sit outside when it rained. They amused themselves with books and needlework whilst Alexine took the opportunity to paint the scene – the dahabiah and its incredible heaps and piles of provisions. The surrounding marsh made it impossible for them to alight. The day dragged on with no sign of the men returning.

First steamer to Gondokoro

Instead, as darkness threatened, a series of enormous floating islands appeared, carried down river towards them by the powerful current. A particularly big one struck the steamer and crashed it against the dahabiah, so that for a moment it looked as if both would be carried downstream – a terrifying prospect, since most of the men were away on the search for wood. But this time, all was well.

During the two weeks in which the flotilla had been making its way through the sudd, several of the crew had become ill. Now Alexine took to her bed. Harriet somehow kept up and about, worrying over everybody else and seldom considering herself. She utilized her spare time to start a notebook she entitled: 'A few general directions for travellers on the Nile.'[32] In it she commented on the need to avoid draughts, the advisability of wearing flannel or at least a bandage round the loins, proper diet – 'an English diet, not too much fruit and well-cooked vegetables' – and the mixing of medicines for various ills, including dysentery and small-pox. Her medicine chest was in constant use as the men came to her with insect bites, fever, and knocks received in arguments. But she had nothing that would cure her own insect bites which made her face and arms very painful; and the ladies were obliged to go to bed early, sheltering under mosquito nets, in an effort to rid themselves of the gnats. The beds were damp and the curtains hung wet from the humidity of the night air, and thoughts of the beautiful house they had left behind in The Hague returned when Harriet announced that they had left home exactly a year before.

Fortunately, this trying voyage soon improved. Enough wood for the steamer was found, and the boats were suddenly favoured by a north wind so that they progressed at a furious rate. The towing ropes continued to break at frequent intervals with a resounding rip that could be heard above the chugging of the steamer.

After three weeks of the Bahr-al-Jebel the expedition arrived at Holy Cross mission station at the end of August. There they remained anchored for three weeks. The mission station was situated in the southernmost part of the sudd area, slightly north of where the station of Bor now stands on the White Nile. The Austrian Roman Catholic Church had been sending out missionaries to the Sudan for some years, but by 1862, when the ladies called at Holy Cross, the missionaries had suffered endless tragedies and were facing defeat. The mission house in Khartoum had been abandoned first, and that of the Holy Cross and another at Gondokoro had been started. Not surprisingly, the missionaries were unable to survive the fevers of the Sudan, and soon the remaining few were to be ordered to return to their home countries.

The Holy Cross mission station did not stand on the banks of the White Nile, but near an inland lake along a canal from the river. On this site were built thirteen straw houses, or tukuls, of which one was a chapel, one a dining-room, one a stable, and one a store-room: each member of the mission had his own room. There were two priests, Don Francesco and Don Angelo, and about seven laymen. The visitors had brought letters and newspapers from Khartoum, and on calling at the mission received a warm and delighted welcome. So touched were they, that emotions almost gave way to tears – for the Dutch ladies had not mixed with people of culture for many months.

Only a few days before they arrived at Holy Cross, the English Consul in Khartoum and his wife, John and Katie Petherick, had passed there. They had been sent by the Geographical Society with food for Captain Speke and Captain Grant whom they were to meet at Gondokoro in the southernmost part of the Sudan. Petherick was travelling a little behind schedule, though not so many months as Speke and Grant. On the White Nile he had been further delayed. Three out of four dahabiahs he had hired had leaked so disastrously that he had been forced to send the supplies overland from Holy Cross to Gondokoro. One dahabiah alone continued on its way up the White Nile. Petherick was desperate to get the supplies to Gondokoro, and in order to obtain sufficient porters he had taken over some of the local inhabitants by strong measures.

Alexine heard of Petherick from the missionaries, and felt sure she could transport in the steamer the supplies for Speke and Grant more quickly up the river. She therefore set off as soon as possible with Don Francesco, hoping to catch up Petherick and his porters at the village of Ador, but by the time she arrived they had gone and it was difficult to know the route they had taken. Petherick was already months behind schedule at this point, and the offer of the steamer would have been a godsend, but it was not to be, and Alexine returned to Holy Cross.

As the missionaries talked of the land that lay away from the river, Alexine became eager to make an expedition overland which Don Francesco offered to join. So off they set. The sudd area did not continue as far as at first appeared, and soon the mirage of a lake turned into a long road which they followed into woods, prolific with flowers on the trees and underfoot. In a strange way these were refreshingly reminiscent of the woods near The Hague.

They were always welcomed and offered hospitality since Don Francesco was widely known to the local people. The first night Alexine was invited to sleep in a *tukul*, but the door was too small for her bedstead, so she slept in the open. At the next village the tukuls were mounted on poles to avoid the white ants, but in spite of this the men managed to lift Alexine's and her maid Anna's beds into them. This was the first night of many Alexine slept in a Sudanese tukul, on an iron bedstead, brought, moreover, from home.

'There seems no danger for them to go or us to stay,' Harriet had noted in her diary; but whilst Alexine was away worries never ceased for her mother. Without Alexine she felt very much alone, particularly as she could not speak Arabic, and 'happen what may I don't understand a single word and nobody understands me'. In this predicament she felt as if she was deaf and dumb, and described the steamer, generally bustling with life, as 'looking like a great coffin'.[3]

One of the hunters got drunk and remained away all night despite the blowing of trumpets, shooting of pistols, and lighting of lanterns. It was almost unbelievable to Harriet when Osman Aga, employed to protect her, wandered off and got lost. She found herself frequently contacting the missionaries for help in these dilemmas. She also enjoyed their garden, but here again to her embarrassment some of her men stole the fruit one night, and though she had them punished she could do nothing to make good the deficit. On top of her many anxieties there was a violent storm, heavier than any they had yet encountered and the White Nile had produced many. Suddenly two claps of thunder burst directly over the steamer, followed by a weird metallic echo. For once in her life Harriet trembled. She was afraid the steamer would be struck by lightning, and also worried over Alexine in the heavy downpour extending along the horizon. Fortunately, after several days the expedition returned safe, and delighted with all they had experienced.

During their stay at Holy Cross the Dutch ladies came to know the missionaries very well. Alexine showed them some photographs she had taken. Although photography was such a new technique that these were probably the first the missionaries had seen, they were more entertained to see the forged money Mohammed Kher had presented to her. Harriet and Addy enjoyed the Sunday Mass, and Harriet commented: 'I really said my prayers with pleasure.' Inside the little straw-built chapel was an ornamental cross, and despite the heat the priests wore ornate robes. It was tormenting to the ladies to leave Holy Cross, and they found it difficult to convey their appreciation and thanks – especially to Don Francesco, who had not only organized the expedition, but been the life and soul of the party during their stay.

They were now on the last lap of their voyage to Gondokoro. Although merely a small village and trading centre, it was known as the farthest point up the Nile which could be reached by boat, for beyond Gondokoro the river passed through many rapids.

A horrible accident occurred just as the boats were approaching Gondokoro. Here the river narrowed and carried a very strong current: it was the end of August and the flood was almost at its height. Until now the steamer had been dragging the dahabiah and the nuggars, the three heavy boats dwarfing their valiant leader, but finally the engine could no longer wrestle with this massive load against the current of the river. A solution was reached by which the sailors were to tow the dahabiah and nuggars with ropes from the river's edge, and for a short time this worked admirably. Then the inevitable happened. The rope snapped, and the men were left standing in the water with the end of the cord in their hands. In astonishment they watched the huge boat lurch sideways, and within moments start to gather speed in the rushing stream. Osman Aga, who was a big hefty man, at once took the initiative to jump into the river and catch the rope of the dahabiah, but just as suddenly as he had entered the water, he sank. The ladies, taken by surprise at his heroic act, were at the same time aghast as he disappeared. He was quickly rescued by the sailors and dragged

First steamer to Gondokoro

ashore, and the boats somehow anchored. Everybody felt sure he would soon revive, but he did not breathe again. Osman Aga had died. The noble janissary who had come with the Dutch ladies all the way from Cairo to protect them on their dangerous journey, was lost for ever.

With great ceremony Osman Aga was laid to rest and given a full Moslem burial on the shore. Although Harriet, Alexine and Addy could not comprehend the meaning of the service they were touched to see him buried with such reverence. They had come to rely on Osman Aga, and his loss was a severe shock. Again, one more of the original party had gone. Moved by his death and becoming increasingly aware of the closely-knit group they had formed themselves into, Harriet and Alexine wrote a delightful poem, 'Osman Aga's Grave.'[4] (See Appendix 2.)

As they approached Gondokoro they felt a great state of excitement for the steamer was the first mechanical boat to have passed up the White Nile. Constructed of iron, it was probably of British make, and had been described by Addy as a 'very little steamer'. It had probably followed the same route as the ladies, and had been taken to pieces and carried by camel between Abu Hamad and Barbar. Then reassembled and sailed to Khartoum to await its owner, Halim Pasha, the Governor-General of the Sudan, who never came from Egypt for long enough to use it. The steamer was later called *Prince Halim*, and became well-known as the first steamer on the White Nile. Naturally, Harriet and Alexine were delighted to be the first to have brought it up the river to Gondokoro, and there was a sensation amongst the local inhabitants when it docked.

The flotilla, having spent nearly five months on the White Nile, arrived at Gondokoro on 30th September 1862. Since it was used as a trading centre only during December and January, there were few people living there. Gondokoro was known as the farthest navigable point on the White Nile, but, typically, the Dutch ladies had to prove this for themselves and soon after arriving set off on an excursion up the river for another five hours before turning back when the river became too treacherous. They achieved this extra distance because the White Nile was exceptionally high that year, as recorded by the eminent explorers who were to reach it early in 1863.

Their plan was to send the steamer back to Khartoum for fresh supplies of provisions before continuing their journey through Africa. The steamer, it was calculated, would take about fifty days to get to Khartoum and back, and by that time a further expedition would have been drawn up. They soon settled down to camp and 'became friendly with the establishment of Gondokoro', as a contemporary account recalls. The establishment probably consisted of two or three merchants and a few local chiefs. The mission had closed down two years previously. When asked why they had come and what they hoped to do next, naturally the ladies said they wanted to continue their journey. They introduced themselves by explaining they had come from the Netherlands, which must have sounded like a legendary land to the local chiefs, and then they would inquire of their hosts where the source of the Nile lay, only to be met with peals of laughter, for in Gondokoro nobody seemed to think there was a source. The fact that there were many little streams entering the river, and rain every day for six to eight months of the year, was sufficient to explain how the water got there.

'They are a fine war-like race, but rather quarrelsome,'[5] Harriet wrote in a letter home, somewhat understating the position they found themselves in. The fact was that all the local tribes had suffered the terror of the slave-traders: the natives referred to all white men as Turks, and it was not safe for a white person to travel unprotected in the vicinity. The Viceroy of the Sudan had forbidden slavery, but porters were a necessity to the ivory traders, and the margin between those natives employed as porters by force and those taken as slaves was difficult to discern. Soon one trader accused another until most of the merchants, good and bad, were under suspicion.

Harriet felt regretful that there was not a better foreign influence not only to lead the primitive peoples, but to take a scientific interest in all that was new. In a letter she described the flowers she saw, which far excelled any she had seen in an English greenhouse, and commented: 'I wonder there is no Englishman spunky enough to come out here and botanize!'

Since the expedition's arrival in Gondokoro Alexine had not been well, and a fortnight later she was laid up with a temperature. Harriet dosed her with quinine but the attacks of fever became

First steamer to Gondokoro

more serious and of longer duration. For five days she became delirious and unable to recognize anybody. Her worried mother was by her bedside day and night, and decided that for the time being the steamer had better not leave for Khartoum. Fortunately, Alexine pulled through, but the experience had been frightening for her mother. Besides, other members of the party had been taken ill in Gondokoro. Addy decided she had had enough of travel in Africa and told her sister she wanted to return to the Netherlands, and the Egyptian servants said they had had enough of the Sudan and also wished to return home. In addition, the Dutch ladies had been warned of unrest amongst the local tribes and the impossibility of obtaining porters if they wanted to travel overland. Indeed, there seemed no other solution to their problems than for the entire party to return to Khartoum. At this stage, too, the idea of building a house on the White Nile was abandoned. Pietro the Mason the Italian builder, his assistant, and their collection of tools and materials, returned as they had come.

After a month spent at Gondokoro the expedition packed up, and the three boats headed by the steamer departed. They had spent nearly five months on their voyage upstream, but took only three and a half weeks to return. Yet it was with but little feeling of regret that they sailed back, for they were immensely proud of having penetrated up the Nile so far, and they described the triumph of their remarkable achievement in a poem they wrote, 'Gondokoro'.[6] (See Appendix 3.)

As the Dutch boats neared Khartoum they passed a dahabiah under the British flag sailing upstream. In it were Samuel and Florence Baker, who were on their way to Gondokoro where they were to meet Speke and Grant. In Baker's own words he appeared to have resented the hiring of the only steamer by the Dutch travellers, and to add to his frustration the White Nile was particularly high and lacking in north winds, and his voyage was to prove very tedious. 'The White Nile is becoming a fashionable tour,' he remarked when he heard about the adventurous ladies. 'There should be a public house built on the Equator, where travellers could stop for a glass of beer.' And then he excused their behaviour and the high price they had paid for the steamer with the comment, 'They must be mad!'

However others might look upon their voyage, the Dutch ladies themselves had greatly enjoyed it. On reaching Khartoum Harriet sent off several long letters, and in writing to the Queen of the Netherlands emphasized the carefree life she had experienced on the White Nile:

This sad termination is a pity, as else I should have been satisfied with the lazy everyday life carried on without the bother of money, an absence of care, a damn-me don't care sort of life, which I value very much.[7]

14
Bahr-al-Ghazal Expedition

Little did the Tinnes and Addy know that their voyage had been widely discussed by the Geographical Society in London, and though no names had been mentioned, news of their arrival at Gondokoro in the steamer had been much publicized in the press. At the time it was estimated that Speke and Grant were nearing Gondokoro from Uganda, having found where the true source of the Nile lay.

Before the boats got back to Khartoum, Alexine had decided that she would like to make a voyage up the Bahr-al-Ghazal, and the twelve weeks spent in the little capital were devoted to plans for the future expedition, which was to be on a far bigger scale for they were going farther this time. To reach the Bahr-al-Ghazal, the river of the gazelles, they would again sail up the White Nile covering about half the distance to Gondokoro, some 300 miles as the crow flies but very much farther by river. Then, reaching the junction of Lake No, they would turn westwards up the Bahr-al-Ghazal.

Where exactly was Alexine aiming to get on this expedition? Research does not reveal the anticipated destination. At the time it may have been widely known, but nevertheless this fact has been left out of the records. However, John Tinne, who later gave a talk to the Liverpool Geographical Society which he called 'Geographical Notes on Expeditions in Central Africa by Three Dutch Ladies', compiled from letters he had received from Harriet, put forward certain reasons:

The expedition had for its object to ascend the western tributary of the Nile, the Bahr-al-Ghazal, explore the several streams flowing into that river, and so onwards by land to the south-westward, towards the highlands of central Africa and the country of the Nyam-Nams, from which direction it is asserted by many geographers that, at some seasons of the year, the largest supply of water is poured into the basin of the Nile.

The Nyam-Nams referred to were the Azande tribe, a Negroid people who live on the Nile-Congo Divide. Many travellers said they were cannibals, and no doubt weird stories based on rumours had reached Alexine. Reports that the Azande were a people with tails, and eyes that grew out of their armholes, were frequently met. Yet she may have known the true facts, that they are a docile tribe, friendly, and skilful in their traditional crafts. Alexine had been nicknamed 'La Reine de L'Equateur' when she travelled through Egypt the previous year, and this might indicate that she hoped to reach the Equator and had spoken of such ideas.

If we look to Addy Van Capellen for information, we learn that the expedition hoped to do a fifteen-thousand-mile round tour via Fernando Po (an island off the Cameroons), the Cape of Good Hope, and Egypt to Khartoum. It is as well to remember that Alexine was prone to exaggerate, and delighted in making statements that would cause more ordinary people to gaze at her in startled amazement. However, the caravan traders covered thousands of miles, and she may have thought she could do likewise; nor would navigation round the coast have been difficult. With such thoughts and recriminations Addy was left to wait in Khartoum, whilst Harriet and Alexine dreamed and worked for the expedition ahead.

They had already voyaged up the White Nile as far as Lake No. What information did they have on the Bahr-al-Ghazal and the land that lay beyond? By 1862 several European traders had pushed into the terra incognita in the hopes of finding further supplies of ivory or slaves, and they would have described their experiences on returning to Khartoum. A French traveller, G. Lejean, published a map of the Bahr-al-Ghazal in 1862, which was later proved to be accurate; but since no note has been left that Alexine had this information, it is more likely that she depended on her crew, some of whom had been up the tributary. John Petherick, the English Consul in Khartoum, had traded for ivory by sailing up the Bahr-al-Ghazal and then travelling southwards in the 1850s. Generally, he found the people friendly, though on one occasion he only escaped death by scaring some Azande by

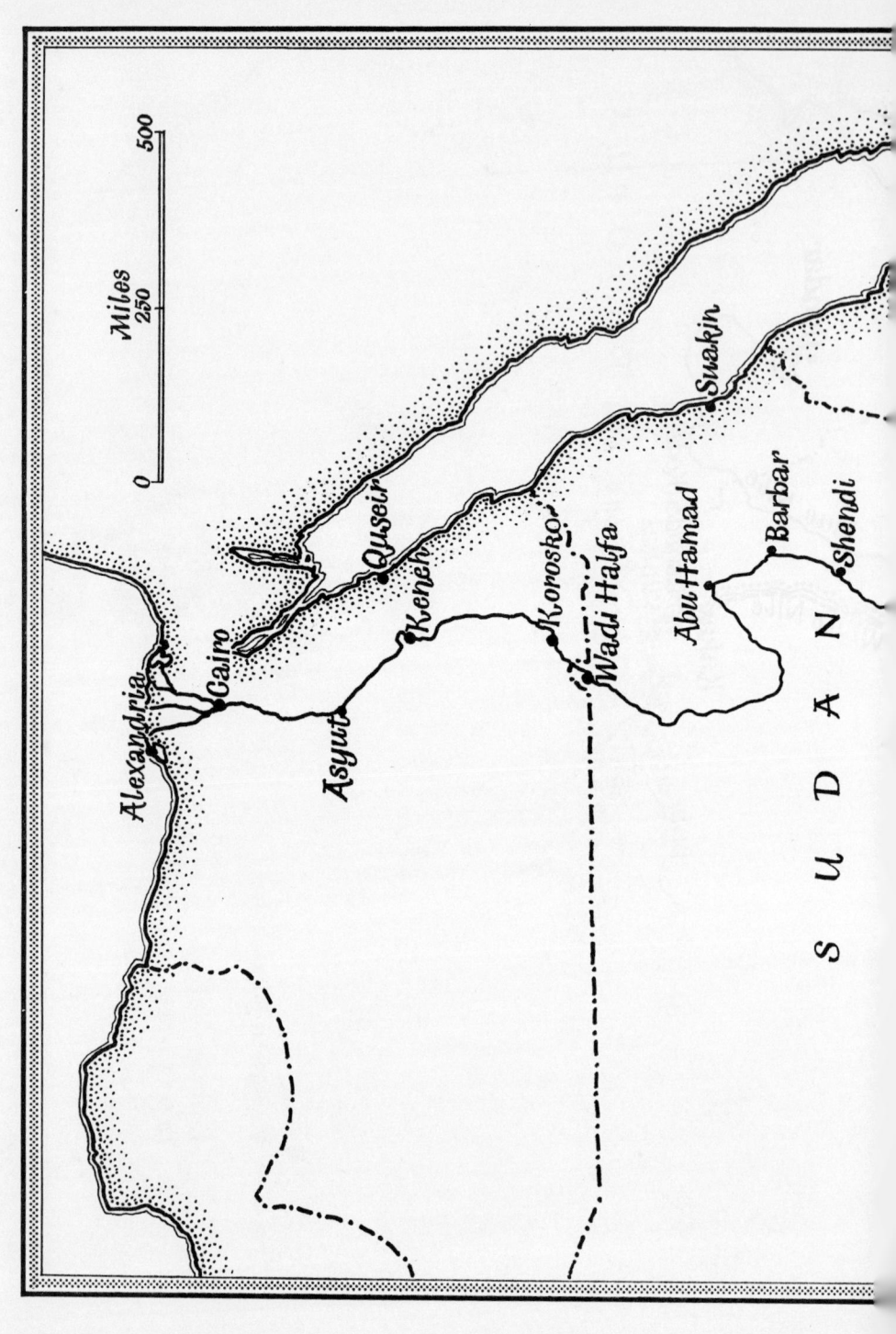

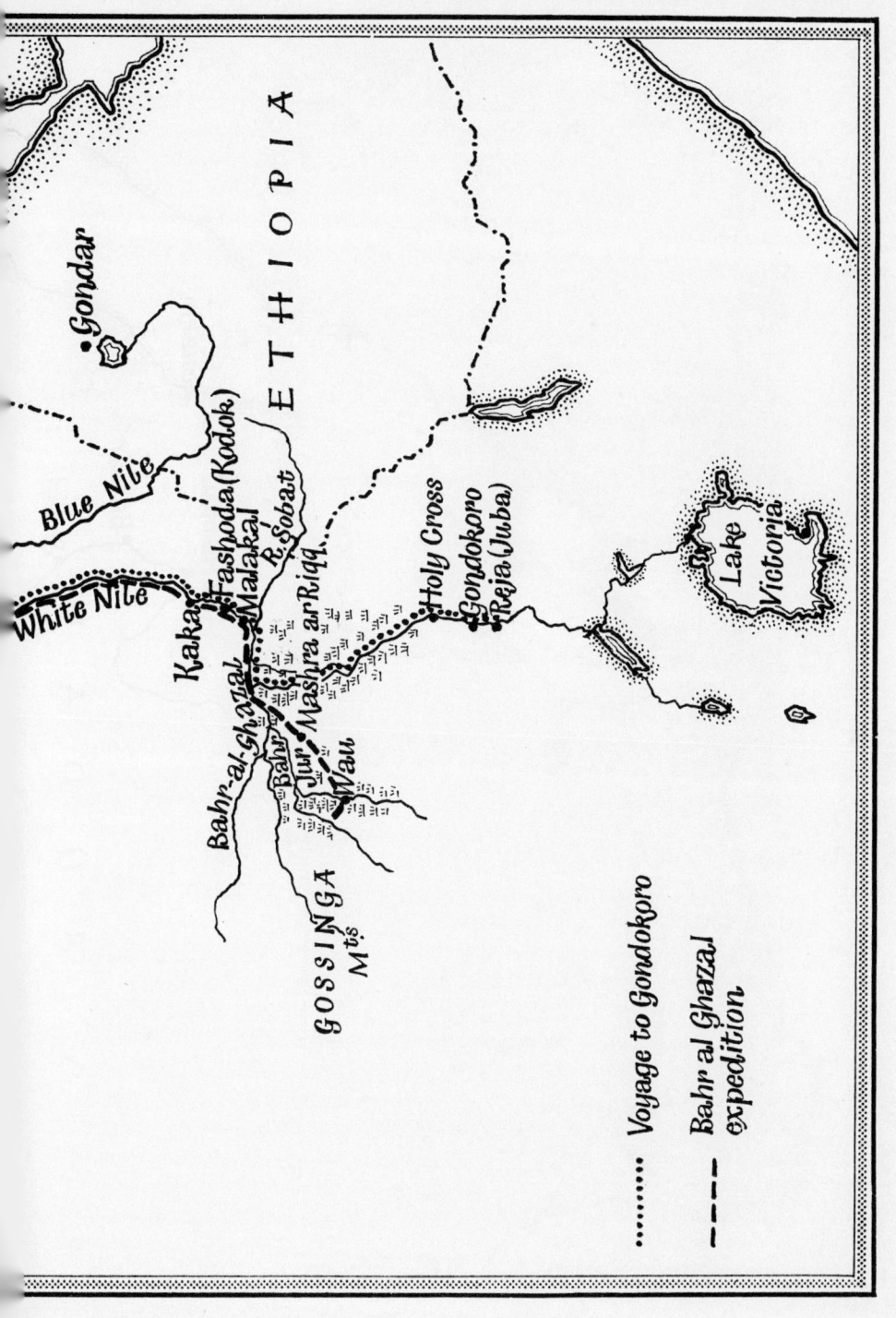

the discharge of his gun. No doubt such a tale of the English Consul added to Alexine's curiosity of the great unknown interior.

Two previous expeditions of discovery in central Africa must have influenced Alexine. Both started from North Africa and must have needed fantastic endurance and courage.

The first of these was carried out by Barth, Overweg, and Richardson under the British Government. In 1851 they travelled from Tripoli, and though Overweg and Richardson died on the journey, Barth succeeded in reaching Lake Chad, then turned westwards to arrive eventually at the caravan centre of Timbuktu, and finally got back to Tripoli after four years. Apparently, Alexine considered that her expedition might reach Lake Chad, since the theory that a tributary of the Nile rose in Lake Chad was commonly held in Khartoum at that time.

Little is known of the second expedition in which Edward Vogel left Tripoli in 1853 to follow up Barth who, he presumed, had been killed. Vogel eventually got to Ouadai where he was held by the Sultan until 1865, when he was murdered. Between these dates search-parties left Khartoum travelling eastwards, following reports that Vogel was being held prisoner by the Sultan of Ouadai. The Austro-Hungarian Consul in Khartoum, a German scientist called Baron Theodor von Heuglin, was put in charge of these. He himself did not set off to look for Vogel, since he was occupied in exploration in Ethiopia and the Red Sea coast, but he sent off a search-party under Beurmann, who may have found Vogel, only to meet a similar fate.

When Alexine and Harriet returned to Khartoum they met Baron von Heuglin. He was very interested in the Bahr-al-Ghazal expedition which was being planned, and no doubt offered valuable advice. Finally, Harriet suggested that he, together with another German called Steudner, should join them: an offer that was warmly agreed to. Heuglin was born in the German state of Würrtemberg in 1824, and as a young man travelled to Egypt where he learnt Arabic. From here he explored Ethiopia with Reitz, the Austro-Hungarian Consul in Khartoum. Reitz died on the way back from Ethiopia and, at the age of twenty-nine, Heuglin was made Consul in his place.

No doubt Khartoum was full of talk over the Dutch ladies'

coming expedition. Everybody realized it was costing an immense amount of money, and several persons asked to join them. Harriet wrote back to her brother, Jules, on the preparations:

> I am happy to say von Heuglin is going with us. He has given so many broad hints of his wish to make this journey that at last we told him we could not offer him a place either in the steamer or the dahabiah, but that there were two other boats going with provisions, soldiers, and animals if he liked to have a cabin arranged for him and his friend he was very welcome, and I wish you could have seen with what pleasure they accepted it. This shows at least what an *interesting* party it is. We shall be fourteen days reaching the River Gazelle. There we shall soon be stopped for want of water and when all is ready to go into the interior I shall send the steamer back with letters and Addy can write as often as she likes.[1]

This is a revealing letter since Heuglin later wrote about the Bahr-al-Ghazal expedition as if he had been the maker of it. With Heuglin travelled his young colleague, Hermann Steudner. Heuglin was first and foremost an ornithologist, and Steudner a botanist, though they were both very interested in geography. The ladies were joined also by a Dutchman called Baron d'Ablaing, whom they had met previously in Cairo and who had since been escorting the Duke of Saxe-Cobourg and his family on a shooting expedition in Ethiopia. Probably Harriet felt it would be safer to take a few men with them, and Alexine agreed, though she stressed that she wanted to lead the expedition herself.

Preparations took longer than anticipated as the vast quantities of articles that seemed indispensable piled up ready to be packed. There were to be six boats in the expedition: the steamer, a dahabiah, and three nuggars financed by Alexine, and Baron d'Ablaing's own dahabiah. Heuglin and Steudner were to travel in one of the nuggars, and d'Ablaing in his dahabiah. The steamer was to tow the dahabiah, a first-class passenger boat, in which the ladies were to travel. Besides their six servants they engaged sixty-five soldiers armed with muskets, and the Mudir then allocated another six soldiers to protect them on his behalf. It was essential that each boat should carry supplies, and every available space made use of, since enough provisions and ammunition had been purchased to allow for six months. One boat was to carry most of

Bahr-al-Ghazal Expedition

the animals, consisting of Alexine's horse, four camels, two mules, and forty donkeys. The dogs came too, and there were quantities of poultry and sheep. As it was impossible to load all these on the animal boat, ten donkeys travelled with Heuglin and Steudner in the advance nuggar.

On 25th January 1863, Heuglin, Steudner and their shipment sailed from Khartoum. It was very early morning when the Germans set off at the junction where the Blue and White Rivers meet. They were favoured with a north wind which lasted for several days. It had been arranged that the rest of the expedition were to follow them the next day, and Heuglin was anxious to keep his lead. Their nuggar was sixty feet long, the shape of an elongated saucer, built of thick planks and had a sail and thatched roof over the stern as a protection against sun and rain. Heuglin was afraid the steamer would catch up very easily, and he would not find enough time to make scientific investigations and notes. He was pleased to have bought in Khartoum a second sextant, a barometer, and a large ship's compass by which he hoped to map the route they were taking. To be sure of accuracy he had asked Alexine to mark down the distance between stations by means of a watch, since the steamer maintained a fairly even speed. Lack of space made it uncomfortable on the nuggar, and difficult to get ashore when it stopped. The donkeys were not allowed ashore because it was too swampy, but they managed to get some exercise in spite of this for each day they broke their tethers, regaled themselves with corn, and had a kicking match with the mules.

Making excellent progress, Heuglin and Steudner reached Lake No, a great sheet of water where the Bahr-al-Ghazal tributary joins the White Nile. Sailing along the Bahr-al-Ghazal, the silence was soon broken by the crew as they spied peeping Dinkas watching through the papyrus stalks. These were tall, lean, black people who would stand even for hours on one leg, the other foot balanced on their standing knee. Though they wore no clothes the Dinkas sometimes covered their coal-black skin with ashes to keep off flies. The nuggar passed villages with cottages built of straw with conical roofs, and gardens that grew maize, tobacco, and beans.

It took three weeks for the advance boat to arrive at the little port of the Mashra Ar Riqq where they were to await the rest of the expedition. During the time they spent waiting there Heuglin and Steudner could not imagine what had held up the ladies with the steamer.

Back in Khartoum the main part of the expedition had met with many unexpected adventures, for the preparations and plans far exceeded any before. The more provisions the party took with them the more men and animals were needed to transport them, and the more men and animals, the more provisions were necessary, and the Dutch believed in plentiful food. Alexine and Harriet busily occupied themselves during those weeks of pleasant winter weather, but neither the Dutch nor Egyptian servants relished the idea of an expedition into the unknown. Fortunately, Alexine's enthusiasm fired their curiosity, for she had a way of stimulating people, while Harriet would tell the servants briskly when they grumbled to her: 'Stir your stumps and be agreeable!'

Finally, departure date came and all was ready, when Anna noticed that the dahabiah had sprung a leak. The hole was soon detected and repaired by the sailors, who were heard to remark that she would have gone under in another two hours. Meanwhile, Alexine and Baron d'Ablaing went off to complain to the Mudir, as the boat had been hired from the government. The Mudir, sedate, surprised and apologetic, returned with them to the scene and, after the dahabiah was mended, suggested they went for a three-hour trial run, but again a leak was found:

> There was again a fuss, and the captain of Alexine's boat was made to own he and the pilot had made the hole so as not to go on the White Nile which he did not like. The hole was again stopped. Four experts were sought for, who all engaged to make us safe, but we are now to have another Captain and another crew.[2]

Another two days passed before a new crew could be selected for the dahabiah, and Harriet was able to visit Addy, who had asked to be left behind. It was a beautiful moonlight evening, and to her delight she found several friends gathered round her sister and singing together in the garden. Harriet had taken Baron d'Ablaing with her. He was usually of a serious nature, but that evening she was able to make him laugh at the absurdity of the situation they found themselves in:

By this fine moon Mr. d'Ablaing and I returned home and we laughed at the idea of being in the centre of Africa, a *nous deux* on donkeys, only attended by an old man, he and a little boy with a lantern!! We were no more afraid of lions and tigers or Negroes than on the downs *chez nous*.[3]

However, ultimately the main expedition was ready and sailed from Khartoum on 5th February. The chugging steamer drew the ladies' dahabiah, followed by the two luggage boats, one holding the animals. They entered Lake No, and from here the steamer edged her way up the almost hidden tributary of the Bahr-al-Ghazal. Some of the crew had been on this voyage before, but for the steamer, as well as Harriet and Alexine, it was a new route. Rumours that the Bahr-al-Ghazal might lead to the source of the Nile had filtered into Khartoum for several years, and it was generally agreed that it provided much water at the rainy season towards the Nile flood. It was not at all easy for boats to discover the main channel. The problem arose because the appearance of the land varies greatly from season to season and year to year according to the formation of the sudd, which does not consist of rotting weeds alone, but floating vegetation, trees and their roots, and the mud in which they grow, building up new barriers.

The steamer, which had not been up the Bahr-al-Ghazal before, was to prove more of a burden than a blessing; for so shallow was part of the river, that the paddles were constantly clogged with water-hyacinth and other floating plants. Whereas the nuggars could sail on the small amount of water, the steamer became incapable of any progress whatsoever. When eventually the Dutch flotilla arrived at the Mashra Ar Riqq, it was a moment of triumph.

Heuglin and Steudner were keeping watch and went to meet the expedition in a canoe. First came one of the nuggars towing Alexine's dahabiah. Then followed Baron d'Ablaing's dahabiah, and lastly came the second nuggar dragging the steamer which was helped along by fifty men pulling the vessel with ropes and poles. Heuglin described the scene in his logbook:

> The entrance of the flotilla into the Mashra was indeed a splendid sight. The boats, about twenty, which were here, all hoisted their flags and received the newcomers with salutes of at least three hundred guns. The salute was suitably returned, whilst from our camp cannons roared.

The Mashra is entirely filled now, so that it would be difficult to introduce two or three boats.[4]

Indeed, when the Dutch squadron anchored there was little water-space in the muddy recess which held mostly nuggars, jammed closely together. This port was the point of departure for several routes. Here merchants' boats waited to carry back slaves, ivory, and other commodities which they procured from the interior. Everywhere the land was interlaced with narrow channels, and on a near-by tongue of land Heuglin and Steudner had installed a temporary camp.

The first action Harriet, Alexine, and d'Ablaing took was to hold a conference with the German scientists. It was first announced by Alexine that the expedition could not move forward without extra provisions, and for this purpose it was arranged that the steamer would return to Khartoum under the command of d'Ablaing. Heuglin then pointed out that the expedition was very numerous to move as a single unit, and suggested that he and Steudner should go ahead to reconnoitre a suitable area where the whole force could spend the rainy season. At the same time they would inquire for local porters who were needed to carry the provisions, ammunition, and the travellers' vast amount of luggage. Though the Mashra was a desolate outpost, Harriet and Alexine made themselves comfortable living on the dahabiah. Upstream on the Island of Kit they had a garden made which they could enjoy during their stay.

It was decided that Heuglin and Steudner should leave at once, and on 23rd March the Germans set off. They crossed the Bahr Jur, a tributary of the Bahr-al-Ghazal, and continued a hundred miles to reach the village of Wau. Until this time both men had kept remarkably fit, and had swallowed regular doses of quinine in the hope of keeping tropical disease at bay. At Wau, Steudner was taken ill. He was a younger man than Heuglin, who was terrified lest he lose his friend. He had already been robbed of his travelling companion recently when Reitz had died in Ethiopia. Steudner's end was equally sudden. One day he became feverish, quickly losing consciousness, and the next day he quietly died. Poor Heuglin was desperate, and fearful over his own state of health. He felt a similar fever coming on and sank into a state of delirium. He awoke, and though weak and suffering from shock he managed to get Steudner buried, and then went on to the west where he had hopes of procuring porters.

On 24th April, a month after leaving, Heuglin returned to the Mashra. He had discovered a suitable caravan route for the expedition to Wau, but his search for porters had been on the whole unsuccessful though he had managed to find some. Most of the male population of the surrounding Dinka tribes had been taken by force by about six traders, who had sold their families as slaves. The expedition could not have arrived in the area at a more unfortunate time, but luckily they did obtain porters by sheer chance. The English Consul, John Petherick, who had been trading in the vicinity, turned up at the Mashra Ar Riqq with offers to help them just at the opportune time.

15

Journey into the Interior

Meanwhile in Khartoum Addy Van Capellen was finding life uncomfortable and lonely, though she cherished a few kind friends. She had long hoped to travel back to Cairo but had not felt strong enough to make the journey. In a letter to her brother, Jules, she expressed her feelings in no uncertain terms:

> I was on the point of starting for Cairo but I was not well enough, as that at least is a place, while this is not one. It is nothing but a mud-hole for frogs. Amongst the 4,000 inhabitants there are only three women that can speak French: the Consul's daughter, a half-educated child of a Negress, the daughter of a Cairo tailor married to a slave merchant, and her mother-in-law who looks, and perhaps was, an actress. But such as they are they are very kind and willing to do anything for me, but I am very tired of vulgar people and savages.[1]

Harriet had found Addy a temporary home, but the windows had no glass, so when it was gusty she kept the shutters closed and the door ajar to allow the daylight in. Even so several birds chose to make their nests along the ceiling. A much better house had been on the market; but, with costs of the expedition mounting, Harriet had declined to take it, especially as the rent had to be paid five months in advance and Addy might be leaving for Cairo. On the other hand Addy found this reassuring, for she sincerely hoped it meant Harriet and Alexine would not be away for long:

> Alexine said she meant to go as far as possible to the south-west, and said she hoped to arrive opposite to the land of Fernando Po, but this as well as her intention of going as far as the Cape of Good Hope are all vain boasting which she does to astonish the people, and many tell me they surely will come back here in a couple of months as then the rainy season will begin, and they will be glad to come away. Anyway,

time will tell what they will do. It is a great pity Alexine has not more reasonable tastes and that she threw away her money in such a ridiculous and useless way, and when there are so many beautiful countries to see she has brought us into this horrid place.[2]

Addy's views on the expedition were not altogether unfounded. She had recently met and entertained Speke and Grant, on their way home after discovering the Nile source in Lake Victoria, and she had taken the opportunity of asking their opinion on her niece's expedition. As Harriet enviously commented: 'Addy has been in luck. She has met the great lion of the day, Captain Speke.' Probably Speke and Grant were equally pleased to meet Addy for, believe it or not, she was the only other English-speaking person in Khartoum.

Speke and Grant had arrived in Khartoum on 30th March 1863. The message on its way to London bearing the news that the 'Nile was settled' had passed through one day ahead of the explorers themselves, so that when they arrived a reception had been arranged in their honour.

They were met by a representative of Musa Pasha who came aboard their dahabiah and embraced them, but since the explorers could not speak Arabic they did not know who he was and followed him ashore wondering what was coming. He insisted on the English officers changing from their well-worn clothes into an assortment of Oriental garments, complete with a fez for Speke, though Grant's head, fortunately for him, was too large to fit. They were then ushered into a room and offered coffee, brandy, and cigars before the élite of Khartoum rushed in to greet them.

It seems these two eminent gentlemen did not fit into Khartoum society with the aplomb the Dutch trio had done, as they spoke neither French nor Arabic. However, they spent much time in conversation with Addy, and soon found themselves at ease in her company, after their servants had entered her house drunk and they had laughed together at the absurdity of the situation.

Addy recognized the fame of Speke and Grant, and she took the opportunity to ask the former for his advice on the Bahr-al-Ghazal expedition. Speke spoke strongly against it, and though this alarmed Addy, she realized she could utilize his opinion to bring the party back. Indeed, she felt it would be wise to get him to write in a letter all he had said to her on the matter. His letter follows:

Khartoum,
11th April 1863

My dear Baroness,

As you have shown so much anxiety with regard to your party on the Bahr-al-Ghazal, and have condescended to ask my advice respecting the feasibility of their being able to accomplish a journey which would tend either to scientific or even pleasurable results, I must frankly confess I can see no possibility of either or the other ending satisfactorily, knowing full well the nature of the African climate. I would never dare travel with more than one companion and should even then be careful in my selection of one whom I thought constitutionally fitted to undertake a harassing march.

With regard to pleasure, sight seeing, and so forth, there is nothing to see anywhere near the Bahr-al-Ghazal of such interest as exists in the regions of Gondokoro; indeed the beauties of Central Africa are concentrated within 4 degrees on either side of the Equator where rain is continuous throughout the year. If a Scientific Expedition was the object at issue, every sacrifice, even life, must be risked for its accomplishment. Then porters should be engaged to carry all property – there is no trust in any animals – and bartering stores taken in sufficient quantity to last two years at least, for there is nothing of any material importance in a geographical point of view to be gained until a march of five hundred miles has been made South by West from the Bahr-al-Ghazal. At that distance the watershed between the White Nile and the Congo may reasonably be expected to be found, and should anybody be fortunate enough to discover the source of the Congo the greatest credit would be given for having unlaid the last feature of interest in Africa.

I sincerely hope your party may be *the means* of discovering the source of the Congo. One man or two might do it, more could not, and if they attempted it I would not be answerable for the lives of any.

Pray excuse the abruptness of my style in writing, but what I have said I mean, and I should be sorry to see any ladies attempt an exploring journey when failure would inevitably be the result, not from want of pluck, but the fearful effects of African climate, which cannot be overestimated.

Believe me,
Yours ever truly,
J. H. Speke.[3]

Addy forwarded this letter by the steamer, hoping it would tempt Alexine and her mother to return at an early date.

The famous explorers had sailed down the White Nile from Gondokoro where they had been met by Samuel and Florence Baker. John Petherick, English Consul in Khartoum, had been commissioned to be at Gondokoro with provisions, and being an ivory merchant and unpaid in his capacity as Consul, he had taken time off to shoot elephants. To the downfall of Petherick, Samuel Baker passed on to Speke and Grant scandalous reports that the English Consul had been trading in slaves. The truth was that Petherick had taken on hired porters. Petherick had arrived at Gondokoro early in January 1863, but Speke and Grant did not arrive until mid-February, sixteen months later than the date expected. It is hard to know why they presumed Petherick would wait for so many months for them in the same spot of Africa, but apparently they did. He returned back from his excursion only three days after they arrived, but he was not received. He at once realized that his post as Consul was in jeopardy and the emotional strain made his young wife ill.

At the beginning of May, whilst Harriet and Alexine were waiting at the Mashra Ar Riqq, John and Katie Petherick arrived, having sailed up from Khartoum. Petherick had been the first European to make a voyage to the Mashra, and had described the Bahr-al-Ghazal in a book, of which the ladies had a copy. He was taken aback now. The river he had sailed up before had been forty to sixty yards wide, but had now shrunk to a series of stagnant ditches. That year the White Nile was more flooded than it had ever been in the memory of man, but the Bahr-al-Ghazal had had exceptionally little water. There had been a drought in the hills that led into the western tributaries, and the fierce heat of the early spring had brought about increased evaporation.

Apparently Harriet and Alexine had heard rumours of the deaths of Petherick and his wife when they were at the Holy Cross mission on their way back from Gondokoro. They must have been very surprised to see an Englishman and his wife at the Mashra, and even moie so to be told they were the Pethericks. In fact the news had come from a rumour carried by word of mouth that Katie Petherick was ill. Later Alexine was able to show John and Katie Petherick notices of their deaths in newspapers. She also lent them the photographs she had taken of Gondokoro and their recent voyage. Such was the extensiveness of her luggage!

Katie Petherick was able to pass on to Harriet provisions and various articles which she felt might be useful. These had come from England and included wine, pale ale, tea, four tins of soup (just what the Dutch ladies wanted – they had never seen any before), biscuits, pearl barley, soap, packets of seeds, pins, needles, cottons, and pens. She also bought from them a gutta-percha inflatable boat, which they later used to cross the Bahr Jur.

Harriet and Alexine enjoyed their stay at the Mashra but had been delayed two months and were, as always, eager to press on and see what lay ahead. In addition, the rainy season threatened to commence any day. They were not sure how long the steamer would be on her voyage to Khartoum for provisions, but they could have started ahead had they had the necessary porters. This was the great hold-up, for each porter could carry 40 lbs. only, and the expedition had a small mountain of personal baggage, provisions, ammunition, china beads as barter, and camping equipment. It had been Speke's opinion that the party should consist of one person or two besides porters, but Harriet and Alexine pleased themselves. As well as a small army of soldiers and several servants, each took a personal maid and plenty of clothes and amusements. It had never occurred to them to travel without what they considered were necessities for comfort and enjoyment. They had brought with them everything they were likely to need, and this produced a monstrous luggage problem.

Alexine obtained eighty porters from a merchant called Ali Almori, and these men were to carry luggage to Ali Almori's zeriba, which lay about a hundred miles beyond Wau. Petherick passed on to them 130 porters who had just brought a consignment of ivory to the Mashra. Heuglin had gathered 100 porters, but these he needed to carry his own supplies, and there were still not enough men to carry d'Ablaing's luggage. He unselfishly offered to wait behind with Heuglin, who announced he was too ill to move. The poor German was suffering from the fever from which his companion Steudner had recently died. The immense expedition accordingly set off, thankful to leave the Mashra and be on its way into the unknown, usually then referred to as 'the interior'.

The rainy season does not start on a regular date of the calendar. Some years it holds off later than others, and it is indeed any man's guess exactly when the first storm will break. From the beginning of May the weather had been threatening to change and it seemed essential to Alexine to make an immediate move since plans had been delayed so long already. Until this time there had been little rain and Harriet and Alexine had slept peacefully on the deck of the dahabiah. The very night they stepped ashore a terrifying storm broke the long period of fine days. It started with a clap of thunder and came down with a vengeance that was cruel. The Pethericks passed a dreadful night in the cabin of their dahabiah, first sheltering beneath an umbrella erected over their bed, and then submerging themselves under a panther skin. Harriet and Alexine sat up all night trembling with cold and wondering if their leaking tents would fall over in the gale. However, the grey skies were blown away before the next day, which dawned as a beautiful African morning. Quickly the sun dried the ground and soon the chaos of the camp was put in order and everything laid out to dry.

Everybody's spirits rose with the sunshine as they prepared to set off. Harriet rode in a chair carried by four porters, and Alexine, Flora, and Anna went on donkeys. Some thirty more followed carrying corn. Being unusually numerous, the expedition caused plenty of comment and admiration from the local inhabitants. There were over five hundred porters, sixty-five soldiers, the Mudir's guard of another six soldiers, and several personal servants of the ladies. They frequently passed through small villages of neat straw cottages with vast quantities of cows and sheep, usually surrounded by high hedges. They were joined by Heuglin and d'Ablaing after the first week. Heuglin was still very weak and d'Ablaing had not sufficient porters, but they were anxious to keep up with the adventurous ladies.

In a few days the vast cavalcade had settled down to a routine which Harriet somewhat oversimplified in a letter home:

> We take very short journeys and always find a village to sleep in about four o'clock. We stop at a place that pleases us and send for the Sheik, who gives his orders and chooses our host who clears out his cattle and his furniture, and we take possession for the night. We have always found them kind and willing to quit a little group of tukuls. There is always one large one for the cows: here I, with Flora, and the dogs put by with the luggage. Alexine and Anna go to another, but the cow house has a deeper door so I prefer that.[4]

Unfortunately, all was not well amongst the men they had hired. The uncertainty of the purpose of the expedition, the lack of maps and a known destination, and the differences between the men engaged in Khartoum and those taken on from the locality, all led to unforeseen problems. The porters complained they had no corn to eat and that the meat they had been given was meagre. A crowd of men threatened to mutiny. It was a frightening experience and the ladies had no one of authority to help them: Sacker and Hendrik, Osman Aga, Halib, and Contarini were no longer with them at this hour of real need. The vakeel who was in charge of Petherick's porters had no control over them. Bravely Alexine mounted a rostrum and spoke to them. She agreed to feed them better, and an arrangement was made that the Petherick porters and the vakeel over them should go to their zeriba where they could collect more corn. For them it was a detour, but she felt a worth-while one.

The remainder of the expedition were setting up the tents and preparing for the night when a sudden storm broke directly over the camp. Lashing rain was followed by hail and widespread lightning and thunder. It was the most sensational tropical storm the ladies had yet seen – and they had experienced many. Alexine, sheltering in her tent which had been carefully tethered, felt it collapse on to her bed before she was able to get out. Shivering and soaked she had to battle against a fierce wind to get it erected to form some sort of shelter. Nor had the worst yet happened. The next morning to their horror Alexine and Harriet were held up at gun point by the soldiers they had commissioned to protect them. The men said they would not tolerate the dreadful conditions they had endured during the night, and threatened to mutiny for the same reason the porters had given, that they had been short of food. Again Alexine got them under her control. She knew their grievances were unfounded, and told them in Arabic that they must obey her. At her command the soldiers laid down their muskets. They then lined up and, one at a time, entered her tent to ask pardon for their behaviour. Although they had been given adequate food, Alexine felt she should provide more. She arranged that one contingent of men should go on ahead to Ali Almori's zeriba, and another she sent back to the Mashra to obtain further supplies of provisions.

Disaster having followed disaster, Alexine was now taken ill with fever. It started suddenly and unexpectedly, but she was soon in a critical state. Her mother did all she could to comfort her, but Alexine scarcely knew her. For three days she rallied, and then her condition worsened with long periods of unconsciousness, and times when she seemed to be rapidly weakening; but miraculously she managed to pull through.

Another week had been wasted, and the expedition had to get to the hills before the plains were inundated by the rains; and for the next few days Alexine was carried on a stretcher by four porters. Yet, despite all they had experienced, she and her mother were soon enjoying themselves again. Harriet, true to form, sent home an optimistic letter, minimizing the hazards that threatened, and describing how they were travelling quite comfortably through beautiful country:

Alexine stands the journey very well. She has a stretcher, arranged with a canopy to keep off the sun, and her mattress on it, so that she rests very agreeably and often takes a refreshing nap. I have a chair. We are each carried by four Negroes. We each have twelve, so they have time to rest. Flora and Anna ride on donkeys. Mr. von Heuglin and Mr. d'Ablaing ride on mules. We now have 120 Negroes for our immediate luggage.

. . . the ground was a rich grey and full of flowers and there were groups of trees so elegant and trim that I defy any part of England to have better.[5]

Harriet and Alexine both had been enthralled by the country they had passed through. The first few miles after leaving the Mashra Ar Riqq had been flat, but the numerous attractive villages of tukuls, surrounded by the domestic animals, had fascinated them. The route then cut through wooded country, rich in colour with flowers and fruit, and abounding with flocks of birds. Following this they crossed into the ironstone district which had grey earth, sparsely inhabited by men, but abounding with wild animals. Although herds of buffalo, elephant, and many other beasts were seen, they tended to move into cover as soon as the expedition appeared. The hunters, having failed to get bigger game, depended on antelope and gazelles for meat, and on a variety of birds including guinea-fowl, pigeons, partridges and bustards. Heuglin, who always walked carrying his gun, frequently fired at any bird that interested him to add to his collection.

After the ironstone district they crossed into the red ironstone area. Here Harriet and Alexine were enchanted with the freshness of the trees, wonderfully coloured by the first rains. Most travellers see these in the dry season. The ladies had had to endure the storms of the wet season, but were captivated by the sight of trees covered with prolific blossom. One entire day was spent winding through a wood of gardenias in full flower over a path of fresh, lush grass, the colour of young corn.

The flowers enthralled Alexine so much that she found time to make notes and diagrams when the expedition halted. They had travelled overland for about fifty miles when they reached the Bahr Jur, a tributary of the Bahr-al-Ghazal. Approaching this river they came to deep ravines filled with tall trees heavily entwined with creeping plants, known as the gallery forests. The undergrowth was dense, giving the warm verdant atmosphere of a tropical forest.

The expedition and all their goods had to be transferred across the Bahr Jur entirely by small boats, and it was a lengthy manœuvre to get everybody and everything across. Like many other rivers in the Sudan, the Bahr Jur varies in its flow enormously from season to season, and the recent rains had swollen it. By the beginning of June the Bahr Jur was wide and swiftly running. Poor Heuglin and d'Ablaing got soaked in a shower of rain; and though they had been amongst the first to get across, their luggage was mislaid on the other shore. The two men stood and shivered in their thin clothes whilst Alexine endeavoured to send messages for their cases, but such was the bulk of luggage they could not be found for some time. Harriet and Alexine were amused to make the crossing in the gutta-percha boat they had bought off the English Consul:

There were little boats of the country to pass the men and luggage, but too small for the beasts who swam over. We had bought a gutta-percha boat off Mr. Petherick, a very old, worn-out concern, losing its wind, but I went over more pleased than in the boats which are only hollowed trees. Mr. Petherick made us pay £35 for the boat, but I will not complain for it has saved us time already to cross water and we have still a river to cross before we reach the place where we mean to put up for the worst of the wet season.[6]

The Gossinga mountains where the expedition planned to install their camp still lay sixty miles ahead, but the travellers were hopeful they would reach their objective so long as there were no further delays. Up to the Bahr Jur they had been going south-west, but now they continued due west. After further gallery forests the country again abounded in flowers. Somehow Harriet managed to find time and place to write long letters describing the scenery and routine of the numerous cavalcade. She told of the Negro porters who carried their loads on their heads. They had employed over five hundred, and not one had caused any trouble, she recorded; but the subject which impressed her most was the beauty of the country they had passed through. With delight she described the immense plains with clumps of trees like an English country park, the prolific creepers falling in cascades, the ponds surrounded by trees whose branches dipped down to meet their reflection; but above all the vibrant colours and delicate textures of the rare flowers were her joy.

By this time Harriet had received Speke's letter which Addy had forwarded. She quite disdained the advice he had given. As if to contradict his warnings, she wrote fully of the success of the expedition to her stepson, John Tinne, no doubt hoping her findings would be made known to the Geographical Society in London. John preferred to avoid publicity, but was pressed by the President to give news of the Dutch ladies, which he decorously recounted, emphasizing that their expedition was for pleasure and was not scientific. In the journals of the Society's meetings, amongst notes from Speke and Grant in Uganda, from Livingstone in South Africa, and from explorers in central Australia, is intermingled information received in long letters from Harriet.

In November 1863 a member of the Society remarked on the need for exploration of the Bahr-al-Ghazal, and was curtly reminded by the President that this was being carried out by the Dutch party. Following doubts on Speke's assumption that the source of the Nile was in Lake Victoria, theories had been put forward that it lay in the region of the Bahr-al-Ghazal. It seems that the expedition, which had set out purely for pleasure and adventure, had been recognized by the experts.

16

The Slave Merchants

Three weeks after crossing the Bahr Jur the expedition came to the red ironstone village of Wau. It presented a dream-like scene set beside a small river, the Bahr Wau, a tributary of the Bahr Jur. Never had Harriet and Alexine felt so far from home, yet they were enthralled with the magical atmosphere they found here, and they experienced a simplicity of beauty such as they never had met before. They were enchanted by the neat straw huts and the fine-looking inhabitants so closely knit in their family life. The peaceful appearance of the village was enhanced by the river thickly edged with ambatch, a curious spongy wood that the people lash together to make narrow boats. The ambatch has bulky stems headed by huge feathery foliage, profuse but strangely delicate when seen against the sky. Towards evening, up the river and its banks swarmed thousands of birds: flights of egrets, geese and ducks, and pelicans flapping on their homeward journey in their hundreds.

Heuglin had already visited Wau the previous April when he went ahead of the expedition with Steudner, who had died there following the sudden onset of fever. It was by now June, and Heuglin showed the grave to Harriet and Alexine. Although deeply grieved they were relieved to think of him lying at rest in such a picturesque African scene. However, they did not have time to ruminate on any dangers which might befall themselves, for they had plans to make for the next part of the journey.

At Wau the expedition were hoping to meet another caravan with which they would join forces, but as no news of it had been received they proceeded across a small river, and three days later came to Buselli's zeriba. This was one of several stations within a few miles of each other which belonged to a group of merchants.

As the beginning of the caravan came into sight of the zeriba, which was surrounded by high poles and had soldiers guarding the entrance, there was an explosion of gunfire. Harriet and Alexine were quite unperturbed at the deafening noise that went through their weary heads. The soldiers who led the way in front of them quickly returned the welcome by firing off their muskets in unison, only to hear again another thunderous salutation. Then the gunfire was exchanged four or five times. After the last report had echoed away over the rolling hills they walked up to the entrance, and had scarcely arrived before Buselli appeared to greet them. The haughty slave-merchant grimaced at the ladies and, after speaking to the vakeel, had a few words with Alexine as official leader of the expedition. He then invited the visitors inside the enclosure. No doubt news of the caravan had reached the chief well in advance of their arrival, but to Buselli the travellers appeared peculiarly out of place. White women had never been seen in this part of Africa, and amongst the expedition of more than 700 they were immediately revealed not only by the colour of their skin but because of their clothes.

As the newcomers entered the zeriba Buselli wondered what to do with them. He had never met such a situation before, and although he had controlled thousands of men in the past, he was disturbed by the arrival of the European ladies. He realized they must be very rich indeed as he threw a glance at the size of the caravan which assembled outside the gates and beyond.

There were six Europeans in the expedition: Alexine, her mother, their two maids, Heuglin, and d'Ablaing. The women wore full-length dresses sweeping the ground, and the men trousers and short coats: probably both men had beards. No description exists of Buselli, but he was not the first slave-merchant who had entertained the Dutch ladies, and may have resembled Mohammed Kher from whom they had received hospitality during their voyage up the White Nile, in looks as well as ways. Like him, Buselli was losing the power he had held over the Negroes of the south, and was growing increasingly anxious about his position – with good reason. He had heard that the new Governor-General, Musa Pasha, had already taken strenuous precautions to halt the traffic of slaves; and knowing the ladies had hired the steamer from him and had been provided with a special guard of five soldiers at his wish, Buselli decided to play

The Slave Merchants

safe. So long as the visitors did not intervene in his livelihood, he was prepared to meet the cost of keeping them.

Therefore he poured hospitality on the newcomers in true Arab tradition, insisting they remain the first night free of charge. The following day he offered to keep the entire expedition as his guests for a few days. Harriet and Alexine discussed the strange situation in which they found themselves and decided they were obliged to stay for two reasons. First, they felt Buselli would be offended if they moved on and might disrupt their porters. Secondly, d'Ablaing was not well and Heuglin complained he felt tired; but for themselves, they had no need to rest.

After one night, surprised and somewhat overwhelmed by the generosity of Buselli, the visitors thought it would be fitting to present him with a gift in return for his hospitality and to give him one of their valuable mules. (The fact that mules and donkeys were exceedingly rare in these remote parts is illustrated by the Italian, Romolo Gessi, who visited the district on his donkey some years later, and related how 'many of the natives believed, not much to my credit, that we were one and the same animal!')

As yet Harriet was trusting and seemingly unaware of the consequences of putting herself into the hands of Buselli; and Alexine, probably becoming suspicious, was apparently confident they could get out of any difficulties by the influence she held over her men. Yet although they had not admitted as much to each other, both were beginning to puzzle over the strange sequence of events. However, Harriet reassured herself that for the time being they were settled to stay because of the rains, and wrote a long letter home telling of the grand welcome they had been given. She finished by assuring her perturbed relations that it was 'very safe'. The fact of the matter was the opposite: it was very dangerous. The brave ladies had already decided to make a get-away.

News then came they could rent a near-by zeriba which although small might accommodate them for a short period. Buselli told Alexine she could have this for 30 thalers a week. Then he changed his mind: the price he said would be 200 thalers. This was about ten times too much and Alexine refused to pay. As for selling *durra* to feed the expedition, Buselli charged twenty times the standard price; but Alexine had no one to side with her and the chief soon got his way. With reluctance she agreed to pay his bill, and the ladies transferred to the near-by zeriba before starting on the next part of their journey which they felt must somehow be managed despite the weather.

Buselli was one of a group of merchants who had set up slavery stations in the vicinity. There were several others within a few miles of each other. Upon these uncouth characters the expedition was dependent for porters. Alexine approached a merchant called Ali Almori who offered her eighty porters at a rate of 6 thalers a man. Her hopes rose as she estimated that if she could get these extra men the expedition would be able to leave for the Gossinga mountains, a march of approximately twenty days. Unfortunately Ali Almori had not finished: having compelled her to meet his price, he insisted that she should hire another 100 men from Ghattas's zeriba, 130 from Petherick's zeriba, which had been left under a manager, and then 250 from himself. The final charge for these porters is not recorded: in any case it was probably never paid. Although the experience had been very unpleasant for Alexine and her mother, they had plenty of money in the bank if they ran short. Reassuring herself, Harriet finished a letter she had been writing on a cheerful note, adding:

> At any rate we are in for it, but I would never advise anybody to come here without a vakeel and *plenty* of money! The expense of travel is ridiculous. You are entirely in the hands of a *set*.[1]

Indeed, they were entirely in the hands of a set of rascals; but having been through so many adventures before and survived, they little realized the extent of the difficulties they had let themselves in for this time. Harriet eased her mind of the extortionate costs by asking John Tinne to continue to transfer £1,000 every quarter into the Bank of Egypt for her during the coming year. It was by now early July and when she heard that the last caravans before the rains were leaving for the Mashra Ar Riqq and Khartoum, she took the opportunity of writing several lengthy letters to her relations. Afterwards there would be no further conveyance for at least four months. She, fearing the future, reflected how they had remained in safety so long by trusting in God, and hoped that a miracle would help them over the next sequence of their adventure. In her last letter she wrote:

The Slave Merchants 147

As I have had this opportunity of wishing you well I may have more, but don't reckon on more tidings for a terrible long time, as once the rain has set in communication is impossible.[2]

Then finishing she reverted to the beauty of the country which had delighted her so much:

Oh, it is a beautiful country and richly repays all our trouble, fatigue, and expense.

From July Harriet and Alexine were cut off from all their friends and relations, alone with two dull men and their lady's maids. Addy was to hear no news of the expedition for eight months, and the relations in England and the Netherlands had to wait longer. Yet the reality of the situation they had brought upon themselves did not worry them unduly, and they harboured no regrets for coming on such a remote tour. Unfortunately, they were in for a series of setbacks.

The caravan had come so far on the assumption of reaching the Gossinga mountains before the rainy season began. Suddenly information was received that the land they were about to cross was already extensively flooded, and water flowing off the hills would soon increase the swamps. They were therefore forced to find somewhere to remain in the neighbourhood for the months until they could travel again. Alexine was deeply upset. The unlucky expedition had been delayed again and again, and had wasted two weeks at Buselli's zeriba, and she felt he had prevented the party from pressing on by his cruel tricks to confuse her.

She now decided to go off with d'Ablaing and Anna, accompanied by a group of men, in search of a site where the entire expedition could camp. During that evening the sky became overcast and Harriet, left at Buselli's zeriba, longed for Alexine to return. Later during the night Heuglin came quietly to her tent and woke her up to show her a note that had been sent back from Alexine by a runner. In it she wrote that there had been rumours from her porters that Buselli, whom they hated, was trying to prevent the party from leaving his zeriba. Alexine, therefore, had written at once to warn her mother. Harriet took the news calmly. Early in the morning she wrote a note to confirm she had received the message, but then realized she could not address it for she had no idea where Alexine was. In exasperation she wrote: 'Mademoiselle Tinne. God knows where!!', and assured Alexine that she would beware of Buselli:

> ... We were all asleep when your note came. Mr. Heuglin brought it. I will inquire tomorrow if Buselli means to play us a trick and if so, you may be sure I will move to the outward tukul. I send the bottle of butter!! Mariam must be careful: we have only four bottles for all the time we remain here! The dogs are well. They ate up your dinner, Mr. d'Ablaing's and Anna's – that is they were well off today. I am glad you arrived safe and trust you will take care of your dear self for my sake.[3]

Harriet and Alexine were not only cut off from the world they knew, they were temporarily divided from each other. Since leaving the Mashra Ar Riqq, the expedition had added greatly to their fame, for they had reached land where no European had ever been before. Yet just when they could claim to call themselves explorers, the whole expedition was brought to a standstill by the rainy season. It was a tantalizing state of affairs.

Their main problem was to find a suitable camping site until they could travel on. Then, they hoped to leave Buselli and his dreaded intrigues behind them. Hearing more rumours of Buselli's plans Alexine wrote to the Governor-General of the Sudan, Musa Pasha, telling of their distress and asking that he would send out a government official 'to keep the merchants in respect'. In case this could not be done at once she asked for a signed letter ordering the merchants not to molest members of her expedition. The new position chosen lay about three miles west of Buselli's zeriba. Alexine advanced with some porters and soldiers, then returned to Harriet and the rest of the men and luggage who were to move a few days later.

Meanwhile the ladies were determined to make themselves comfortable, and although they felt unfamiliar in their surroundings, this had often been the case on their previous excursions. Little did they foresee that their precarious situation was destined to take a still more serious turn.

Up till this time Harriet had never been ill; if she had been poorly she had never succumbed. She had remarkable physical endurance for a woman of sixty-five. Several years before, when her travels with Alexine had begun, she had once written in her diary that she was really 'too old to travel', but since that time she had accomplished journeys remarkable by any standards. Not only had she cheerfully, patiently and bravely withstood the novel ambitions of her daughter, but she had been able to enjoy herself. She had talked and laughed with the people she had met, marvelled at the scenery, and overcome disasters with practical common sense. Although the Bahr-al-Ghazal expedition was bigger and bolder than any travels she and Alexine had ever experienced, she had been determined to join in whole-heartedly and with a feeling of vision, as well as excited anticipation.

Addy and Alexine had both been seriously ill at Gondokoro, and Alexine again more recently. The poor health of Flora and Anna had caused concern since leaving the Mashra, and Heuglin and d'Ablaing had suffered from tropical fever. With perseverance and determination Harriet had always kept up and about. Now she felt weak and feverish and for the first time was obliged to stay in bed.

In a letter to John, Alexine described the sequence of her mother's illness:

We had not the slightest idea of anything being amiss. On 16th July she took the quinine Mr. Heuglin had ordered but unfortunately there seemed to be something relaxing in its composition, for many people who took it immediately had diarrhoea, and it gave it to Mama too, and made her very ill. From that time she had a burning thirst which augmented till the last, and from time to time she wandered a little, though generally perfectly sensible. Her thirst was dreadful. Nothing could satisfy it. We gave her cold tea, wine and water, lemon-essence and water, and arrowroot with wine. On the 17th she was a little better and had some chicken broth which she took with pleasure. The 18th and 19th she was in about the same state, thirsty and irritable but sensible and taking interest in all that happened around her, even in a gazelle the chasseur had brought and such little things. It now seems strange but not she herself nor we had yet any fear.

On Saturday, 22nd, everything was ready, all her things packed up when on that very morning she slept unusually late. I went several times to see, but would not wake her, till at last the servant looked closely and saw she was dead![4]

The shock was immense. Harriet had been the pillar of strength to the whole expedition, not leading it or running it but always in the centre of the picture, a composed and lively person with a solution to put forward for every problem. While everybody was profoundly hurt at the sad news, Alexine was hardest hit of all. It was a shock she never got over. The poor girl was so overwhelmed that at first she could not absorb the reality of the situation. She felt lost, weak and confused in a world so remote that she could hardly believe it existed. When the dawn appeared she stared through the opening of her tent and recollected how her mother had enjoyed the journey. Yet now, the day before seemed like the distant past. The daily round would never be the same again: she would never see the person who had been closest to her heart, never again be able to ask her questions to be patiently answered, and see her sweet face light up with laughter. It was the end of a chapter of her life.

Even months later she could not bear to recall the succession of events. Ever since her birth she had seldom been parted from her mother for a day. Alexine had always had her way and her wishes in life up to this time. As she cast her thoughts back over the past days, the unhappy truth reappeared like a cruel delusion as she kept on wishing she could step out of the tragic situation as one can awake from a bad dream.[5]

Yet the saddest repercussion Alexine had to shoulder was not the memory of her mother's death, but a sense of guilt and self-blame. Harriet had, of course, died from natural causes on an expedition she had chosen to join; but poor Alexine was persecuted by the reprobation that would fall on her, not only from herself, but from others. Although the true story penetrated to her immediate family, it was too sad to be accurately told to the many friends and acquaintances in The Hague, many of whom had talked of the expedition with such contempt. Wicked allegations were made against her, and not infrequently it was said: 'If only it had been Alexine instead of her mother!'

The outcome was that Alexine was too shamed ever to return home. She was tormented from the day of her mother's death with the thought that, had she never persuaded her to come on the Bahr-al-Ghazal expedition, she would not have died. It was a humiliating recollection, and one that Alexine could never rid herself of. Yet we know Harriet was confident until her last brief

The Slave Merchants 151

illness. Had she not written back to England only three weeks before her death:

> Oh, it is a beautiful country and richly repays all the trouble, fatigue and expense.

What now was to become of the expedition caught in the rainy season? In this sad and relentless scene time did not stand still for Alexine. She realized that although the danger of Buselli had been momentarily forgotten in the shock of her mother's death, the entire expeditionary force must be transferred to the new camp without delay. A grave was dug beneath a tree outside the enclosure, where Harriet was buried until such time when they could return to The Hague with her body, and Alexine ordered a rota of soldiers to stand guard by it. To those entering and leaving the camp it served as a painful reminder of the gallant lady who had been esteemed and valued as a friend by so many of the expedition.

The sudden loss of Harriet did not affect only Alexine and her future plans, but also Heuglin and d'Ablaing. Alexine decided that she and her party should at the first opportunity go back to Khartoum; but although she felt the urgency to return, she realized that Heuglin and d'Ablaing would wish to carry on the journey of discovery they had envisaged. Heuglin had already made extensive inquiries about the next stage of the expedition. He wanted to travel westwards until he reached the Azande people, known as the Nyam-Nams: those strange Negroes of curious cultures of whom so many rumours had circulated in Khartoum but whom no white man had so far encountered.

The decision to return, having come so far, was a severe disappointment to Alexine, but she never doubted this was her duty. She assumed, moreover, that Heuglin and d'Ablaing would choose to go on, and pressed them to leave her and her retinue to return back alone. By now Heuglin was a very sick man, his former enthusiasm and vigour lost. With Teutonic thoroughness he had worked on plans for going ahead, yet reluctantly he knew he could not face the risks that threatened. Painfully he recollected how he had striven to earn his fame as an explorer, to travel where no European had ever been before, to discover the country and map the mountains of the Nile-Congo Divide. The wretched man was torn by conflict. For him, the goal of a lifetime was nearer than ever before, yet he knew he was too sick to attempt it.

Heuglin hoped that with rest and careful diet he would regain his strength of body and mind. As he tried to relax he felt frustrated that he could not get about to make an accurate map of the surrounding district. Even if he had been fit enough it would have been impossible to do this during the rainy season. Fortunately, his efforts towards geographical research were not wasted: he managed to draw a map from his notes of the area the expedition had covered since the Mashra Ar Riqq, and to add further details from conversations with the porters. He marked the present position of the camp as 'Establishment A.T.'. Installed in comparative comfort within the precincts of the camp he felt, as he stared at the large unfilled areas, as if he was playing blind-man's-buff in making plans for his future journey. To add to his problems he had not brought sufficient geographical instruments to make his plan of the district, even so far as it went, strictly accurate; and though he had been short of money and the means of transport, he regretted not bringing the necessary equipment with him.

With rest Heuglin was beginning to recover his health, when a message reached him that Schubert, a fellow German scientist, who had travelled out on a previous expedition some distance south, had died of a fever. This came as an ordeal for Heuglin, and he wrote in his notebook that he was:

... Confined to bed with fever and dysentery for two months at Establishment A.T., the last frail member of the German expedition, with apprehension for his own existence.[6]

He had already decided that if he was to continue he must return to the Mashra for further supplies; and now he made up his mind to join Alexine and her retinue at the first convenient opportunity.

During this difficult period of waiting Alexine occupied herself with organizing the day-to-day routine of the camp. She had received particular kindness and loyalty from Flora and Anna since her mother's death. They at least had helped to heal the pain of the tragedy, and Alexine had fallen back on their faithful support with thankfulness. Flora was about sixty years old, and had been her mother's maid for longer than Alexine could remember. As Alexine had observed, age had changed her very little, for she complained whether she was in The Hague or on their travels. She was always complaining. In fact Harriet and Alexine had long ago learnt to turn a deaf ear to her grumbling. Harriet once had described her as 'always the same: always as cross as a bear with a sore head'. Yet although Flora was full of complaints she was a splendid servant. Hard work and high standards seemed to come to her naturally, and above all she had proved herself at Harriet's death. Silently Alexine blessed Flora for all she had done at this melancholy time.

On 20th August another blow fell. A month to the day after Harriet, Flora died. In every way her death resembled Harriet's: she took to her bed with a slight fever, but her end was sudden and totally unexpected.

The additional shock to Alexine was cruel. At the time of her mother's death she felt she had lost everything she had to live for; yet within the stress and suffering that had followed, Flora's integrity had shone as a flame in the darkness. The loss of Flora, on whom she had depended, drove her nearly mad as she struggled to surmount this second blow. The same ritual took place as for her mother, and Flora was buried next to the grave of her mistress. This time, just as Flora had cleared up Mrs. Tinne's belongings, Anna set about packing up in Flora's tent. Poor Alexine sank into a depression of deep sorrow and conflict over the expedition which she had initiated, but found in Anna a companion to console and give her moral support. For Alexine, the girl who had always had her way, worse was to come, but the agony of further events was as yet unforeseen.

17
Survivors return to Khartoum

In Khartoum, Addy and Mr. Thibaut were worried, for they had heard no first-hand news from the expedition for several months. Addy had never felt fit enough to return to Cairo by herself. As time went by, slowly and painfully, she became more and more agitated about her dear relations, and often wished she had accompanied them – for then at least she would have known their whereabouts. As matters stood she knew nothing, and although rumours were rife in Khartoum she clung to the hope that they would presently return. Furthermore, cruel rumours to the effect that her relations had bought slaves on the White Nile came from a party of French travellers. Of course, Alexine had bought a family of slaves, but only to free them; and in any case they had run off or been recaptured shortly afterwards. Addy reflected how Harriet had chatted of their friends and the Dutch Royal Family when she had last seen her, as if she might never live to return.

As the months passed by she became almost delirious with anxiety; and her letters, written in a scratchy and detached style, made her relations realize how confused and agitated she had become. Within a year she had almost run out of money, but at the same time she heard that the banker in Cairo had advanced Mr. Thibaut £1,500 on behalf of Harriet. Little matters tended to upset her. The pretty cage birds she had been given had been a fine collection which she had delighted in, but the cat had killed them some months back and now the empty cage was another sad memory.

Besides staving off her loneliness by writing letters, Addy received frequent visitors, though not of a sort she would have chosen. She greatly appreciated the mission church; and although the services were Roman Catholic and she was a Protestant, she joined in whole-heartedly. Here, every Sunday there was a considerable gathering of people from widely different backgrounds.

The harmonium was played by Martin Hansal, the Austro-Hungarian Consul who had taken over from Baron von Heuglin when he had joined Alexine's expedition. Hansal wore full Consular uniform with vast epaulets. Coupled with Mr. Thibaut, who was always resplendent in Turkish attire, he apparently liked dressing up despite the heat. Addy, tall, handsome, but sadly thin, must have felt hot and restricted in the clothes she was accustomed to wear: her dark bonnet, buttoned boots, long-sleeved dresses and serge coats, for she had no alternative.

Once at the mission, at the christening of a Sudanese girl, Addy was asked to be godmother and Captain Speke was made godfather. During the ceremony, which was well attended, loud bangs were heard as friends of the girl celebrated the event by firing guns in her honour outside the church. Yet nothing could divert Addy's anxiety over her sister and niece. 'Everyone tries to make me believe they have sent no messages because they hope to come very soon to Khartoum,' she wrote home, frightened that she had received no news.

The months ticked by. Addy met most of the few Europeans who had come out to Khartoum. Some Frenchmen talked to her of their project to build a railway from Cairo to Khartoum, and how she wished it had already been completed! The English Consul and his wife, John and Katie Petherick, were unfailingly kind. They offered to take her back to England with them when they went, and did all they could to relieve her misery. The person upon whom she depended most, however, was Mr. Thibaut. He had tried to re-engage the steamer for Harriet following her instructions by letter, but completely without success. He had since heard that the steamer had gone up to Barbar carrying slaves. As the end of 1863 approached, Addy and Mr. Thibaut became seriously concerned, for they felt certain the expedition was in difficulties.

Now, surprisingly, it was Addy who was to send help to Alexine. Somehow during those lonely months in Khartoum, when to some people she appeared half out of her mind with worry, she had the ingenuity to obtain, either by influence or with the promise of money, some seventy-five soldiers and a group of porters, together with enough provisions to save Alexine and Heuglin from starvation.

Alexine's expedition had started on their return journey at the beginning of January 1864. At Wau they were met by the search-party initiated by Addy, which was to be Alexine's salvation. The most difficult and wretched part of the journey was still to come, but the prospect of moving towards safety and security seemed all that mattered, and Alexine silently blessed Aunt Addy: Addy whom she had laughed at and who had been such a despondent traveller, always patient and polite, and willing to talk to the most boring visitors.

The relief party came as a godsend. The sight of their arrival must have been electrifying to Alexine and Heuglin, for by this time the problems with porters and soldiers was desperate. The newly arrived contingent brought fresh hope to the expedition: without them the chances of getting back to Khartoum had been slim; with them there was every hope of success. At Wau the soldiers Addy had sent procured some extra porters. Negotiations were made with a chief, then the barter was completed and the chief kept in custody until the men were delivered as promised. At the same time a letter was received from the reis of the dahabiah Alexine had travelled out in, saying it had arrived at the Mashra Ar Riqq. The message was written on a screwed-up bit of paper in an indistinct hand, saying that this was the first boat to arrive at the Mashra in the season, and that it had taken forty-five days to make the voyage from Khartoum. The reason for the delay was unexplained, and Alexine and Heuglin wondered what condition the Bahr-al-Ghazal would be in for their return voyage.

On 14th January the first part of the sorrowful expedition led by Alexine turned back from Wau on their long trek, and on 22nd January there came yet another unexpected death. Anna, Alexine's maid, died of a fever in much the same manner as Harriet and Flora. Alexine, already numb with sorrow, unable to distinguish fantasy from reality, knew only how much she would miss the Dutch girl who had been so close to her in all her recent difficulties. The men carried the bodies of her mother and Flora in rough-hewn coffins, and now another was made for Anna, so that she too could be buried in the Netherlands.

The way back to the Mashra was tedious, and on some days pitifully little progress was made. The porters were unco-operative and excitable owing to suspicions amongst themselves that they were later to be sold as slaves. The villages that had once welcomed them turned hostile. As the expedition approached, the inhabitants left their homes, filling the wells with sand. It was sometimes late into the night before the wells were dug out and a little dirty water eventually obtained. The advance caravan consisted of 450 people to feed and water, and each day satisfying them appeared as an insurmountable ordeal for their young leader.

By the time the straggling band of travellers reached the Mashra Ar Riqq it was the middle of February, and there were twenty boats in the port. Alexine learnt that the steamer had been sent to Barbar carrying slaves, and that Musa Pasha, the new Viceroy of the Sudan, had delayed the boats ordered by Mr. Thibaut by not allowing them to leave Khartoum until exorbitant taxes had been paid. At this she was mad with anger. Months before she had written to Musa Pasha complaining of the molesting and torment she had suffered from Buselli, and she wanted to bring a lawsuit against the slave-merchant when she got back to Khartoum. It seemed unbelievable that the Governor-General himself was causing her further delay, and she decided to take her complaints to his higher authority, the Viceroy of Egypt.

A few days after Alexine and her party reached the Mashra, Heuglin and d'Ablaing and their retinue arrived. The two men, halted by their weak and weary bodies, had been carried on stretchers by a rota of porters. To board the boat, however, they had to fend for themselves, for it was necessary to half-swim, half-wade through the dense swamp of water-covered vegetation. There was no time for modesty, and, seeing their goal of the two dahabiahs a few hundred yards away, the men stripped off their clothes to make the crossing. The mud was soft and where the water seemed clear the current ran swiftly forcing them to lose balance. Eventually, after four and a half hours of trudging through the swamp, they reached the dahabiah.

When at last the expedition had assembled, it was the end of February. They packed their luggage into two dahabiahs and a nuggar, and soon set off down the Bahr-al-Ghazal. The river was still extremely high and fast-flowing, and the outlook from the boats very different from that they had experienced the previous April; for the ambatch trees which had lined the banks had been snapped off and washed downstream leaving short jagged trunks and broken branches in their place. The sky was always overcast, and the heat of the day broken by frequent thunderstorms. With an eerie quietness the downpour would start, the wind and lightning inevitably followed by ferocious cracks of thunder and drenching rain beating against the boats and their sails. Fortunately, the storms were brief; and as the sun came out the dahabiah would be enveloped in a fine mist as the water evaporated from her decks to show the two other boats slowly following in her wake.

After one night of incessant rain both dahabiahs became waterlogged and were forced to a standstill until the deluge stopped and they could be bailed out, but worse than heavy weather was to befall the expedition.

At Fashoda, now known as Kodok, the White Nile was completely blocked from one side to the other. It appeared from first sight that the barrier had actually been built, and Heuglin wondered if it had been designed to prevent slave-dealers' craft from using the river. He later realized the barrier could only have been formed by nature, such was its strength. The reed was so firmly packed that hundreds of workmen would have been needed to build such a dam. Already the dahabiahs had been pushed and pulled along with poles and boathooks, and they had frequently cut away blocks of land to make a way in the river. Now the Mudir of Fashoda ordered over 150 of his men to assist the boat crews in cutting a canal through the formidable barrier. Heuglin recorded the episode:

Whilst one part of them pulled at two lines, the other part worked with boathooks. The partially made canal was widened by others with hooks and hands immediately before the boat, and so the fettered reed was at last, after two days, tolerably broken through. The canal being scarcely fifteen to eighteen feet wide, the current was enormous like a waterfall, but in spite of it the river was only two feet deep. The underneath was paved with half-decayed weed.[1]

At Fashoda Heuglin noted that, given time, the current would more likely force a new path through a neighbouring swamp rather than break the dense barrier. Another closure the expedition had come to in the Bahr-al-Ghazal had led Alexine to dis-

Survivors return to Khartoum

covering an alternative channel which was, and still is, named after her, as the Miyah Signora. Indeed, some sixteen years later a Russian explorer, Johann Junker, reported:

> We found to our amazement that the whole breadth of the White Nile at the so-called Miyah bita Signora (a backwater named from the intrepid traveller, Miss Alexine Tinne, who was the first to explore it) was obstructed by a grass barrier over 300 yards wide. The new formation had accumulated during the last few days since the vessels had descended.[2]

An Italian officer, Romolo Gessi, who was under the command of General Gordon, suffered terrible disaster in 1881. Gessi and many of his men were stricken with malaria in the Bahr-al-Ghazal when his convoy of boats were trapped for weeks in the floating sudd. Many of the men died from starvation and Gessi survived the ordeal only a few months.

Hardly had the expedition passed through the canal at Fashoda and were sailing downstream to Khartoum, when the unforeseen happened and they were held up once again. A search revealed that five slaves had been hidden in the hold of the dahabiah. They were set free and the guilty reis was severely reprimanded by Alexine who told him she would have him imprisoned. However, soon after, the reis cleverly captured three sailors from a pirate boat.

This happened because Alexine wanted to get a letter to the Mashra concerning the transport of the remainder of her luggage, and, meeting a line of four pirate boats going upstream, she hailed the first of them to stop. The vessel deliberately sailed on. Likewise, the second boat was about to pass, when the reis and two sailors from Alexine's dahabiah were lowered into a boat and towed towards the pirates who were towing a nuggar in which sat three sailors. Taking no notice of threats, the men from Alexine's dahabiah were soon under fire, but unperturbed they adroitly cut the tow rope of the nuggar. Luckily, a sharp breeze carried both boats downstream. The protesting sailors were neatly captured, and were taken under guard to Khartoum to be tried in court.

Inquiries were made at landing places to obtain supplies of food, as provisions were becoming scarce, but the markets had little or nothing to offer. Eighteen months previously the same merchants had pressed the ladies to buy from them on their voyage to

Gondokoro. Now many markets had closed down and food was scarce everywhere. They passed Kaka, the village of Mohammed Kher, who had entertained the Dutch visitors with such ceremony, but this was quite deserted. Mohammed Kher had fled to the mountains to save being savaged by those he had so cruelly maltreated.

The sad little flotilla progressed slowly homewards. At places Alexine's dahabiah made a better speed than the others which would become separated, usually to catch up by the evening. Almost daily they passed three or four pirate boats anchored together. Eventually, the weary and hazardous voyage through the sudd was finished and the boats sailed more briskly down the final straight reaches of the river. In Khartoum Addy was distraught with anxiety and, shortly before they arrived, was to have a dream that Harriet had died.

18
Tragic journey to Cairo

During the period Addy had been left in Khartoum she had found a sympathetic companion in Katie Petherick. Katie was very anxious over Speke's rejection of their supplies, and still did not know if her husband would be summoned. He had already been dismissed as Consul, following the allegations that he had used slaves. Addy was equally worried by uncertainty. She had had no news of the Tinne expedition for many months, and longed for Harriet, upon whom she had been so dependent. As the days passed by her fears mounted. She had no guide as to when they might return, and it was hardly surprising that she gradually became ill with distress. The kindly Pethericks tried to comfort her in every way they could, and told her again that she could travel with them to Cairo; but poor Addy had lost much of the will to live by the time Alexine eventually returned.

One night shortly before Alexine sailed into Khartoum, Addy dreamt of the shape of things to come. For a while Katie had been seriously worried over Addy's frail condition. 'Miss Van Capellen is an angel . . . and I pray God will let her remain yet awhile,' she wrote in a letter to her sister, and then recorded the story of Addy's dream. 'Oh, Mrs. Petherick, I must tell you my dream!' Addy had said. 'Last night I saw my lovely mother and my dead sister holding out their arms from the clouds to take me there also, and I was *so* happy. I awoke from this dream but later when asleep again I had a dream of Harriet – she was DEAD.'[1] Katie tried to reassure her older companion by telling her that dreams were often contrary to fact, and they passed the afternoon reading to each other.

Towards evening John Petherick came home to announce that the Tinne expedition was coming down the river. Addy was overjoyed at the thought of seeing Harriet and Alexine again, and after dining with the Pethericks she returned home. They had promised to send a messenger should the boats arrive during the night. At three they were awoken. The dahabiah of d'Ablaing and Heuglin pulled into the shore and was tied fast. John Petherick hurried to meet them and, hearing of the tragic deaths, told his wife to return to bed. But she met the reis and was told the worst: Mrs. Tinne had died last July, her maid in August, and Alexine's maid in January. As soon as the sun was up d'Ablaing and Heuglin, together with Katie Petherick, set off on horses to tell Addy.

The expedition returned to Khartoum on 29th March 1864. They had been away fourteen months. A few weeks earlier rumours that disaster had overtaken them had got into the European newspapers. Recently John Tinne, as well as giving information to the Geographical Society in London, had read a paper to the Liverpool Geographical Society on his relations' travels in the Sudan. Without mentioning who the travellers were, he entitled his talk 'Geographical Notes on Expeditions in Central Africa by Three Dutch Ladies', and for this he made a detailed report based on Harriet's letters. The result was purely factual, and showed little of the drama and adventure the expedition had experienced. Until he heard more John did not feel he could publish his talk, and he had received no direct information since Harriet had written in July 1863. As Alexine was enduring her return journey he wrote to Hora Siccama, Harriet's brother-in-law:

Thank you for your letters. I return them to you again along with a corrected and I hope interesting account of their travels, which I have been requested by one of our literary societies to read to them. Whatever I may do in the way of preparing such a paper is one thing but my reading it publicly is another, and depends on events, which at present cause us all great anxiety but which I have every reason to believe are unwarrantable and cruel rumours only as to the fate of our dear relations. I have in fact dates from Khartoum down to 12th January last, which are later than any that have been received from that quarter as far as I learn and there is no mention of any such disaster as has now been propagated and circulated in the Dutch, Belgium, and now English newspapers.[2]

Evidently John had been in close communication with Petherick in his capacity as English Consul. Petherick now sent news of the deaths by messenger to Egypt and thence to England by telegram.

Alexine could not bear to stop at Khartoum, which held so many memories, and ordered her dahabiah and luggage boats to proceed north where they moored by the Island of Touti. Addy wondered what sort of reception she would get from her niece, but was welcomed warmly. She was surprised to find Alexine so calm, but obviously relieved to unburden her afflictions on her patient listener. The poor girl was still obsessed with the thought that her relations and friends would blame her for bringing back her mother as a corpse. Addy, kindness itself, did all she knew to comfort her.

Later that day they were joined by Mr. Thibaut. Alexine was tormented over the money he had spent on her behalf. She felt it had been unnecessary to give in to Musa Pasha's exorbitant demands, and distressed that there might be further debts. Mr. Thibaut explained meticulously that nothing could be done to regain the money already spent, but this did little to quieten Alexine. It has not been recorded what charges Musa Pasha made on the Dutch ladies, but evidently he took from them an extortionate sum. Without warning, he demanded excessive taxes to be paid on the outward voyage as well as the homeward one. The money was handed over by Mr. Thibaut, who was not allowed to send boats to collect Alexine and the remaining members of the expedition until he had paid. Valiantly he protested, but to no avail. The boats were kept waiting until he had paid up fully on behalf of the ladies he had taken upon himself to protect.

For the present Alexine felt compelled to economize to the hilt. Her efforts, being temporary, were rather absurd. She and Addy discussed the vast cost of the expedition, the return voyage, and future plans. Since the three of them had been in the Sudan a sum of between £10,000 and £15,000 had probably been spent, possibly far more. Now Alexine spoke of her wish to get away from Khartoum, and of the ideas of going to live in Barbar or Syria which she had been considering. How Addy must have yearned to return to The Hague, yet she put Alexine's needs first.

Seven weeks later Addy was taken ill, and a doctor was called; but he was not unduly worried over her condition. Alexine was told, only half an hour before she reached the scene, that Addy had died; and again this was an acute shock, for she had already become dependent on her aunt's companionship. The next day a funeral service was held on the Island of Touti. There was a large gathering, and all the Europeans Addy had come to know over the past two years were present. They were as cosmopolitan a group as any, yet united in sympathy. Despite the heat all wore their funereal best. Alexine headed the mourners with Mr. Thibaut by her side, but even with the tension of the occasion she resented his presence. Yet as the river flowed peacefully by, all was not quiet, as more curious onlookers arrived to be hushed by the gravity of the ceremony. Later a memorial service was held in the Roman Catholic church which Addy had so often attended, and a sermon preached by one of the missionaries. In her will she left money to these people who had given her strength and courage to endure her lonely existence.

Sorrow had followed sorrow, but Alexine was not one to be downcast for long. The first step she had taken on returning to Khartoum was to write a long letter to John recording the disasters in detail, knowing he would inform the rest of the family in England and the Netherlands. Although she was anxious to get the news to him before anyone else, he had already heard from Petherick. Another description of the catastrophes came from Heuglin: Alexine had pressed him to write explaining that the calamities had been unpreventable. She also sent a map Heuglin had drawn showing the route taken to Buselli's zeriba.

Alexine had never written many letters, but now she found time to write several to her relations, giving them a detailed account of the expedition. She felt alone, and had nobody left to confide in, and no doubt found tranquillity in putting pen to paper. In a letter to her aunt, Jemima Van Capellen, describing her anguish and remorse, she concluded:

I was so sick of sorrow that I lay for days on my bed, trying only not to think. There was something too monstrous and unearthly in such a rush of sorrows, and I got very ill. Aunt Addy, who had been well for a whole year, died at my return. Your sorrow will be dreadful, but I think even you cannot imagine the unspeakable sorrow it was for me. It was all so sudden that I could not realize it and in my very sorrow, the new unhappiness with the old, one forgot its cause, and I got myself every moment expecting her or thinking of telling her something. Then the truth came on me each time afresh: she is gone too. They are all gone![3]

Alas, before the letter reached its far-off destination in The Hague, Aunt Jemima also had died!

Since Alexine had been away on the Bahr-al-Ghazal expedition for fourteen months, many changes had been made under the stringent rule of Musa Pasha. Previously, she and her mother and aunt, as wealthy and distinguished visitors, had been treated with every attention. They could rely on assistance whenever required from the French Consul, Mr. Thibaut, and in Khartoum had been treated as honoured guests. Within a year the situation had been reversed. Alexine returned to find all Europeans treated with contempt – intrigues being staged to make them suspicious of each other, and the Consuls carrying little prestige and no power to help.

In a letter to Uncle Jules, which she described as a 'long tirade which came out of itself', and which she wrote because she was 'bursting with indignation and had nobody to tell it to', she specified the difficulties Europeans in Khartoum were facing. 'I could not have been more astonished if I found Holland burning Jews,' she wrote; and then described the malicious bullying some of the Europeans and their servants had endured. For reasons which are manifest, she herself had suffered no interference:

> I have not luckily been so insulted yet, and a scrape they will get in if they do, for I certainly won't stand it with the patience of philosophy, as they call it, of the colonists here. And when they have the alternative of being shot or shooting me they will be confused, for insolent as they are, they don't dare yet *openly* to murder Europeans![4]

Musa Pasha had inflicted massive taxes, with the result that he had harmed commerce, leading to the closure of many local markets and a desperate food shortage. To make matters more serious for Alexine she heard there was famine in Egypt. This drove her to writing to her Uncle Jules at The Hague with a long list of provisions, which she asked him to send to the Consul-General in Alexandria. 'Khartoum is like a desert,' she woefully remarked after struggling to get enough for her journey by every means she could devise. The necessary supplies were not available at any price, and to add to her dilemma she was, for the first time in her life, short of money.

Despite worries over the future, and even though Alexine was weary from the series of disasters that had befallen her, she was determined that Buselli and other slave-merchants should be punished for impeding the expedition by withholding porters and food. Besides which, her vengeance against Musa Pasha surpassed even her anger against the slave-merchants. Against him an official complaint was filed, but the Governor-General of the Sudan was not to be roused, and by refusing to admit he had received her communications, he made her even more angry. She was exasperated at the excessive taxation, wild at being labelled as a slave-merchant, and in desperation decided to carry her complaint to the Viceroy of Egypt. Her quick mind was soon at work to produce an effective method of attack.

She would again write to her Uncle Jules, an eminent Admiral in the Dutch Navy, and get him to air her grievance to the King of the Netherlands. Brightening at the idea, she soon felt confident that if the King were informed personally, he would be obliged to see that her complaint reached the Viceroy. Uncle Jules, her mother's youngest brother, was a benevolent extrovert, and Alexine had only to ask to gain his sympathy and assistance. In a frank and detailed letter she explained her dilemma and told at length of the injustice of the taxes, and of being granted no protection against the tyranny of Buselli and the other merchants. She claimed that they should be made to pay fines:

> It may strike you as rather strange that I ask money of these merchants, but it is the only way to punish them, for prison is a farce here, and I cannot ask for their execution. I think I will give the money to some mosque, or to the government, to show I wanted it only for right's sake.[5]

As has been mentioned, news of the Dutch expedition had appeared in newspapers all over the world, and no doubt Alexine had received some of these notices amongst her post. Brooding over how she could repay Musa Pasha in every way for his insolence, she decided that publicity of his injustice towards her

Tragic journey to Cairo 167

would damage his prestige and offend him most. She therefore wrote to John requesting him to send details of her complaints to the Press. Alexine no longer had her mother to ask, and henceforth she showered her long-suffering half-brother with her insoluble problems. But her protests against Musa Pasha appear to have got little publicity, and, finding she could do no more in Khartoum, she made arrangements to get to Cairo, accompanied by Heuglin.

During the late afternoon of July 5th 1864, Alexine sailed in the dahabiah in which she was already installed, with a second to carry her luggage. Heuglin followed in a third dahabiah. The same evening John and Katie Petherick left Khartoum, discreetly choosing to moor their dahabiah some distance from the position Alexine had chosen. Five days later the boats arrived at Barbar. Alexine settled in a pleasant house overlooking the Nile and surrounded by a garden on the outskirts of the town, whilst Heuglin chose a house nearer the centre.

She had hopes that it would be easier to get provisions at Barbar, but the food shortage was widespread. Here she witnessed greater hunger amongst the people than she had yet seen, but eventually she managed to buy corn from Khartoum. Large quantities of food were necessary for the next part of the journey as she still had her retinue of about eighteen servants. Camels were very scarce, and a large caravan was necessary to cross the desert – for Heuglin and Alexine had a vast amount of luggage. Both had brought back many scientific specimens. There was an incredible quantity of wooden boxes, tin trunks, and bulky leather cases, and in addition they had the four coffins carrying the dead back to their homeland. About fifty camels were used to take Alexine's belongings, and Heuglin probably needed as many again. Fortunately they succeeded in hiring enough, though at a high price. John and Katie Petherick were not so lucky. They, wishing to cut across the desert from Abu Hamad so that they could sail by the Nile to Cairo, bravely set off on donkeys on a search for camels. Failing, they realized they must make do with bulls to carry their luggage.

Alexine could not abide making the journey by the Nile route she had taken on the way out, and therefore planned to return by the desert crossing from Barbar to Sawakin on the Red Sea, a distance of 250 miles. Heuglin travelled with the same caravan, but Alexine found no geniality in her staid companion.

To travel by camel is the most leisurely means of transport, and during this time she must have reflected on the journey out, when there had been so much to look forward to. Now she had lost her mother, Addy, Flora, and Anna. Sacker and Hendrik had been with them as far as Khartoum and then fled home. Osman Aga had drowned in the rapids approaching Gondokoro. Even Matruka, her treasured dog, had died giving birth to puppies on the White Nile. Poor Alexine kept the weight of her sorrows to herself, but, stunned by the series of misfortunes, she was thankful she had Heuglin to accompany her back to Cairo even though she gained little sympathy from him.

As the days drifted by and she began to recover from the burden of her grief, she became persecuted by guilt. The outcome of the expedition had been cruelly disappointing, and it seemed that a lonely life lay ahead. She had witnessed many atrocities in recent months, and never ceased to air her disapproval in public in the hopes of getting authority to act. Noticing the crowded and stinking conditions on a slave boat which anchored at Barbar, she and Heuglin, together with the Pethericks, had tried to get some of the miserable, half-starved creatures freed, and sent letters of protest to the local Governor and the French, English, and Dutch Consuls in Alexandria. Yet although no effort was spared, the endeavours seemed fruitless.

Heuglin busied himself making notes and taking measurements along the route, for he wanted to make a map of the crossing. This was later published, as was much of his work, in the German geographical journal, *Petermann's Geographische Mitheilungen*. The specimens he had diligently collected filled so many crates, he worried how he could afford to transport them back to Berlin.

Towards the end of October, after two months of arduous travel, Alexine and Heuglin reached Sawakin. It was a feat to arrive alive, and they were both worn out and weary with the heat and discomfort of the desert crossing. Usually the sky is clear and the sun hot, but when Alexine arrived she found no view of the hills and even the buildings were hidden in mist. Here she was fortunate enough to receive hospitality and simple comfort at the French convent.

Tragic journey to Cairo

Everywhere about the town were hordes of Egyptian soldiers, and here, at last, plentiful provisions could be purchased. The port, shimmering like a jewel at the edge of the azure water, and backed by rose-coloured mountains, was well-known for its slave-market. From the time of the Pharaohs, merchandise had been exported from here to the East: ivory and valuable hides, ostrich feathers, gum arabic, millet and sesame. Yet the fine oriental buildings and residences of the town had been built with money from the sale of tens of thousands of slaves exported to Arabia and beyond during the last hundred years.

Soon the English Consul from Suez arrived, congratulating her on her journey and offering to help: later the French Consul also arrived. There was little she needed from them, but what gave her pleasure was to see that the local people respected and saluted them, unlike Khartoum where the Consuls had been treated with contempt.

After two weeks Alexine and Heuglin boarded a freight steamer, *The Gladiator*, for Suez. Usually the voyage took six days but they were not so lucky: a violent head wind held them up for another four days. It was cold and wet, and the rain persisted every morning. Alexine and her servants were miserable and kept to their bunks in an effort to keep warm. An uncouth crowd mingled on the deck whenever the weather looked like clearing, and at one stage clouds of huge locusts were blown on to the steamer, being seized by the passengers who devoured them with gusto. As always, Heuglin was absorbed in taking notes, and worked assiduously to draw up a correct list of the places they passed. Near Suez, several lighthouses had recently been built, and he learned of the port's improvements: new docks, a railway connected to the town, and a sweet water canal, all constructed since his previous visit.

Many ships were in port as *The Gladiator* docked. Alexine was met at the quay by a messenger sent by Mr. Ruyssenaers, the Dutch Consul-General in Alexandria. She was told that he himself had promised to set off immediately he received news of her arrival. A telegram was sent to Liverpool; and when John and Margaret Tinne heard that she had got to Suez they made plans to travel to Cairo to meet her.

At last Alexine realized she was on the final lap of her long journey. Had she not written from Khartoum six months ago in a letter: 'Suez will seem so close'. Yet although Cairo was only four hours by train, and would be familiar, how far it was from the house in Lange Voorhout and all those dear relations she had not seen for so long. A pile of letters awaited her which she eagerly read. In her haste she picked the more recent first, and was horrified to read that Jemima Van Capellen had died some weeks previously. She knew of her aunt's illness, but this loss was quite unexpected. She answered, wrapped in blankets, unable to get her hands warm, but determined to answer them, though she could not conceal her sadness:

> Such a succession of misfortunes, which generally happen at long intervals, is too cruel, and it will require all the kindness expressed in the letters of you all, to cheer a little of the gloom of my arrival.[6]

For the time being Alexine could not foresee her future. On her return journey she had resolved never to visit places where she had been with her mother; but she hated Suez. Where could she go but Cairo? She asked Heuglin, who went ahead, to find her a suitable house; and meanwhile she purchased some warmer clothes for herself and her servants, and bought further supplies of provisions. There was no need to open the parcel of food sent from The Hague which was awaiting her. A month after arriving at Suez, Alexine went to Cairo. Here she found a warmer welcome. She met John and Katie Petherick again, and was pleased when John and Margaret Tinne arrived to be with her.

Yet in spite of their kindness Alexine was obsessed by the idea of revenge against Musa Pasha. She was still angry and hurt, but a wall of officialdom had prevented her getting any satisfaction. Mr. Ruyssenaers could only promise to press the complaint against Musa Pasha right up to Ismail Pasha, Viceroy of Egypt; but this seemed to be an ineffective approach. Probably John and Margaret tried to quieten her, knowing nothing would come of the complaint. John, logical and practical, could not make sense of his flamboyant and temperamental half-sister: the damage was done, Harriet and Addy were both dead, and now it was best to let the matter rest; at least, so John tried to persuade Alexine. Still puzzled, he wrote to the relations in The Hague:

Tragic journey to Cairo

What is your opinion of those last letters sent by Alexine? I cannot say (*entre nous*) that I am quite satisfied with her part of the case. It strikes me there has been as much a quarrel about money as love![7]

After a few weeks John and Margaret left Cairo to return to their big family in Liverpool. It was Alexine's wish that she should be left alone.

All the way from the Bahr-al-Ghazal expedition Alexine had preserved and brought back in her luggage the skilful botanical drawings, paintings, pressed specimens, and even seeds and plants of the flowers she and her mother had collected. These she sent to the eminent botanist, Theodor Kotschy, of Vienna. The seeds and plants were to be passed on to the Imperial Herbarium of the Court of Vienna. Kotschy was amazed with the quality and the large number of new species in the collection. Alexine had made systematic notes as to the development of many plants, and several of them were more remarkable than Kotschy, who had travelled extensively in the Sudan himself, could believe possible. He asked permission to publish a selection, and employed a colleague, Dr. Peyritsch, to copy and lay out the illustrations of the flowers.

The book, *Plantae Tinneanae*, was subsequently produced. Because of its immense proportions, it is seldom examined though carefully preserved in many libraries. It measures two feet by eighteen inches, but is less than an inch thick; and within are printed twenty-seven plates of flowering plants which have been hand-painted with exquisite delicacy. Their profuse growth, their weird yet wonderful shapes and vibrant colours, which bloom and wither so quickly in tropical Africa, serve as a reminder of the magical qualities nature propagates in the southern Sudan. At the beginning is an account covering the Bahr-al-Ghazal expedition, and notes on the flowers written in French and Latin; and on the first page is a picture of Harriet Tinne, to whose memory the *Plantae Tinneanae* was dedicated.

PART FOUR

North Africa

19
Cruise of the Mediterranean

Amongst her mail at Suez Alexine received a letter from her uncle, Vice-Admiral Jules Van Capellen, to whom she had written regarding her complaint to the Viceroy of Egypt. In the first place the Admiral had had a talk with the Foreign Minister of the Netherlands. Then he approached the King. With diplomatic foresight he told of Addy's recent death, and waited for the King to ask after Alexine. He thus obtained an opening to expatiate on his niece's plight, and her complaint of how badly she had been treated in the Sudan. Alexine had already received a charming letter of sympathy from the Queen, and now the King said he would take her complaint in hand. He promised that he personally would direct instructions to the Consul-General in Alexandria, who was familiar with the case already, and also write to his minister in Constantinople asking for their influence. Yet they met with no success apart from making her case better-known, and she heard nothing more.

When Jules wrote to Alexine he appealed to her to return to her home country, if only for a short time. Following the recent deaths of three of his sisters, he sincerely wanted to see Alexine, for he wrote:

> The less we grow in number, dear Alexine, the more we must stick together, to make up for that kind and treasured affection for ever gone. I hope time has borne off a little of the sorrow. Bear up, take courage and trust in God![1]

In the same letter Jules remarked that he had no commitments, apart from escorting a member of the Prussian Royal Family who was coming to swim at Scheveningen. But Alexine never returned to her homeland.

Years later, when Jules represented the Dutch Navy at the opening of the Suez Canal, he must have pondered over the extraordinary adventures of his niece and wondered how she had mustered the courage to achieve her fantastic travels. Like her, he never married, yet he was extremely sociable, and his charm did not bypass the ladies. In fact a story relates that he was very amicable with the lady next door. Apparently rumours abounded that a builder had been called to cut a connection between the two houses. However, the couple were meticulous in their care never to be seen walking together, and if they wished to take a stroll at the same time he would follow at least fifty yards distance behind her. Unfortunately for them, suspicion of the close liaison was aroused, for their two dogs played in the space between the couple as if well-known to each other.

Alexine moved to Cairo as soon as Heuglin had found her a house. She then changed to a quaint residence in the old part of the city, not far from where Shepheard's Hotel then stood. Her house had been built as a harem and had a wall of frosted glass that allowed a filtered light, keeping the room comparatively cool. As the year wore on and the summer heat penetrated the thick stones of the house she decided to change her bulky, heavy clothes for Arab dress. She put aside her well-worn boots for a pair of local sandals, and felt more comfortable and more part of her new home.

A German artist called Wilhelm Gentz frequently visited her house. Gentz, who had already travelled extensively in Nubia, was interested in making drawings to illustrate as many tribes of Negroes as he could find. He was introduced to Alexine, who was renowned for having collected – at different stages of her travels – a retinue of eighteen coloured servants. No doubt Alexine had chosen some for their looks alone; and now, having little to do, they were pleased to pose for the artist.

Later Gentz was to write a description of Alexine's house in his book of reminiscences. He recorded how it was approached by an unusual flight of steps descending to a lower floor, such as he had not seen before in Cairo. Passing through a yard where servants lazed and children played, he was frightened by two enormous dogs leaping from the shade towards him.

When Alexine appeared he was surprised to see her dressed as a woman of the locality with a cloth over her head. They proceeded down a passage piled with many boxes of relics from the Sudan, some of which were partly unpacked and lay unarranged along the walls. As they passed through several darkened chambers he saw more and more of the vast ethnological collection which had been transported out of the heart of Africa. He described how he saw: 'Queer weapons, stuffed birds, horns of all sorts of antelopes and rhinoceroses, implements of Sudanese people which lay piled on one another.'

Alexine was living quietly in her rented house, but she was overspending her income. The household was a large one and she wanted to keep it that way. During the last year there had been massive expenses. The cost of bringing some twenty people all the way from Khartoum to Cairo had increased at every stage of the journey, besides the expense of transporting the enormous quantity of ethnological specimens. However, she felt confident she could curtail her expenditure if she settled in Cairo, at any rate for some months. Alexine had long wished to live in Egypt, and she now decided to build a luxurious house in superb surroundings on an island in the Nile. She felt she would find security in a home she could call her own. To enable her to make plans with an architect and to start building, she wrote to John asking him to make her a transfer of a bigger allowance, but he was reluctant to allow this, foreseeing she might change her mind. He therefore stood firm, though in a kindly way, and suggested that some of her capital should be invested in alternative stock which would bring additional income, and that she should engage a reliable man from England to carry out the supervision of the building, and let her know in advance the costs of maintenance.

It seems that when Alexine required an answer she was capable of catching the post. She at once wrote off to John with instructions for a man 'who shall be paid in a way that I do not scruple to employ him and whom I may consult on the value and management of land, who will help me to select a site of land, take the necessary steps for purchasing it and who will help me to build a house and manage my land or garden'. She also enclosed a piece of paper on which she had signed her name a dozen times in case he had need of her signature!

Though plans were made and Alexine enjoyed imagining the finished house and even dreamt of living there, it was never begun. Probably she fell into difficulties in buying the site through her recent contretemps with Ismail Pasha, for to the Viceroy

Alexine was well-known. Both from Khartoum and since she had been in Cairo she had exasperated him with details of the injustice she had suffered in the Sudan. More strength to her cause was heaped upon the Viceroy by backing from the King of the Netherlands; but Ismail Pasha, though she caused him the desired concern, held Alexine off with an insurmountable wall of officialdom. The hostilities were, moreover, never fought out, for Musa Pasha died in 1865.

The summer of 1864 had been exhausting in its hottest months, and now that Alexine saw no prospect of getting permission to build her dream house she decided to make a move. The thought of living near the Nile had greatly appealed to her, and captivated with this romantic idea she thought the most satisfactory alternative would be to hire a yacht in Alexandria and go to sea. No sooner had the plan of action been sown in her mind than it began to germinate. Life once again seemed to be looking up. After eighteen months in Cairo she cleared up to start on fresh travels. She had the entire collection of ethnological specimens shipped to John Tinne, who placed them in the City of Liverpool Museum. (This collection was almost entirely wiped out by Hitler's bombs, but fortunately the catalogue remains, quoting some three hundred items from war-clubs to wash-tubs, and from carved calabashes to ostrich-feather headdresses.)

It has been recorded that whilst in Cairo Alexine was admired and befriended by many of the local people to whom she spoke in Arabic, and was known in local parlance as the 'Contessa Olandese'. Always a sentimentalist about animals, she could not abide the sick donkeys, and would dress their sores and nurse them with simple medicaments. A fable soon circulated round the district that the Contessa Olandese kept a donkey hospital.

Before leaving for Alexandria her philanthropic endeavours had to be curtailed. All her animals were sold: that is to say all but two or three dogs which she could not resist keeping with her. She knew if she dismissed any of her servants they would be taken immediately into slavery, so somewhat reluctantly she felt obliged to take them with her. Later, she was to talk of the 'potpourri of nations composing my household', and in France and Italy the young Dutchwoman with her large retinue, some of them coal black, drew plenty of comment.

The steam yacht Alexine hired in Alexandria was called the *Claymore*. Probably of English origin, it had accommodation for herself, twelve to fifteen servants, and the crew who were Egyptian. Few letters exist to tell us where Alexine sailed in the *Claymore*, but it is known she visited Crete, Greece, Italy, France, Sardinia and Malta during the summer months of 1865.

In October she arrived from Candia at Naples. She had anticipated spending the winter there. Meanwhile John Tinne in Liverpool, and the relations in the Netherlands, wrote to and fro trying to make out her whereabouts. In attempting to keep her money matters in order and attend to the ceaseless inquiries, John numbered each letter he wrote her. From Naples Alexine sent her long-suffering half-brother a plea to send money urgently, but she did not acknowledge its arrival for several weeks, and then wrote in her usual casual manner:

I just received your letter No. 157 and letter of credit for £400, and I can understand you are rather astonished I did not write sooner from Naples but hope you will excuse me when I tell you why: that is partly I waited till I heard if you had received my letter from Candia, not wishing to repeat for nothing all those long and not pleasant details about my being absent from Egypt, steamboats, etc.

I must, of course, return to Egypt, but in the meanwhile I cannot tell you exactly yet what I shall do for the present. I had meant to spend the winter in Naples, but since my arrival here the cholera has been officially declared. Now I am not a bit afraid for myself but I don't like at all the idea of going through all the trouble and anxiety I have had with sick people in my house in Cairo, and the gloom and disturbed state of a town suffering from cholera.[2]

Besides which, Naples held no fascination for Alexine. The Dutch Consul she found extremely hospitable, but most of the people she had been given introductions to were living out of the city. Amongst her papers there exists a letter of introduction to Garibaldi, but it seems she never made use of it. The city dwellers she saw as a morose and miserable lot, whilst the fearful tales of brigands and murders could not fail to shock her. In view of the likelihood of being attacked and robbed, she never ventured out without taking her entire retinue along with her, including the cook, armed to the teeth. Apparently the party caused some lively entertainment to the locals. In a letter Alexine wrote:

> If Naples has not struck us much I may say without vanity that we have struck Naples. I am so accustomed to Arabs and Negroes that I quite forgot they could be found extraordinary but my first walk in Naples soon made me aware of the fact. They were so mobbed that I have been obliged to dress them in European clothes. But the Neapolitans are good-natured people and the sensation they made seemed to be a pleasant one for they were everywhere admired and made much of and the photographer of the place asked to do their pictures. Abdullah's wife is particularly admired. She certainly is a little beauty. If I were not afraid they would perforate it in the quarantine like the letters I received I would send you her picture though it does not do her justice. As I care less about my own I send you one. The photographer made me have it done by force. I only send it you for the sake of contrast with my Egyptian one.[4]

Alexine was quite right. The contrast between the picture she had had taken under her own supervision in Cairo when she stood posed with her horse, and that taken in the Naples photographer's, is all the difference between good and bad. Later her relations had an opportunity to see the work of this photographer, for he published the pictures, together with appropriate captions, in a German illustrated paper.

Three of Alexine's retinue suffered from light attacks of cholera, and aware of the cramped quarters on the *Claymore* she decided they must leave Naples, having enjoyed during her stay visits to the opera at San Carlo and a journey to the summit of Vesuvius. The *Claymore* sailed to Ischia at the beginning of December during a spell of magnificent weather, though inadvertently she returned to Naples before the year was finished. From Ischia the yacht sailed to Malta and then on towards Sardinia when the warm weather unpredictably turned to thunder and lightning. Suddenly a terrifying gale struck, such as Alexine had never imagined possible in the Mediterranean, and rocked and buffeted the *Claymore* without ceasing for two or three days and nights until it seemed certain that she would be wrecked. Somewhat miraculously she proved big enough to compete with the massive waves and eventually entered the Bay of Naples. Even on the last

Vice-Admiral Jonkheer Jules Van Capellen

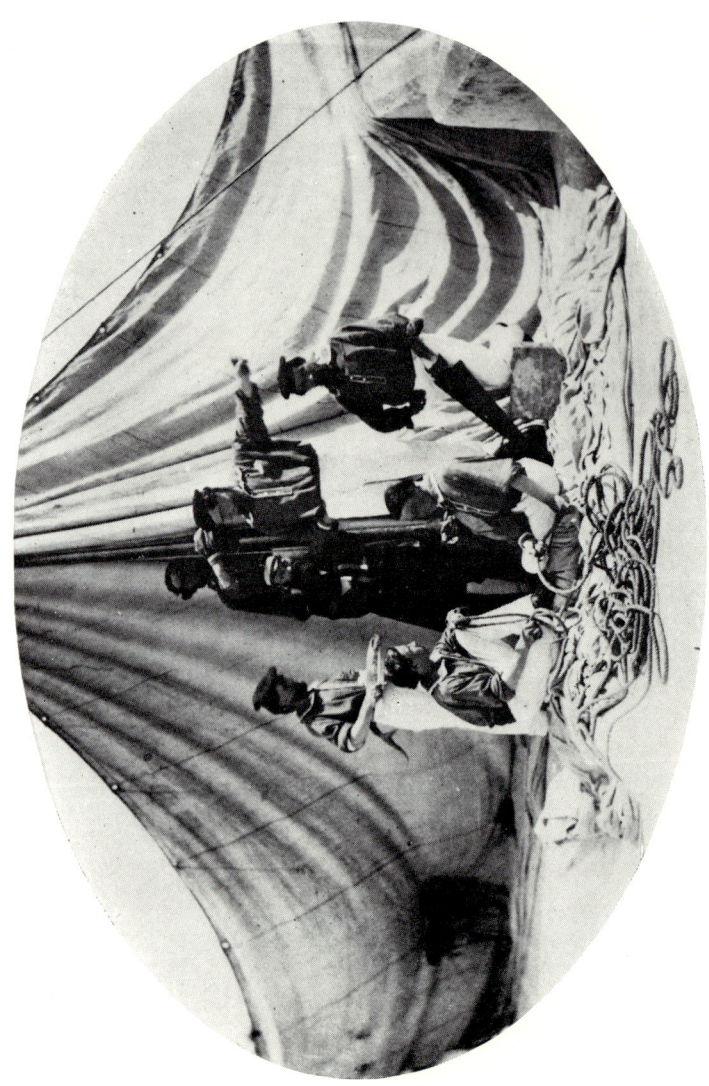

The Dutch crew photographed as sailors by Alexine, Algiers, 1867

stretch they appeared to be fast approaching some rocks, but after a hazardous night a tug boat came to their rescue when their distress flag was seen in the morning light. Early in 1866 the *Claymore* reached Sardinia and went on to Barcelona, then back to Leghorn in March, and Genoa in April.

There had always been a close affinity between Alexine and Sara Sandbach, her mother's younger sister who had married Philip Tinne's partner. Aunt Sara was a particularly affectionate, sympathetic person, and had for some time fostered a desire to travel out to meet Alexine. It was a bold step, for since her marriage she had never ventured out of England. As Sara had been a favourite Lady-in-Waiting to Queen Sophia, probably the Queen urged her to go to see to Alexine's welfare, for though absent from The Hague she had become one of the biggest topics of conversation. It is little wonder that Sara never joined Alexine, for she found it impossible to track her down. Always preoccupied with more pressing matters, she would write letters just as she was leaving a port, often concluding that she had many more things to say but was in a tremendous hurry and must finish.

Her relations were prepared for surprises, but she now wrote to John with a request that was totally unexpected. Previously, when she had stated her intention to sail in the Mediterranean, he – knowing her dislike of the sea – imagined this would not be a drawn-out phase of her travels, and therefore had advised her to hire a yacht. Yet six months later Alexine asked that he should buy her one in England and have it sent out for her to collect at one of the French Mediterranean ports. John was pleased to attend to his half-sister's commissions, but the complications in purchasing a yacht were immense, and were increased with the buyer being Alexine. Although 'comparatively so much nearer' as she described the south of France, she apparently had no intention of returning to The Hague, though she kept on the house in Lange Voorhout. The yacht was to be bought by instructions through the post.

After much time and trouble spent travelling about England by train and stage-coach at a time when he did not want to leave his comfortable home, John found a suitable yacht for sale at Cowes. She had been built in the Isle of Man three years previously, and weighed 200 tons. He was pleased when he discovered her compartments naturally divided into four sections which he thought would be suitable for Alexine, the Captain, the servants, and crew. The yacht was little used. She had only sailed to Cherbourg and back, before rendering her unfortunate owner bankrupt. Owing to his need to sell quickly, she changed hands for £1,950, complete with masts, sails, anchors and other necessary equipment, which, John wrote, 'you will think a great bargain and so it is'. Being an astute businessman, he was extremely pleased with his purchase. He might have guessed that it was inevitable that Alexine would hold a contrary opinion.

The real problems began after buying the yacht. First she announced she preferred a Dutch crew, and to sail the yacht under the Dutch flag. She also wanted to be in charge of her vessel and to give orders to the Captain herself.

'Would it be in order,' wrote John, besieged with her requests, to Jules Van Capellen, 'for the yacht to be registered at the Royal Yacht Club of Rotterdam under Alexine's name since she is a woman?'

Jules answered there was no reason why not so long as Alexine was Dutch, but was she? As with so much, Alexine had never remained constant. She was of English and Dutch parentage, as her father had taken on English nationality; but now she had to decide between the two. She immediately posted a statement to John simply bearing the words: 'I declare myself to be Dutch.'

The cost of sailing the *Seagull*, as the new yacht was known, to the Netherlands was considerable, and John was not prepared to pay the sum of £70 which was demanded for the use of an English crew. Eventually, the yacht was checked as sound; and was, after negotiations, sent to Rotterdam, where a crew, carefully chosen by Jules, and on contract for more than a year, took over. Finally, there was indecision on Alexine's part whether to meet her new treasure at Marseilles or Toulon.

In May the yacht arrived at Toulon. From the start Alexine was disappointed. With alterations and redecorations, and the crew dressed and installed, together with delivery costs, the expenditure had risen astronomically. Soon Alexine was writing to her Cousin Yetty: 'Fancy wasting £4,000 on a yacht!'

In any case Alexine wished to do the yacht up herself. She wanted plenty of comfortable and spacious accommodation for herself, and not so much for the crew; but although the new yacht was bigger than the *Claymore*, she had less room. There was insufficient space for Alexine and everybody else to live at sea, and she realized that her half-brother had purposely meant that she should go aboard by day and spend the nights on shore. 'Besides, her shape is hideous,' she wailed in a frenzy of dissatisfaction and disappointment. One might have hoped Alexine would mellow to appreciate the trouble she had caused John and Jules, but she never changed her opinion. The truth was that the yacht which had pleased John so much when he had chosen it at Cowes, bored Alexine.

Soon after taking over her yacht, Alexine sailed from Toulon. The name *Seagull* was translated to *Meeuw* when it sailed under the Dutch flag. It was the beginning of June, and the *Meeuw* followed the coast to Marseilles for a brief period before crossing to Algiers. Her new owner, whilst waiting, had already been thinking of travelling in North Africa. Once she arrived in Algiers, Alexine had no desire to take to the sea again. She moored the yacht, and decided to find out about crossing the Sahara. Meanwhile, she rented a house and found accommodation for her retinue. Her crew, headed by the jovial Captain Wilhelmie, quickly made friendships in their new environment, some of which were to lead to romances. Summer drew on to autumn and passed into winter, and she felt relaxed – settled once again on the African continent.

Though she had missed the horror of the cholera epidemic in Naples, a worse fate was to hit Algiers, for in January 1867 a sudden earthquake shattered most of the town. There was dreadful suffering amongst the poverty-struck population, and the cholera soon became widespread. Appalled by the squalor and disease, Alexine, who never turned a blind eye to human suffering, did what she could to help and restore order. For many years she was remembered by these people for her kindness and courage. About this time many outbreaks of cholera were recorded that occurred amongst the poor due to inadequate living conditions. The dreaded disease had ravaged Liverpool and several other English towns two years previously.

From Algiers into the Sahara

After Alexine had lived in Algiers for some months and it became evident that she had little intention of utilizing *Meeuw* again, Captain Wilhelmie, who had been engaged to lead the crew, approached her. Would it be possible, he politely asked, for his wife to come out from the Netherlands to join him? This may have seemed a big favour to seek but Captain Wilhelmie had only based his request on his observations. Alexine's African servants all had their wives with them, kept by the lady they had attached themselves to so confidently. Moreover, Abdullah, her head servant, had recently shed his former wife in a legal divorce, and taken on a younger woman. If they had their spouses with them, why should not Captain Wilhelmie?

Settled in Algiers, Alexine felt blissfully happy. The house she had rented was not particularly attractive or comfortable, but the household had become a homely centre. As, during the day, her retinue turned up for their duties, often accompanied by wives and children, it resembled one enormous family – such was the informality, contrasting strangely with the hierarchy of many a Victorian residence. She had become familiar with her surroundings, but at the same time had plenty to occupy her thoughts and engage her lively imagination and curiosity. However, she had never been resident anywhere for long, and now her real ambition began to take shape. For many months she had dreamt of making a journey south across the Sahara, continuing either towards Timbuktu to the west, or Lake Chad to the east, and now this long-held ambition of crossing Africa seemed possible to fulfil. Reliable information and plans were not easy to come by. Several people in Algiers offered conflicting views, so that she began to wonder whom she could trust. She needed to buy new equipment and supplies. Barter in the Sahara consisted of provisions and valuables which were virtually unavailable in Algiers, but plentiful

From Algiers into the Sahara

in the Netherlands and England. Alexine had no hesitation in sending off long lists of large orders which were to be shipped out to her. Meanwhile, she spent much time reading: she learnt to speak Tamachek, the language of the Tuareg, and settled down in earnest to her hobby of photography.

To Captain Wilhelmie's request she replied in the affirmative, and it was not long before Mrs. Wilhelmie arrived. Accommodation was arranged and the united couple appeared satisfied. Unfortunately, the coming of Mrs. Wilhelmie was to prove the turning-point in Alexine's relationship with her Dutch captain.

Before many months were up all the six sailors remaining from *Meeuw* were married, and the strange assortment of nationalities who looked after Alexine had once more increased. She was very much amused by the romances which had so rapidly succeeded each other, and picturing that she would later settle in Egypt after her travels, where they would all be able to live quite cheaply, however many, she wrote off to her Uncle Jules:

> We are all flourishing – *all* my sailors married! Yes, all!! except me. All those wives I hasten to say are not going with me, except the one I already told you of who is to be my lady's maid, and they are to remain here till I am settled with their husbands in Egypt, and then they come to live in that country.
>
> There is not a day Captain Wilhelmie does not split his sides with laughter at the funny family we make and the queer navigation he has fallen in with. His principal work of late has been acting father to his sailors and bringing them to church to be married. Every week there has been a wedding. Oh dear, oh dear, it is such a funny set with all those terrestrial sailors, Arabs, blacks, and French wives all pigging together. It is certainly rather expensive but at least one gets a laugh for the money.[1]

Furthermore, to illustrate her terrestrial sailors, Alexine enclosed some photographs she had recently taken of what she entitled 'L'Equipage à Bord' and 'L'Equipage au Désert'. For the first of the two sittings taken in the desert outside Algiers she rigged up an enormous mast with sails and had the Dutch crew wearing their seafaring clothes. For the second the same men formed a similar group but were dressed as bedouins ready for their journey across the Sahara. They are most skilfully posed, and the photographs are remarkable for their clarity and distribution of light and shade. They have several times been shown in exhibitions. No doubt the ordeal of preparing for such pictures caused everybody concerned much merriment; and watching the photographer in action was quite an entertainment in itself.

Alexine had been advised to move to Tunis or Tripoli to start her Sahara crossing, so that she could follow the principal trade-route south through the Fezzan. Before she made final plans to sail eastwards she was persuaded to explore the M'zab region to the south of Algiers, for by the time the camels were procured, and camping equipment and provisions purchased, it was autumn. In Tunisia the rainy season threatened, and Alexine, unable to forget the fate of the Bahr-al-Ghazal expedition only four years previously, felt it was essential to wait before starting a major journey.

Upon her decision to make an excursion to the M'zab, some 300 miles south of Algiers, and because she knew better than to plan a return journey, she first had to collect together all her luggage in order to pack what was needed, and to distribute her obsolete belongings. She tried to make light of the task of tidying up her household effects, but it was difficult to sort out the necessary from the unnecessary. She bought new equipment for the expedition one day, only to find she had to rid herself of something the next. Her biggest headache was to unburden herself of *Meeuw*.

The yacht had never been a success. Before it had arrived, Alexine had had enough of sailing the Mediterranean, and when the alterations had been made the yacht seemed no more spacious. and she had no desire to cut down on crew or servants. Sadly, in less than a year after the yacht had been collected from Toulon, she was delivered to Malta to be re-sold, and a letter was dispatched to John asking him to deal with the discarded toy. It was no easy task for him to sell a yacht moored in Malta when his business lay in Liverpool, but he never reproached Alexine. Besides which, he received minimal gratitude for his trouble. He had made extensive efforts in having major structural changes made to the yacht to suit his half-sister's exact wants, only to receive frequent complaints that *Meeuw* had been expensive in maintenance and had required many repairs. She had finally written to Jules:

From Algiers into the Sahara

It is so frail that in a short time it would require more repairs than it is worth, and I use it so little it is a pity to keep it on for nothing.[2]

In a jocular mood John wrote to Jules Van Capellen suggesting, as a last resort, that one of the Dutch relations might take up yachting, as he was anxious for a quick sale. The request fell on stony ground for Jules also had been given his share of worries by Alexine, for she had asked him to reinstate most of the crew he had engaged so carefully under contract. The Captain and six of the crew stayed on with Alexine, and even so that was too many. The superfluous sailors from *Meeuw*, probably about eight, had to be paid off. It was hardly surprising there was widespread discontent amongst them. They had been employed to work at sea, and had found themselves living in dock for months on end. It was a way of life very different from what they had expected, and they found little to do in the hot and dirty port of Algiers – except find wives! Even Alexine, who had so easily adjusted herself to North Africa, had nothing but contempt for the people she had so far met. In a letter, she described the difficulties she had come up against:

In Algeria one cannot venture in safety half an hour out of a great town, and the might of the French can hardly make the Algerians conceal their fanaticism and hate to Christianity, and then the travelling! Nobody seems to travel in Algeria, no caravans, no African mode travelling even. There is no life, no traffic, no ability, nothing. Everybody seems to rot (forgive the inelegant but true expression) rolled up in his rags where he was born, ignorant and careless of what goes on two days from him . . .[3]

In fact Alexine had decided she had had enough of Algiers. Her craving was to explore the unknown, and she would have felt the same anywhere along the North African coast which is well implanted with European customs and civilization. To meet Africa proper one has to journey south to get beyond the influence of the Mediterranean, and then with the Atlas mountains behind and the Sahara desert ahead the norm quite suddenly changes. This vast, mysterious land has for centuries been criss-crossed by caravan routes, especially since the Arabs introduced the camel from Egypt and beyond. To enable the traders to travel it was essential to keep open certain wells along the way, and most of these were under the domination of a people called the Tuareg.

Alexine had obtained a recent book published in Paris, *Les Toureg du Nord* by Henri Duveyrier, in addition to studying their language. At the age of seventeen Duveyrier had been on holiday in Algiers, and had made a short excursion southwards. Fascinated by the Sahara, and eager to explore it, the young Frenchman had gone to London to seek the advice of Heinrich Barth, the brilliant German explorer, who had crossed from Tripoli to Lake Chad and had reached Timbuktu on expeditions sponsored by the British Government. Of all the Europeans who had taken part in expeditions to cross the Sahara, Barth was the sole survivor. When he met Duveyrier he was so impressed by the French boy's candour and diligence to gain scientific skills, that he gave him every encouragement.

The following year Duveyrier made a successful tour of the M'zab where he met a strangely-dressed man in Ghardaia, who he was told was a Targui. He had a passion for finding out more about such people, of whom he had gained some knowledge from Barth. Within a few months, in 1861, Duveyrier, only twenty years old, had persuaded the French to send him on an official mission to meet and examine the Tuareg. He left Philipperville, a port 200 miles east of Algiers, and travelled south to Constantine and Ghadames, where he met the supreme chief of the Ajjer Tuareg, called Ichnuchen, who was later to take a fancy to Alexine. Duveyrier realized the danger of continuing to cross patrolled territory of the Tuareg, but bravely he went on to reach Ghat. At Ghat he was so badly and roughly treated he was thankful to get away alive. So far he had discovered much but felt he had only made a beginning. Unfortunately, he never travelled again in Africa, for on his journey to France he caught typhoid, became seriously ill, and suffered loss of memory from which he never recovered. Fortunately, his notes were written in such fine detail that it was possible to publish his book three years later.

Alexine was captivated by the romance and courage of Henri Duveyrier. She could not resist the idea of travelling to the places he had been to and meeting the curious people he described so colourfully. Before starting, she was held up waiting for goods which she had ordered from France, of which the guns and ammunition were vital, but as far as the Djelfa she was assured it was safe to travel unarmed. Therefore, she sent off an advance party to cover the first stage of the journey as far as Djelfa, a centre on the high tablelands of the Atlas Mountains, where they were told to wait for herself and her retinue.

It was Alexine's experience that the only satisfactory way to prepare for an expedition was to have a trial run, and as the advance party set off she saw what a novelty the travellers appeared to be. For the first part of the route along the mountain pass that leads south along the wooded slopes of the Atlas range they probably walked, some leading horses and mules to carry their luggage. What amused Alexine was to see her six sailors dressed up looking like a typical assortment of Arabs until they began to move, when their postures and gesticulations all at once seemed very Dutch, and their serious expressions and guttural speech seemed comic with their bedouin clothes.

It was late autumn and the climate was pleasant. Alexine was relieved to be left with only three servants: Abdullah (an Egyptian servant she had come to rely on), his wife (a Negress who acted as her lady's maid), and one sailor boy. It had been arranged that her party would soon follow the others to Djelfa, then they would form a caravan to travel farther south to the M'zab.

As usual there were more delays than Alexine had foreseen, and several weeks had passed before her small party started. It was some time in December, but the date did not interest her any more than she knew the time of day. The travellers would simply follow the sun for the time to rise, the time to journey, and the time to make camp for the night. She enjoyed the route through the fortress town of Medea, and winding alongside and over the mountains. A sense of excitement grew as they passed through treacherous gorges over rough roads of pebbles or rock, the vegetation becoming more scanty the farther they rode. Occasionally she glimpsed a gazelle or saw a monkey scuttle away, but there was little noise other than the wind playing ceaselessly on the rocks, and the roar of waterfalls and fast-running rivulets.

The distance from Algiers to Djelfa was seventy miles, and as they travelled there Alexine looked forward to organizing the caravan for the next stage of her journey. She had been informed that she would be able to hire camels, get provisions from the market, and buy anything else she wanted from Djelfa, but she had not been prepared for staying in one of the most desolate habitations the world has ever known. 'We are anchored,' she moanfully recorded in a letter, 'in the ugliest and horridest little place in the world, Djelfa.'[4] Her sailors could hardly be sincere in their welcome. Captain Wilhelmie and his equipage of men were evidently very dissatisfied with the discomfort they had encountered. Djelfa was a squalid collection of single-storey mud houses situated 6,000 feet above sea-level on the high tablelands. At night the cold was penetrating, and every morning they had to hammer and break down ice to obtain water. In addition to enduring the agonizing cold and wind, severe sandstorms were a frequent hindrance especially to cooking and cleanliness. The bleak little town was deserted as well as forlorn: most of the nomads who frequented it had left to winter in areas to the south where the climate was not so extreme.

It was evident from the moment of Alexine's arrival that her expeditionary force was frustrated to distraction, and she decided to leave as soon as possible. As well as the worries of her servants she had her own discomforts to bear: the tents she had purchased so expensively in Algiers had shrunk with the wet weather, dust now penetrated the seams, and with the gusty winds she wondered when her tent would collapse. 'It is having to be uncomfortable for nothing,' she wrote in her distress, bravely enduring her aches and pains to set an example to her expedition, and went on:

Then we have the African plague of sandstorms. Yesterday we were nearly buried alive, and nobody could move from his tent and for variations we have wind and rain! The worst in my opinion is for all this suffering there is no compensation, as Djelfa is a newly-built French village with a French jardin public, and nothing to remind one one is in Africa but the discomfort.[5]

Though Djelfa was a dejected town it commanded a second-to-none panorama to the south, overlooking the vast loneliness of the Sahara. Alexine was enraptured when she looked beyond the nearby palm trees and shepherds grazing their flocks, to the infinite horizon of ever-changing colour beckoning her with its secret mystery. Thankful to leave Djelfa, and fortified with the view that lay before them, the party soon set off for the M'zab. The caravan probably covered about twenty miles a day. It is not known how many the expedition made up in numbers, perhaps twenty or thirty people at this point. As usual, Alexine did not travel light, and probably the caravan consisted of over fifty baggage camels besides riding camels and three horses.

From the beginning this was to be a journey beset with problems and delays. On the move, all went well; but, unfortunately, bickering and arguments amongst the people seemed to crop up at every stopping place. There were frequent setbacks before they came to the small town of Laghouat and a crisis was reached when one of the sailors was so ill that they had to rush the last miles to get him into hospital, and one of the Algerians also. By the time the caravan had waited while they were nursed back to health, an Arab woman appeared to be giving birth imminently, and Alexine had not the heart to go on. Meanwhile, she decided they needed more camels and had to wait for these.

It was at Laghouat, 250 miles from Algiers, that Captain and Mrs. Wilhelmie asked that they should be joined by their son of fifteen, and no sooner had Alexine agreed than they pleaded for their daughter to come as well. Although the Wilhelmies paid their children's fares from the Netherlands, Alexine was put to considerable delay in making arrangements and sending telegrams off to get the children sent out. It seems that she could only add to her party, and the numbers never failed to grow at every stopping place. Then to be safe she would make fresh purchases before the provisions were much depleted, necessitating more camels and more guides.

At the beginning of 1868 the caravan reached the M'zab, a well-known area of the Sahara containing seven walled towns, each nestling in its man-made oasis. The small but important population depended entirely on the trade carried on in their markets, especially in Ghardaia, the capital, between merchants coming from the north and the south. Here they did not stay long and perhaps Alexine was disappointed with the astuteness of the M'zabites. Although Barth and Duveyrier had found the walled towns, each surrounded by hundreds of palm trees, a haven after the aridity of the desert, she may have had reason to think otherwise. For she found the women were hidden away, seldom to emerge. Even at the present time they wear veils completely enveloping their figures in billowing fullness, and allowing only a tiny diamond-shaped hole for one eye to peep from. Alexine would have felt embarrassment walking through the town, she could not surrender herself to being an exception, and before long the cavalcade set off travelling east to another town of the M'zab called Guerrara. Again they stayed but briefly. Often the water was salty and muddy, for the M'zab is an artificially made area of irrigation, and the wells are sunk tremendously deep, some to 300 feet. Rain falls rarely, sometimes not for years on end; then it may come as a torrential downpour. The unfortunate expedition, dependent on tents as their only cover, were now to experience such a rainstorm.

Already the tired travellers had seen much variety of landscape on their tour. They continued riding north-eastwards towards the little town of Touggourt where it was necessary to cross over *ergs*, the vast sandy wastes which are interrupted by drifting dunes. With few landmarks, they had to steer by the direction of the sun and stars. Any sign of a track had been eradicated by the sand being blown and shifted by the ceaseless wind which never relents in its molestation of the traveller. Alexine tried to remain confident, but although her guides were in charge she felt an increasing responsibility towards the long line of people that followed behind her. The lack of perception of all that the mind is accustomed to, and the phobia of being lost and abandoned, is experienced sooner or later by all Europeans who are brave enough to travel long distances by camel. For some it has to be resolutely fought against day after day. The desert is a medley of moods, of fear and safety, the enigma of the unforeseen.

Alexine seems to have been at a loss to understand her sailors who did not enjoy the beauty of the desert and who only counted the discomforts. She controlled her disappointment over their reactions by telling herself she could leave 'some of the luggage and weak people at Touggourt', whilst I cruise amongst the Tuareg, as she wrote of her plans in a letter.

Alexine rode in a palanquin, a linen-covered fixture attached to the saddle and arranged to protect the incumbent from sun and sand. It was a curious form of enclosure more like a tent than an umbrella, and so large it gave a curious top-heavy silhouette to the form of the camel. The edge of the cloth might be finely woven in colours and braid hangings would fall beneath, to knock against the camel's legs as it lumbered along. The top-knot would be a bunch of ostrich feathers or gaily coloured ribbons which fluttered in the breeze. Mrs. Wilhelmie also travelled in a palanquin, which later was shared by her husband. In a third palanquin the Wilhelmie son sat on one side and their daughter and Jasmina sat on the other.

Already Alexine was inspired with the glowing and ever-moving shades and shadows of the desert that led her on: she felt a satisfaction in the simplicity of the routine the expedition followed. After the day's weary ride she would look forward to the cool of her tent when she could reflect on the spiritual beauty of the country, those breath-taking scenes of movement and melody. Poor girl, every evening when she wanted to be left alone she would hear approaching footsteps and raised voices, and standing at the tent door would be a band of her servants with a dispute or grievance for her to listen to. On the whole the sailors had settled down well in their changed environment with the exception of Captain and Mrs. Wilhelmie. Alexine felt it better to sort out differences on the spot, and did her utmost to fall in with the Captain and his wife, even at her own inconvenience. On a big expedition arguments over provisions are inevitable, for when there is quantity people will be extravagant. Ample stores would be allocated to last a month, but they would disappear after a few days, and then the blame would be passed from one to another. As Alexine sadly defined the loss, 'nobody has had them!' She knew that Captain Wilhelmie had been too generous in his distribution and that the fault ultimately lay with him. He in turn complained that he had been accused unjustly of being stingy and did not deserve the caustic comments that were being made behind his back. At Laghouat Alexine asked the advice of the Commander, a French colonel, who understood her dilemma, common to all who go on expeditions, and recommended that she should have the provisions allocated in rations and packets to be served out week by week. The quantities of foodstuffs which Alexine systematically listed seem massive. Each day for the Europeans, excluding herself, it would include six kilos of potatoes, two kilos of flour, two kilos of sugar, raisins, butter, milk, salt, olive oil, besides ample orders of meat and two bottles of wine or Madeira. But still there was not enough, and as Alexine wrote:

> Throwing away money is a pleasure to no one, and it is just because I hate to be mean that I wish to do all in the best way, to be able to satisfy all.[6]

However, Captain Wilhelmie found other matters to complain about. At first he had ridden on a camel and after a while decided he did not like the motion, so very different from what he was used to. He had then changed to share a palanquin with his wife, and at first found this a pleasure. Perhaps he came into too close proximity with Mrs. Wilhelmie who had not found it easy to adjust to desert travel, but before long he asked Alexine if he could ride one of the horses. She had brought three horses with her. They had been expensive to buy and feed, but were necessary for catching stray camels and for carrying messages. After the first day on horseback the Captain was extremely sore. He was reaching middle age and was not a good horseman, and found the day long and the saddle hard. That evening he came to Alexine's tent and flew into a temper. He had found the horse worse than the camel or the palanquin, and announced that 'he was not accustomed to walk!'

Alexine felt hurt but withstood his remarks none the less. Perhaps she thought Captain Wilhelmie was behaving like her mother's old manservant, Jan, who was always threatening to leave, but never dreamt of going; and she told him:

> ... that if there were divisions and jealousy in the crew then any discontented sailor was free to go, and I had not engaged them by surprise. They knew all about it when they came when I told them enough.[7]

Mrs. Wilhelmie seemed to drown her sorrows in the evening when, without actually getting drunk, she would hold forth with a curious discourse on the rights and wrongs of the world in front of the assembled audience. She was a stupid rather than spiteful woman, and she bore a grudge that her husband was no longer being treated as captain of the equipage. That was hardly surprising: the desert journey could scarcely be compared to navigation on the open seas; but Mrs. Wilhelmie evidently expected it to be so.

Then Wilhelmie became offended because the servants went

direct to Alexine without consulting him. Also, 'he says all letters for me should be brought to him first, which is the first time I have heard it!' He told Alexine that he should be in charge of her money and accounts. The large coffer had a big lock that she was unable to open herself. In camp it was stored under her bed, and when she needed money she would follow the procedure she had taken to in Algiers. Formerly she had Abdullah, her Egyptian servant, to make payments on her behalf; but he had introduced a young boy into the domestic establishment and she had taken to asking him to help her open the money box. Simply for her convenience she would get the boy to write on her behalf in the account book, and Wilhelmie took offence at this. In the first place he told Alexine that it was not right that the boy should enter her tent and, to add injury to insult, mentioned that the boy had been dishonest in his handling of the account book.

In fact Captain Wilhelmie was cutting off his nose to spite his own face. She knew he was not completely honest and that the consumption of wine had not fallen in with the ration. She spoke Dutch to her sailors, and encountered an explosive vocabulary from her captain in the sequence of his complaints. She was not familiar with such language, and though she laughed at the adjectives he had dared to use, she felt humiliated over the deterioration of their relationship. She sympathized over his grumbles about their Algerian servants, as she found them aggravating herself; but over many hours of discussion she pressed him to co-operate and make do. It is all too common to fall out with fellow travellers during the strain of desert journeys. Had not the conflicting personalities of Richardson and Oudney, and of Barth and Overweg, come to such heart-rending discord that they had ceased to communicate and lost each other in the Sahara to go their own ways?

When the expedition reached Touggourt, Alexine looked longingly at the caravans leaving for the south, but felt she had no option but to travel towards the Mediterranean. It was a bitter disappointment, but she could not go on, and a fresh attempt at a Sahara crossing could be made later. Alexine had withstood the crossing from Barbar to Sawakin and she found the physical conditions no harder now, only she was harassed by her retinue.

The way was slow and difficult. They were still in Algeria when they reached Biskra, a little town of whitewashed buildings at the edge of a mountain range, surrounded by hundreds of palm trees. Here, after many months, Alexine expected mail, but there was none. She could only deduce it had got lost, but it was another disappointment. The caravan wound its way through the narrow lattice-work of mountains, and set off once again over stony, undulating country. This journey was as much as Captain and Mrs. Wilhelmie could stick. They became so disagreeable with a endless array of fatuous and nagging accusations, that Alexine longed to be rid of them, and finally suggested they should return to the Netherlands, for, as she commented:

'Wilhelmie cannot eat mutton – the only thing to get here, can't ride, expects the camels to march as an obedient crew, grumbles at the tents, the desert, and the carelessness of the Arabs.[8]

Because the Dutch press had already carried some far-fetched stories about her expedition, and because she imagined Wilhelmie would exaggerate his grievances when he got back, Alexine took the opportunity to write a letter to Uncle Jules explaining at great length the state of affairs that had arisen. During three days of heavy rain she wrote twenty-eight pages on the difficulties she had endured, and then laughed at the absurdity of the situation. Indeed, she described the letter as an 'avalanche of paper', and having aired her feelings wrote:

I laugh thinking of your stupification at this enormous, this incommensurable letter, and looking in dismay at all those papers and wondering what can be the matter. I employ three whole rainy days writing, and have cramp in my hand and back. You will perhaps think of my minuterie and trouble ridiculous in relating so much at length, every little thing and dwelling so on nuisances and rows, but I have often reflected what fuss was Anna's family and in other circumstances, and how people talk. What was *not* said of our journey in Sudan?[9]

The deluge of rain that had fallen during these three days flooded the camp. In some parts of the Sahara heavy rain is a sufficiently rare occurrence to be unexpected, and the tents and equipment were quite inadequate for such weather. One night the heavy fall led to a torrent of water passing through the camp, and everybody was obliged to stand in their tents. As she contemplated her curious surroundings, waiting for the night to pass,

The Dutch crew photographed as bedouin by Alexine, Algiers, 1867.
(Jacobse who attempted to save Alexine is in the centre)

Alexine and the women servants she took on her yacht, Algiers, 1867

From Algiers into the Sahara

Alexine was reminded of a storm at sea, and her imagination pictured the camp being washed away and her sailors swimming for their lives. As the patter once more increased to an icy downpour, she finished her letter:

> Fancy, how funny, here I am in the Sahara, bothering about the intrigues and arranging of a Dutch crew and seafaring men's lives in detail, and the only danger has actually been the fear of being drowned![10]

Painfully, slowly, the caravan followed the route to Constantine, and comparative comfort and cleanliness. Here the parched travellers could enjoy any amount of water brought from the hills by aqueducts built by the Romans. They stayed briefly, then continued north to reach the port of Philippeville where the caravan was disbanded.

The supplies and equipment that had been so carefully chosen were shockingly damaged or broken, and much had to be thrown away. Everybody was tired and ill after six months of desert life, but within a week Alexine and her servants set off for Malta. It was June and she felt nostalgic for a European community. The climate seemed relatively cool, so that she found herself staying several weeks, for she realized she must replenish her health and strength before setting off into the desert again. She was happy in Malta and no doubt the vendors welcomed her into their stores and bazaars, for she had not been shopping for many months, and this was always a pastime that momentarily drew her attention away from every domestic worry.

o

Final attempt to cross Africa

During the time Alexine had been in North Africa she had frequently kept in touch with her friends and relations both in England and the Netherlands. As she still had the house at Lange Voorhout in The Hague, perhaps had she lived longer she might have returned to it for her retirement, but for the present she would consider living nowhere but Africa. The house had been left empty for over eight years, and now Charlotte de Tuyll, a friend of Alexine and her late mother, asked if she could rent it. Alexine thought it absurd not to come to some agreement, but did not like the idea of letting it furnished. She wanted the house and garden to remain as it had been left, but Charlotte de Tuyll begged to use it and said she had been ill. Finally, Alexine agreed so long as the best furniture in the middle storey was removed and no other changes were made. Meanwhile, the garden was kept up, and still a few servants lived on in the deserted home.

How easy and pleasant it would have been for Alexine to return to The Hague after this passage of time, where she surely would have been made welcome. Her family had so many connections with the Court and Queen Sophia still had a sympathetic interest in her achievements. But she cannot have thought very seriously of returning to her homeland, for she already had ideas of settling in Egypt sometime in the future; and for the present she was occupied with arrangements for her next Sahara journey. Meanwhile, she came to appreciate the beauties of Tripoli, which she infinitely preferred to Algiers. In a letter to John she wrote:

Here I have found again something of the *bonhommie* of Egypt, which even fanaticism cannot check. The people seem happy and healthy, and where are seen the awful scarecrows that shocked one's sight in Algeria? Great cordiality seems to exist amongst the natives and the Europeans. The scenery also is original and reminds one of Egypt, and

Final attempt to cross Africa

the people are most kind to me. Mr. Testa, in particular, so that altogether all looks so favourable I cease not regretting that I did not come to start from here a year ago, instead of losing my time in that horrid and uninteresting Algeria.[1]

Alexine had arrived in Tripoli from Malta on 13th October 1868, and lived there until 30th January 1869, yet during these three months a legend was woven round the rich and daring young Dutchwoman. It took only a glance at the size of her household and how they lived, to deduce that Alexine was immensely wealthy. In making inquiries she let it be known that she wanted to cross the Sahara with her own caravan. This naturally caused widespread surprise, as a private caravan was a novelty never before envisaged. When she asked Mr. Testa, the Dutch Consul, for information, he automatically assumed that no expense would be spared. Alexine found Mr. Testa extremely helpful and took an immediate liking to him. Through him she met all the notable personalities in Tripoli, including Ali Riza, the Governor-General, who offered her protection throughout his territory. She also met Dr. Gustav Nachtigal, who was on his way to the Sultan of Bornu carrying presents on behalf of the King of Prussia. She found this young German modest and communicative, and it was decided they might join forces to form one big caravan to go to Bornu.

Tripoli stood at the northernmost point of the trade-route that ran through the Fezzan to the 'countries of the central Sudan', as the spread of the continent from west to east was known. It was a difficult, treacherous crossing, a hazard to human life, yet merchandise had been carried through the centuries with the camel, and before with the ox. From Europe and North Africa was sent such merchandise as cloth, rugs, garments, minerals (including copper-plated vessels and needles), firearms and ammunition, horses and mules. There were salt mines at widely scattered points in the Sahara, and salt was also carried from Europe to satisfy the Negroes, some of whom treasured it more than gold. Many luxury goods went north: skins of leopards and lions, and ostrich feathers; also many sacks of dried dates.

Yet the transport of salt, dates, and all the other commodities put together was small compared to the biggest export from central Africa, the traffic in slaves. A hundred years ago they were driven to Tripoli each year in thousands. Numbers had been greater during the seventeenth and eighteenth centuries. Indeed, those who arrived were counted as fortunate. The majority of these wretched people, who were captured by surprise in their primitive villages, died on the journey. They could not sustain the march of a thousand miles or more of desert – the heat, the lack of sustenance, and the scarcity of water.

Alexine had had her eyes opened to the slave traffic, both on her Nile travels and whilst she had been in Algiers. What she saw in Tripoli surpassed her imagination of the misery and malnutrition of these desolate blacks, still a long way from Arabia where most were to be transported. She was outspoken in airing her opinion on such human suffering, and beside the house she had taken she rented another site and set up a home for liberated slaves. She never informed her relations of this, but it was plain for those who passed by to see, and Nachtigal amongst others admired her courage in so bold a venture.

Alexine decided to begin by following the same route as Duveyrier, towards the Tassili d'Ajjers. From these mountains she would journey on to Lake Chad and the mystical territory of the Sultan of Bornu, and on through Darfur to the Nile at Khartoum. It was then an exploit as brave as reaching the moon in modern times.

Indeed, Alexine was aware of up-to-the-minute inventions and trends. She read the newspapers, and could not resist an occasional purchase by post. She must have caused a stir by ordering one of the newest bicycles, but soon gave it away, as was mentioned the *The Times:*

> ... Miss Tinne recently imported into Barbary a velocipede of the latest Parisian manufacture: but finding it not adapted to the sands of the Great Desert, she presented it to the Pasha of Tripoli.

To Alexine the first priority in planning an expedition was safety. Ali Riza, the Governor-General, had assured her she would be protected in his territory, but could not promise influence beyond his frontiers. However, he offered an introduction to the supreme chief of the Tuareg of the Ajjers, Ichnuchen. Before leaving Tripoli letters were sent to and received from

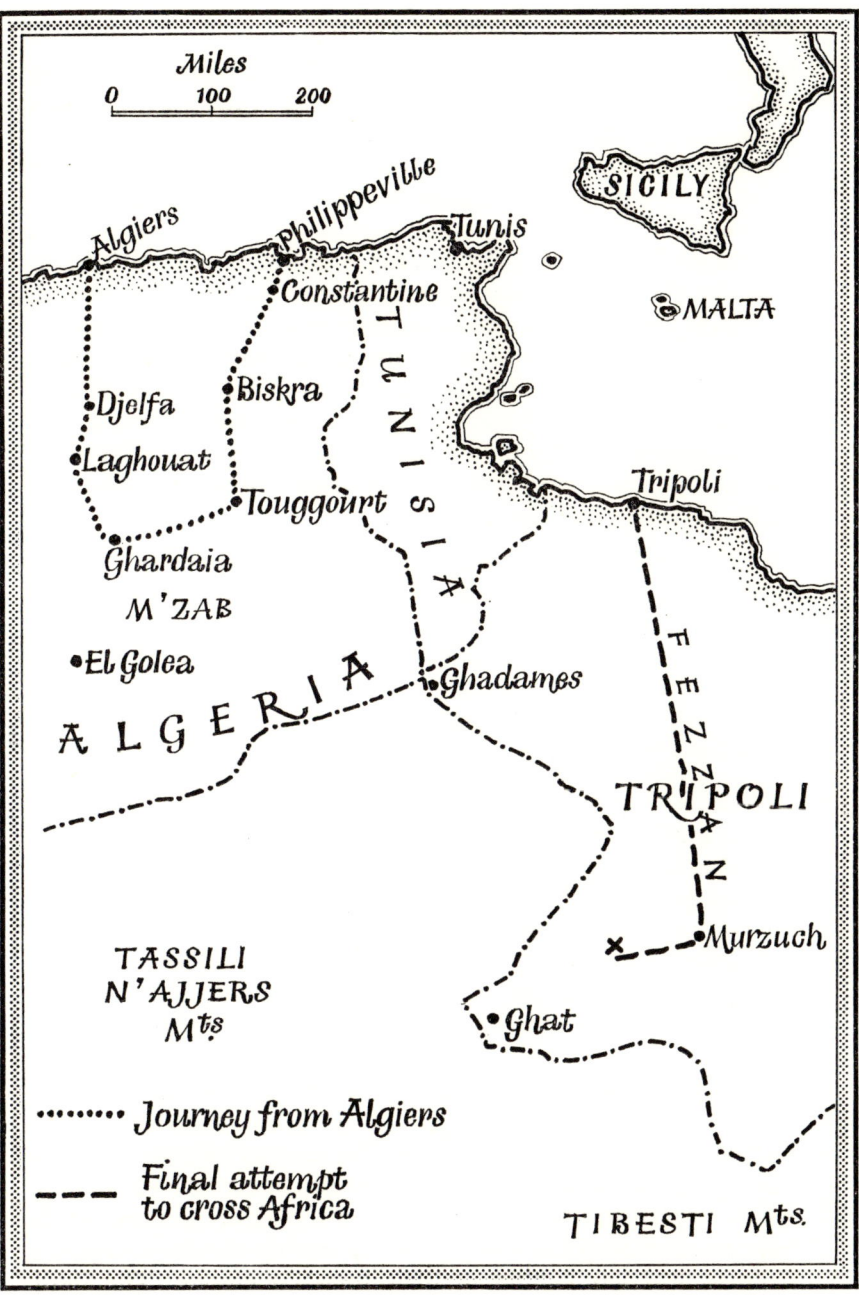

Ichnuchen. In a courteous reply to Alexine he explained that he would be visiting West Ladshal, to the east of the Tassili mountains, during the summer, and offered to meet her. He had formerly entertained Duveyrier, and was obviously curious to meet the first European woman brave enough to penetrate the Sahara.

On 30th January 1869 the caravan rode out of Tripoli. To her relief the Wilhelmie family had left, but two sailors still remained with her. Alexine had made no attempt to cut down on numbers because she knew there was safety in a more numerous expedition. She was only concerned with precautions of sufficient arms and provisions, and enough men to protect her in case of attack. As well as supplies for her own equipage, she had purchased quantities of foodstuffs, cloth and valuables for barter. In a letter to Uncle Jules she explained:

I have ordered seventy camels which should come in about twenty days, and I am busy whilst waiting making preparations which are as curious as complicated. It seems to travel in the interior here one must be quite a grocer. One has to take all sorts of groceries of different qualities and give them according to their value to more or less grand folks. Then one has to take also cotton stuffs, knives, needles, beads, red mantles, Turkish caps, no end of things. It is a complete study![2]

From the beginning the caravan seemed orderly. Each day they got to work very early, and she found it painful to rouse herself from her hard bed long before any sign of daylight. The nights were bitter, with icy winds, and the frosty dawn did little to dispel the cold, so that the travellers were obliged to move quickly to keep warm. At first the camel men caused delays as they rearrangd the loads on their grunting, moaning beasts, but soon a routine was set up and the caravan maintained a steady pace throughout the day.

Each morning before setting off the caravan was kept waiting, sometimes just for one or two of the expedition. Then they would ride off, to lengthen out in a line. The caravan jogged on in the blazing sun, seldom halting, until they reached a well where they would unpack and set up their tents for the night. Alexine would have liked to stop to look at some of the derelict buildings the Romans had left behind in their forsaken empire. The most extensive ruins were at Bondjem and here she was able to explore the deserted town, which she wrote of in a letter:

> There is also at Bondjem fine remains of a Roman town, and it is most curious to see in that lonely spot stately archways and buildings of immense stones. It struck us the more as we have not seen any architecture so massive and grand since Malta. There must be valuable things under the sand that has nearly covered the whole. I had only time to collect some bits of Roman pottery, so distinguishable by its fineness and peculiar red colour. I wonder no tourists have come here.[3]

As well as pieces of Roman pottery, Alexine enjoyed collecting together the different flowers she discovered in the little oases. The brightly coloured clusters of heath and succulents were a balm to the eyes, but quickly withered in the frozen atmosphere of the night. She picked as many varieties as she could find and pressed her collection to send to Liverpool.

She found the constantly changing scenery of the desert different from Egypt and Algeria. In some areas the incessant wind had wrought havoc with the rock structures and left hills of weird and unpredictable proportions, as Alexine remarked in a letter:

> The mountains near a well called Om il Abid look as if giants had been hurling rocks at each other, and had put the whole ground in confusion.[4]

Here one of the Dutch sailors, Arij Jacobse, imprudently strayed away from the camp, collecting coloured stones. He looked round for the marks of camels and found that in a few minutes his footsteps had been covered over. Frantically he ran along the rocks shouting and praying that the caravan would wait for him, but it was a long time before they found him, exhausted from heat and strain. Alexine had felt desperately anxious: Jacobse was her right hand, and, fearing him lost, she became aware how much she depended on him. The constant theme of conversation between herself and her sailors had been the contrast the present caravan from Tripoli made to their disappointing experiences in Algeria.

The expedition planned to go to Ghadames and Murzuch, where arrangements would be made with the supreme chief of the

Ajjer Taureg, Ichnuchen, for his protection during the next stage of the journey. They passed several other caravans travelling north who hailed them to exchange news and hospitality. Alexine enjoyed these invitations, the like of which she had never met in Algeria, but she was appalled at the sight of the slaves tramping along in their hundreds. What astonished her was that such gross injustice could be carried on so openly, apparently without shame. Most of the slaves were women, and perhaps she associated herself with them. Although the French and British had stopped trading in slaves, she realized that they could do nothing to curtail the Turks, and the Fezzan was under Turkish rule. In a letter she described the horror of seeing a weak and ill woman falling and being beaten to make her get up and walk on. 'But enough of that,' she added, 'that subject always makes me *too* angry.'

Stopping at the little oasis of Benolid, Alexine had an opportunity to write some letters. She explained that whilst on the move she would be too busy, but would write more on reaching Murzuch. Such was the novelty of the expedition that she found it difficult to describe except at length, and in her first batch of letters she gives way to feelings of nostalgia of her home intermingled with cheerful expectation of what lay ahead. 'Follow me if you can!' she finished her letter to John.

22
Delayed in Murzuch

Thirty-six days after leaving Tripoli the caravan reached Murzuch having covered over five hundred miles. The news of Alexine's arrival was reported in *The Times* eleven weeks after she got there, and it also appears to have reached the United States and caused quite a sensation there. She was, after all, the first European woman to attempt a Sahara crossing.

Alexine felt exhilarated to have reached the little fortress town from where they would set off into unmapped country to meet the Tuareg. She did not manage to write to John for two weeks despite good intentions, and could even then hardly believe they had arrived, for in her first letter she commented:

I am so distrustful of arriving at where I mean to go, and so disgusted at announcing tidings that never take place, now I can tell you I have reached at least one of my destinations.

At first they camped outside the ramparts of the decadent little fortress town, and from the start Alexine hoped she would not stay long, and described why:

Murzuch is a queer little place, built of mud, or rather of salt. It looks as if some dreadful earthquake had taken place, so crooked and tumbledown look the houses, but that is its normal state. The only danger one is in risk of here will make you laugh: it is of having one's house melted on one's head! So when it rains here which luckily is seldom, one has to go into camp as if some dire catastrophe was happening![1]

Here Alexine met Sheikh Ibrahim ben Alkia, who she described as the 'burgomaster' of Muzuch. He gave valuable advice freely, and she came to rely on him, meaning to reward him later with gifts. It seems incomprehensible that this elderly Sheikh, who was treated by her with an esteem approaching affection, should be blamed only six months later at the trial for intrigues leading to her death. In contrast to Algiers where she had often suffered a mixture of amazement and contempt in reply to her inquiries, Sheikh Ibrahim encouraged her to travel south. Altogether in Murzuch she found it easy to gather information, and nomads she talked with told her they knew India and China, and Zanzibar: they considered Zanzibar next door! She probably suspected them of bragging, though long journeys lasting over years rather than months are known to have been carried out by such nomads.

Living in Murzuch was not an attractive prospect, as it had been one of the biggest slave-markets in Africa; but it was a necessary stopping place. The house Alexine rented was in the very centre of the walled town, on the south side of the main street. The houses were all of two or three storeys in height with walled roof-terraces. The walls of the buildings were thick and porous, and on the ground floor were no windows, only a door. Some of the houses had two or three upstairs windows. Alexine's bedroom had no windows, but she had a courtyard where she could sit.

There were many shops though only one main street, and the ramshackle town was dotted throughout with palm trees. Though there were several varieties, the majority were date palms supplying Murzuch's most important export. What water there was was brown, sandy, and salty. Alexine did not know whether this was to blame, but she suddenly became ill. Sick and in pain she took to her room, and was relieved to hear that Gustav Nachtigal, the Prussian doctor she had met in Tripoli, had recently arrived. He called on her despite suffering from a fever himself; but though he soon recovered, she did not. Later Nachtigal diagnosed an inflamed appendix.

During most of April and May Alexine was seriously ill and could not move from her bed. Afterwards she remembered little except staring endlessly at the four walls and her bedcover. However, after several anxious weeks she recovered; and, typically, as soon as she began to regain her strength she made plans to travel to Ghat, her next port of call. If necessary, she told Nachtigal, she would be carried on a stretcher to her camel! She was for ever grateful to the shy young doctor who had saved her life, and readily used his precious medicines. In a letter to John she commented:

Like you, I begin to distrust all African travellers, though I am one of them, but he seems an exception: discreet, unassuming and honest.²

As has been mentioned, Nachtigal was on his way to the Sultan of Bornu carrying presents on behalf of the King of Prussia. Little was known of the Sultan of Bornu except that he was reputed to have a huge harem. His kingdom was the first Alexine and Nachtigal hoped to reach in the Sudan, having crossed 1,300 miles of deserted country by way of Lake Chad. The gifts the King of Prussia had selected included two life-size portraits of himself and the Queen in heavy frames, a magnificent velvet and gilt throne, and a harmonium. These being extremely heavy and bulky articles, Nachtigal required particularly strong camels; but how these things were loaded each day surpasses the imagination, for most camels need their load divided into two equal parts. Yet the mission was successful, and the gifts were delivered and admired by the Sultan of Bornu.

Alexine likewise hoped to impress the Sultan on behalf of the Netherlands, and she began to make a list of articles she could use as gifts. First she scanned the advertisements of newspapers she had brought with her and reflected on what was modern and practical. After much rumination she wrote to John asking him to buy, have packed and sent to Tripoli a list of presents she felt would be appreciated either as valuables or for their novelty. Like most donors she wanted to give presents that the Sultan and other chiefs along the route would not be able to buy for themselves. She also fancied articles that would be colourful and attractive, and if possible entertaining. If they were ingenious enough to cause surprise as well as pleasure so much the better. The King of Prussia chose gifts of great value, but she preferred to impress the Sultan with inventions of the scientific age. Alexine's list was, in fact, highly imaginative, and, characteristically, compiled as her ideas arrived. It certainly proved a formidable shopping list, and she told John he might have to go to Paris or Brussels for some things. The list was:

1. A microscope, not a very dear one, but good enough to astonish a person who has never seen one.
2. Two ice machines and powder to make it. I would prefer, of

course, light ones as I hear they are now making them to require very little powder.

3. A sewing-machine of a simple kind that is worked by one hand only, and not by feet. I bought one at Marseilles for 60 francs, and they are cheaper in London and Paris. It must be ready threaded as I don't know well how. It need not be a durable machine, only one to look well for a time and do a little work, for it will soon be broken in His Majesty of Bornu's hands. There must be thread and extra needles.

4. A reveille matin or clock that, wound up in a certain way, wakes one at a precise hour by a noise. Some I am told light a candle at the moment they wake one. This would be preferable and directions how to wind it up.

5. Eight pieces of silk of bright and gaudy colours. An old-fashioned pattern might be chosen so as to get the articles cheaper. The silk must not be bad, as it seems they know well the good qualities. By pieces I mean whole pieces of 20 yards or so. Breadth is not of much consequence to them so chose narrow pieces and more in length. I fancy a Scotch plaid of red and yellow, as I have seen some would please. Better that all the pieces should not be alike.

6. Some bottles encre sympathetique, a chemical ink, which does not appear on the paper unless heated, and disappears again when the paper gets cool.

7. Some magnifying glasses ... six of these will suffice. Mr. Heuglin used to amuse the natives by lighting his pipe that way. (By catching the sun's rays, they light and burn.)

8. An appareil photographique Debroni if its price does not exceed 100 francs. and is easy to manage and small, as the papers say, and requires scarcely any chemicals. If not it must be accompanied by directions.

9. A looking glass, 48 centimetres broad, 1 metre long with a gaudily guilt [*sic*] narrow frame. It must be carefully packed, the outer planks not touching the glass or its back. Length is of more consequence than breadth.

10. Twenty-five yards of fine scarlet cloth.

11. Twenty-five yards of black cloth, good also.

12. Four pieces of bright-coloured red, yellow, and one black piece of velvet. I send a sample of velvet to show quality. It must not be inferior to that. When I say a piece, I mean about 18 yards long of each.

13. A chest of good green tea.

14. Some bonbons of sorts in about twenty of those gaudy things the French give to children on New Year's day, and are called cornets. They are of gilt and coloured paper with a silk bag on the top.

15. Twenty-four gaudy cotton handkerchiefs.

16. Twenty-four gaudy silk handkerchiefs, not first quality.

She then continued to list articles which she wanted not for presents, but for her own use. Evidently she felt it necessary to make this clear since they included guns, a cannon, and personal requisites!

17. Twenty tins of Liebigs extract of meat. There are other sorts, but none are so good as his. Mind it is not essence of beef only.

18. Fifty guns of the cheapest sort consisting [*sic*] with safety. Belgium is the place I believe for this sort of thing, lots of capsules and some moulds.

19. A different thing which I most prize! A sort of little cannon or obusier not exceeding 160 kilos each. It must shoot straight, not in a curve and have exploding balls or shells. With such an implement I ought to go anywhere, I am told, and I wish for this article almost most of all. This must be something more than the guns I asked for at Algiers. Ample directions must be with them and moulds for casting new projectiles. I saw on the Nile an Englishman with something of this sort for shooting several ducks at once. That is what I require, only more powerful.

20. Send me some tooth powder and tooth brushes.

21. Some James's fever powder, quite genuine, for that medicine is useful when real.[3]

However, more important than all the foregoing was Alexine's request for money. She needed money to feel secure, and now she realized that she must have enough to last her several months. Large sums could not be transported over the desert without a very large caravan for fear of being attacked or pillaged. Once she left Murzuch it would be impossible to have more sent on. Already she had come too far, but she decided to send Abdullah back to Tripoli to fetch both the money and the articles she had asked John to buy her. Abdullah was an Egyptian of about thirty. He had been in Alexine's service longer than anybody else and, in a subtle way, had probably influenced her. She had come to rely on him and she trusted him with her money although she knew he could not count to more than ten. During the frequent arguments between the camel drivers, Abdullah would stand beside her whilst she tried to establish a routine, and she knew he would protect her. A few months later when all was over people were to say: 'If only she had had Abdullah with her he would never have allowed it to happen!'

Alexine asked John to send Maria Theresa dollars to the value of Fr.45,000 to her banker in Malta, who would send them on to Mr. Testa, the Dutch Consul in Tripoli. These dollars were to be packed in two strong boxes 'so as not to chink and reveal their presence while on camels'. She also asked John to send Fr.15,000 to Mr. Testa immediately, so that Abdullah could make purchases in Tripoli and could arrange to buy extra camels and other necessities for the expedition.

Alexine was aware that Mr. Testa had done very well over changing French francs into Maria Theresa dollars which were commonly used as currency. When questioned by John if she trusted Mr. Testa, she answered:

... one sees such strange things as one advances in life and particularly in the East where consciences are proverbially elastic that one does not know exactly what to think. A man may not be capable of a very bad action, but weak and led by others into doing an indelicacy, and that is what I most fear.[4]

Already Alexine was anxious about Mr. Testa's casualness over sending on her post and messages, but she knew of no one else in Tripoli she could depend on.

Before her letter arrived John received a telegram cancelling some of the order!

NO SEND RED AND BLACK CLOTH. LINE ALL CASES CAREFULLY WITH TIN AND LOCKS NOT NAILED.

If this made two items less there was still a great deal of work in buying the extraordinary collection. She had ordered the red and black cloth to make herself and servants each a burnous – a long cloak with a hood invaluable as a protection against heat and cold in the desert. However, realizing how long they would take to make up and that she had no lining, she wrote to Mr. Houdas, a Tunisian tailor she had previously met, asking him to send some ready-made. Mr. Houdas duly set out to bring them himself, but only got a short distance from Tripoli before he was met with news of the disaster, whereupon he turned back.

23
Meeting the Tuareg

Alexine was glad to set off westwards to Wadi al Gharbi where it was planned she would meet Ichnuchen, who was unwilling to come to Murzuch as he was on bad terms with the officials there. Sheikh Ibrahim ben Alkia, who she referred to as the 'burgomaster' of Murzuch, had arranged the introduction with Ichnuchen, who was the supreme chief or Asgar of the Ajjer Tuareg. If she could get Ichnuchen's protection she felt she could travel safely, and she looked forward to meeting the venerated old warrior, of whom she had been told so much.

In a sense the Tuareg are nomads, but their family life is sedentary. Usually they move their camps little: their wives and children live in ragged tents with few possessions. Round about will be seen their goats, mountain sheep, and the camels which are not on tour. Some of the men would be travelling with goods and might be away for months on end. These people controlled the wells of the desert and thus upon them every traveller depended for his survival, that is if he did not succumb to the natural hazards of the country.

Alexine took with her a varied set of retainers including her two Dutch seamen, some Negro servants whom she had collected in the Sudan, Arabs from Tunis and Algeria, and freed Negro slaves from Tripoli who hoped to make their way back to where they had originated. The caravan started on 5th June 1869. It was evening, and the first camp was set outside the walls on the west side of the town.

The next morning Gustav Nachtigal came to see Alexine off, shaking her hand very warmly before she mounted her camel. Secretly, both wondered if it would be the last time they would meet, for he was going to Tibesti, a journey of considerable danger. He was relieved to think she was setting off under seemingly safe conditions herself, as they talked once more of joining their two caravans together. In three or four months they hoped to start for Lake Chad, riding across more than a thousand miles of deserted country.

As Alexine rode off after her guide she felt slightly heart-sick on leaving Nachtigal. He was a retiring young man, and she guessed him to be about her own age. He was in fact thirty-four whilst she was a year younger. She looked forward to seeing more of this genial, good-looking, German doctor who seemed friendly and unobtrusive, and so different from Theodor von Heuglin whom she had found stiff and unapproachable on the Bahr-al-Ghazal expedition. Indeed, the journey to Bornu held similarities, for again she was setting off on a very long journey and quite uncommitted as to how many months it would take.

The chosen meeting place with Ichnuchen was to be in the Wadi al Gharbi, a valley lying to the west of Murzuch. The caravan had travelled for five days when they came to this oasis. They had met small groups of nomads who assured them the Asgar was in the neighbourhood, but exactly when or how he would appear was anybody's guess. He might come today, tomorrow, or in a few days, but such was his prestige that everybody was ready to receive him whenever he chose the time.

When the Tuareg rode into sight they surpassed even Alexine's expectations. She had often been told of their splendour and magnificence, but she was immensely struck with the pageant of colour and movement. Her immediate reaction was that such a dramatic scene ought to be recorded by a painter, for it surpassed description. As the warriors rode their camels towards her caravan she felt excited, curious, proud, but so charged were her emotions she could only shiver with the thrill and wait to see what would happen.

Alexine and her men had been on the look-out for some hours, and the first sign they saw was a small group of riders on the horizon. The Tuareg, on viewing the camp, quickly formed a row abreast and charged, brandishing their spears, and shouting at their superb camels to quicken their pace. Alexine saw the sand rise behind the stampede in a cloud. She had never realized camels could move so fast. These were arregans, racing camels, not large but bred for their speed, and as they came nearer she was able to observe the riders, who appeared to be wearing black visors with an opening only for their eyes. Their flamboyant robes were a galaxy of beautiful colours, red, purple, blue, and gold, against the creamy coats of their steeds.

They charged in an alarming manner, shouting wildly, waving their spears and looking as if they would never stop before they reached the camp. As they came nearer they did not slow down but seemed to accelerate their pace, so that suddenly to everybody's amazement they found the intruders amongst themselves, nearly knocking into them, and then dismounting.

Alexine had wondered for a few anxious moments if the spectacle would lead to bloodshed. It seemed nothing short of an attack, but as the Tuareg slid to the ground from their mounts, cheerful greetings were exchanged. They at once spotted the lady who was the centre of attention, and surrounding her, told her in their high-pitched voices that the mock war was purely a show to honour her, and for her entertainment. Alexine was astounded to find the newcomers, colourfully dressed with their black veils like strange masks, and flashing burnished steel here, there, and everywhere, utterly friendly. They held to no formality and spoke as if they already knew her. Soon they had explained they were a detachment sent by Ichnuchen and had come to prepare for his arrival the next day. The Tuareg were eager to look over the camp but restrained their curiosity until the Asgar arrived.

The detachment remained at the camp overnight when all was quiet. Well before daybreak everybody was astir and making preparations for the great day. Alexine rode in her palanquin, and no doubt she had dressed up to her best advantage to meet the venerated Asgar, Ichnuchen. The detachment of Tuareg led the way, then came Alexine, followed by her caravan, who were pursued by a crowd of people who, as it seemed to them, had appeared out of the desert. Before long an astonishing sight came into view.

Ichnuchen was surrounded by 300 Tuareg all dressed in magnificent robes, wearing black veils, and riding splendid arregans. They all held spears of a great length, and the harness of the camels was richly decorated. Alexine was incredulous at the sheer splendour of all she saw, which must have seldom been experienced by a European. In a letter to John she wrote:

Meeting the Tuareg

If the sight of the little troop of the previous day had already so struck me, I cannot tell you the impression the scene of Ichnuchen in his strange stately dress, and of all his followers made on me, old traveller as I am. I may say, with that stern wild valley I already mentioned for scenery, I never saw a grander and handsomer sight, those variegated colours, martial appearance, singular trappings, and elegant dromedaries with long snake necks. One cannot describe it! But it was a blood-stirring scene, and if they came to Europe so in full glory I am sure the heart of many a young girl would beat for the handsome Tuareg, barbarians as they are, and many a youth would long to join them![1]

Amongst the aura of speculation that surrounds any long-awaited person, the Asgar stood out. Although his veil showed only his eyes and the bridge of his nose, there was much in the old man's expression which assured Alexine of a kindly interest. It has been recorded that Ichnuchen lived to be over a hundred, and it is certainly true he was the Asgar of the Ajjer Tuareg for a great many years. He may have been eighty when Alexine met him, but his weather-worn hands and creased eyes were little to go by.

Ichnuchen appears to have been amused to meet Alexine. He probably treated her as a very costly doll. He thought her picturesque, and admired her; but he knew she was dependent on him for her ultimate safety and success in crossing the Sahara which was all she now cared about. After Ichnuchen and Alexine had exchanged prolonged salutations, the Asgar and his immediate following of tribal chiefs dismounted and were offered accommodation in two tents. Meanwhile, the rest of the Tuareg he had brought with him settled themselves in the vicinity of the camp. A European woman had never been seen so far into the Sahara before, and the Tuareg were incredulous not only of her but also of her retinue. Soon their curiosity got the better of their courtesy, and they were peeping and prying everywhere. They became so obstreperous that eventually Alexine felt compelled to point out to Ichnuchen that his men were disrupting all her people, and he ordered them to keep away.

Ichnuchen stayed with Alexine for four days. In the course of this time she met and talked with the Asgar's heir, his eldest sister's son, called Bu Bekker, and heard about his grievance. A hundred years ago, to the people of the Tuareg a blood feud was a common form of dispute, as it was to the Arabs. The Tuareg were an arrogant race who got their serfs to do agricultural and domestic work whilst they themselves were very loath to dirty their hands, except with blood. Savage fighting was constantly breaking out within the Tuareg tribes, and the loss of their best men was frequently the latest news.

Bu Bekker was a young chief of much promise, but he was a frustrated man because Djabbour, another chief who came under Ichnuchen's rule, had killed his younger brother. Bu Bekker had asked Ichnuchen to avenge the murder, which the Asgar agreed to do eventually. But meanwhile Djabbour, fearing he would be attacked, joined forces with another chief called Tenmrassan, so that their united strength might protect them. It was a critical state of affairs, for the two sides were both certain of their rights and were both supported by many men.

For the time being all three chiefs, Bu Bekker, Djabbour, and Tenmrassan enjoyed the hospitality of Alexine under the wing of the great Ichnuchen. Alexine was told of the feud, but she could not believe such bloodshed could take place. She had learnt Tamachek, the language of the Tuareg, and was already beginning to speak freely. She begged them, as they ate and drank at her camp, to forget their revenge and live in peace. Incredible though it may seem, by the end of the evening, as the camp fire dimmed and the chiefs' faces were hardly discernible one from another, they had merged into a truce under Alexine's diplomatic handling.

Before Ichnuchen left he pressed Alexine to come with him at once to Ghat, but she was reluctant to do so. Somehow she felt it was unwise to travel unless further agreements were officially signed. Probably Sheikh Ibrahim ben Alkia, from whom she had gained so much information of the Tuareg, had given her this advice. In any case she chose to return to Murzuch, and pleased the Asgar by telling him she must go and fetch her luggage because it contained all the presents she had brought for him. When she got back to Murzuch she called on Sheikh Ibrahim and asked him what written arrangements she should make. He proposed approaching a sheikh who was held in such esteem that he was 'venerated as a holy man by the Tuareg', and asking him to make out papers on behalf of Ichnuchen, that could be signed by both the Asgar and herself. Until these were in order she could not meet him again at Ghat.

Whilst waiting in Murzuch she took the opportunity of writing several letters. In one she skilfully expounded her views of the Tuareg. The year was 1869, and apart from fragmentary information from Barth and Duveyrier, nothing was known of the Tuareg. With her usual ability to like and understand people Alexine showed great insight into their characteristics and customs:

> The Tuareg are evidently a quite different race from the Arabs, tall, powerfully-built men, without that thinness or rather slimness of the Arabs, and with nothing of that hooked nose, rather apish and anxious face. They seem to me, however, not at all to be of European origin as is said: they are too brown. They have such a peculiar laugh, that once heard remains in your ears, and all our people could not help imitating them the whole day, as when one hears a new song one keeps repeating it. They have also a queer squeak they use for exciting their camels, but from force of habit introduce into conversation also.
>
> Unlike Arabs they are lively, take interest in all they see, live very rough, and have none of that Oriental effeminate softness. And though their curiosity to see us was so obstreperous that we had a quarrel about it with them, it denotes to my idea, a certain inquisitiveness of mind that would be a good quality if trained to polite proportions, and is better, not for the tourist's comfort, but for the human race, than a dull apathy.
>
> Their reputation of pride is also not exaggerated. They, without doing positive harm, evidently consider themselves a superior race, and treated the Arabs as a Turk would treat a fellah, as a soldier a *pays conquis*, and bullied about the natives of the place.
>
> They at first were very nice with us, though rather too curious, for if we were surprised at their sight, *ils vous l'ont bien rendu*, and group after group came to wonder at my Algerian women, 'so white and so neat', they said, but at last they became too free and I got very angry and complained to Ichnuchen who immediately put strict order, and stopped the nuisance. Ichnuchen was very civil. I only saw him in greater ceremony, but he gave me assurance of his good will, to take me anywhere, to Kano, if I liked.[2]

The history of the Tuareg has always been in dispute. They themselves do not know where they originated and have no wish to know. However, Europeans have put forward many and varied theories. In appearance the Tuareg are like the crusaders. Their strange head-dresses look like black armour from afar, and their huge shields, and crosses on sword-handles and in front of their saddles, carry a marked resemblance. There is evidence that they are of African origin and of a Berber type. Their veils are not mentioned by the earliest travellers, though this strange form of head-dress separates the Tuareg from the rest of the world. The women go unveiled. It is the men who wear the *teguelmoust,* made of a band of about ten feet of cotton wound over a turban. This is usually indigo blue and may stain the parts of the face which show, giving a weird appearance. On formal occasions the opening in the veil is made as small a slit as possible. Whatever the origin of the teguelmoust, which appears to have been worn only since the sixteenth century, it serves as an admirable protection against sand and sun, allowing moist air from the breath to cool the mouth and nostrils.

The chief's eldest son does not inherit, but his eldest sister's son. The men take on their wife's station of life on marrying, and indeed the women are greatly respected. Alexine commented that one reason why she wished to meet the Tuareg was because the women were the best provided for in the world.

They are very proud, and walk with a strange stride and swagger. In physique they are tall but lean, with muscles like springs of steel. There are many clans within the tribes, and though there are often feuds, the Tuareg consider themselves a united people. The familiarity with which they treated Alexine is typical, and since their means of existence are meagre, they accept everything they can get hold of as their due, and often behave like beggars, yet never show gratitude. Ichnuchen must have had greedy hopes of what gifts Alexine would give him; and, indeed, one wonders what she had in mind. She had ordered two ice machines. Was one for him? Or was his present to be the microscope, the alarm clock, the Debroni camera, or the chest of tea?

At this late stage Alexine took the step of sending Abdullah with part of the caravan back to Tripoli to bring the goods and

Meeting the Tuareg

arms she had ordered. She had meant to send him off before, but had kept him to see what else she needed.

In Tripoli, Abdullah was to buy sixty more camels, a horse, and a big quantity of wheat, besides her order which was being sent and the money. He carried on him a letter for John he was to post in Tripoli. It was Alexine's last. In a touching manner she asked that her retinue should be looked after should anything happen to her, and at length she apologized for her over-expenditure. 'Burn this letter,' she told him. She explained that the people she had employed from Algiers and Tripoli had been sent back as an economy, and from now she would take local people at a very low cost: but, she added, 'one must be numerous in these countries'. Of all her servants she cared most for her two fellow-countrymen, and she wrote:

> I don't like to be always talking of dying, but one can't help thinking of it in these wild countries, and if it should happen pray be very kind to my two poor faithful attendants.[3]

On 21st July Alexine left Murzuch to meet Ichnuchen at Ghat. She had taken on a guide called Sheikh Ahmed to lead the caravan After three days the travellers arrived at a charming little oasis called Wadi Shergui. To Alexine this was paradise. As she wrote in her last letter, she felt enthralled with the surroundings and more satisfied with her retinue than she had for some weeks. After the desiccated country they had passed through, this was marvellously fertile and alive, and she was reminded by the orange sand and black rocks of the second Nile cataract.

The rest of the tragic story was reconstructed later by Alexine's nephews, from accounts given by the survivors.

After camping at Wadi Shergui for a week because of its pleasant situation, the caravan left one afternoon to follow the Ouadai Aberdjoush. The next day they continued towards Ghat, and set up camp in the usual way.

In the morning, when the sun was already hot, there was some consternation at the sound of visitors approaching. There were six Arabs and nine Tuaregs on camels; and Alexine, watching through the flap of her tent, may have recognized Bu Bekker amongst them. They rode directly to the centre of the camp, where two of them dismounted. She then heard them say that Ichnuchen had sent them from Taharat – half-way to Ghat – to accompany her on the next part of the route. Bu Bekker added that he had been asked to lead the caravan. At this point, Sheikh Ahmed went off: he, too, had been asked to lead the caravan, and now said that he would either do so or depart. Bu Bekker was a bitter man in a dangerous mood, determined to spite Ichnuchen for not taking revenge against Djabbour, the man who had killed his brother. He knew that Ichnuchen had taken a fancy to Alexine, had treated her as a protégé, and would be sorry to lose her. Besides, she was rich, and would be worth pillaging.

As Alexine sat in the comparative cool of her tent, she heard the voices of the new arrivals raised against her Arab servants, who shouted back. The new escort seized her own camel-drivers' weapons, as if to defend themselves in a mock battle. Soon, they were all yelling and screaming at each other; and in another minute they were fighting and tussling. Unless someone acted quickly, there would be bloodshed.

Arij Jacobse boldly marched forward to separate the contenders; but suddenly one of the Tuareg threw his massive lance, which pierced right through the sailor's body, and wounded a servant behind him. Alexine, seeing Jacobse fall bleeding to the ground, came out of her tent and held up her hand as if to command a truce. One of the Tuareg brought his sword down on her forearm, severing her hand. Then there was a shot, and Alexine fell.

That was all the survivors knew.[4]

There was chaos in the camp. People were screaming. There were further shots, until it seemed that half the caravan were dead, and half alive. Soon after Alexine was killed, Cornelius Oostmans, the second Dutch sailor, was also shot. It was blinding madness. Nobody knew what was happening.

Then the shooting stopped. The victors – if victors they could be called after carrying out so cold-blooded a slaughter – sorted out the spoils and made off. They took with them nine camels from the caravan, and helped themselves to everything of value. Then, leaving the dejected survivors, they started briskly back towards Ghat.

Did any soul care for the dead or dying? Did Alexine die quickly, or did she linger in the heat of the August sun until the blood had drained out of her body to relieve her of all suffering?

The few survivors had been left six camels. Somehow, they collected themselves together and set off on the way they had come, back to Murzuch.

24
'La Croyante'

COURRIER APPORTE LETTRE D'UN DOMESTIQUE DE VOTRE SOEUR DISTANT. MADEMOISELLE TINNE ET DEUX DOMESTIQUES EUROPEANS TUES PAR TOUREGS PROBABLEMENT PREMIER OU DEUX AOUT. JE DONNE ORDRE AUX SURVIVANTS RETOURNER TRIPOLI. ABDULLAH ET HOUDAS SONT ICI. DONNEZ MOI VOS INSTRUCTIONS.

The fateful telegram from Mr. Testa, the Dutch Consul in Tripoli, arrived late in the evening of August 18th 1869. The news, which had taken two and a half weeks to reach Tripoli from the scene of the murder, took less than twelve hours to travel to Liverpool. John immediately showed the telegram to the family. Feeling, perhaps, that they could somehow have prevented the tragedy by exerting more influence on Alexine, and anxious to avoid any further self-reproach, they planned to take immediate action. The word murder was almost too cruel to be whispered in the Victorian drawing-room. Yet each member of the family imagined Alexine's death. They doubted whether she had fallen with the first blow, for they knew her as a woman who would defend herself. As each one tried to obliterate such a picture; the vividness of the scene of the murder reappeared.

John went to The Hague a few days later to settle Alexine's affairs and see to her house. Of his sons, Fred went to Egypt to wind up the belongings Alexine had left in Cairo. Theodore and Ernest travelled to Tripoli to carry out the necessary investigations and deal with her luggage and equipment.

Stopping in Malta, Theodore and Ernest met *The Times* correspondent and were invited to revise his lengthy statement before it was posted to London. Most of the details of this had been supplied by Mr. Houdas, a man who quickly introduced himself, and to whom they took a profound dislike. Houdas was a tailor from Tunis, and had been on his way to Murzuch with the burnouses, or cloaks, Alexine had ordered. He had not got far before he met with the news of her death and at once turned back.

On arriving in Tripoli Theodore and Ernest were met by Mr. Testa, the Dutch Consul, who had arranged for them to stay in Alexine's house. What had seemed everyday to her, their Aunt Ally, seemed very strange to them. From the windows they could watch the Negroes she had bought out of slavery, who had built themselves houses of palm leaves. Their good looks and tidy ways were remarked on by Theodore and Ernest, who had found plenty of fleas in their own beds. They met Abdullah, Alexine's Egyptian servant, who was about to set off in a determined effort to find her grave, and felt that, in his bitterness, he was contemplating revenge. The load of valuable goods he had been commissioned to transport out to Murzuch was to be disposed of by Theodore and Ernest together with Alexine's other luggage.

They were asked by Mr. Testa to call and interview Djabbour, the man who had killed the brother of Bu Bekker, the suspected assassin of Alexine. Djabbour appeared with a companion. When the two Tuareg walked in, soldiers took away their lances, ten feet high with barbed tips, but allowed them to keep their daggers which they wore attached to the left arm. The sequence was an argument that soon got out of hand, for it was impossible to distinguish between fact and fiction. In a letter home Theodore described the absurd form the interview had taken:

> ... it was rather interesting to find that Djabbour was in town and that we could have our interview with him. Our communication was rather intricate at first, for we went to him with the Vice-Pasha and the Governor and the interpreter. We spoke in French to the Italian interpreter who handed it on in Turkish to a go-between, who turned it into Targui, then Arab, then Turkish, and then French.
>
> We sat in a kind of circle and it was rather amusing to notice how the 'round game' (so difficult to keep up at first when Djabbour merely answered with a grunt) gradually struck across the circle until one interpreter after another being left out, Mr. Testa spoke directly to Djabbour in Arabic![1]

Obviously, Theodore and Ernest had a great sense of humour and were high-spirited young men. Whilst awaiting the sale of Alexine's things, they tried out her camera, which they referred to as 'Aunt Ali's photo-machine', and saw round Tripoli on donkeys. During their stay Mr. Testa told them the Governor-General had ordered all survivors from the fateful expedition to return to Tripoli, and that a trial would be held at his expense.

The trial that eventually took place lasted from January to April 1870. It proved to be drawn out, involved, and illogical. Two of the Arab servants, who had seen Alexine's murder, had lived to tell a distorted tale by hiding from the raiders in their mistress's tent. The language problem did not ease the complications, and the blame was passed to and fro until it eventually fell on an absent witness, Ibrahim ben Alkia, the kind old Sheikh who had helped Alexine in Murzuch, and of whom she had expressly asked that he might, should she die, be given presents by way of thanks.

One can but hope that Sheikh Ibrahim earned a reprieve from his unjust accusation. The most likely version of what happened is described in the previous chapter, which was deduced by Theodore and Ernest from the people they met in Tripoli. By the time of the trial almost every fact had been twisted, and it seems to have served no useful purpose. Whatever the verdict, the general opinion was that Bu Bekker murdered Alexine; and that this was widely acknowledged, is demonstrated by Erwin von Bary, a German explorer who travelled disguised as a Turkish doctor. Years later, when he was asked to treat Bu Bekker, he recognized Alexine's assassin, and although the ill man wore a tormented expression, he firmly withheld his medicines.

To John Tinne's family in Liverpool Alexine was the last link with the Netherlands, and they were sad to dispose of her house at 32 Lange Voorhout. Many of her belongings were distributed to her relations, and some are still treasured. It was not like sorting out the house of an elderly person, for Alexine had been thirty-three at the time of her death. Anna Berthon, John's eldest daugher, caused consternation within the family by remarking that, after all, Alexine might be still alive. In view of this, the house was not immediately sold, and an arrangement was made for it to be used as an extension of the Royal Library, to which it was adjacent.

Her memorial in The Hague, given by her relations, was a new building for the English Episcopal Church. This was bombed in the Second World War, and another church has since been built.

In Algiers, a window and memorial brass were erected in the church she attended. As the years ran on the Tinne family tended not to talk about their adventurous ancestor. They could not, of course, forget her, but following the spectacular news of her death which had been so widely publicized, they preferred to let further comment lie dormant.

Until the bombshell of 31st July 1895: for then, quite out of the blue, appeared a story in *The Daily Telegraph* reporting, after all those years, that she had survived! Twenty-six years after her death, came an announcement that she had been captured and sold to a Targui called Eghmissea, by whom she had had three children, two of whom were still alive, a son and a daughter in their twenties; the daughter being married. The news reached the Netherlands within hours of being published in England. Yetty Constant de Rebecque, Alexine's cousin, who had been brought up alongside her as a child, was deeply concerned. As Alexine's body had never been retrieved, she had reason to be frightened. Yetty, now nearing sixty, with grown-up children of her own, at once wrote to the reporter, called Djebari. He replied that he had not stated that Alexine was still alive, but that he had seen her tomb in the mosque of a little oasis ('not shown on any map but twenty-five days' journey from Agades in the direction of Bibtako'). He added that this had a cross of palms placed on it, and that Miss Tinne was referred to in these parts as 'La Croyante', whom they much respected.

The news of Alexine's reappearance had first come in a pamphlet written by Djebari and published in Tunis, entitled *The Survivors of the Flatters Mission*. Some years before Colonel Flatters had led a French military expedition to explore the project of laying a trans-Saharan railway. The expedition had been cunningly divided and ambushed by Tuareg, who rightly foresaw that the railway would take away their livelihood. Those of the eighty Frenchmen who had not been killed at once, had starved to death on their way home. The horrific outcome of the Flatters Mission had put a stop to further French expeditions, yet now Djebari claimed that several of them were alive, including their leader who had become a nationalized Targui!

Was Djebari mad or was he speaking the truth? All these years afterwards one can only surmise that the Tuareg, delighting in satisfying a stranger with tall stories, got the better of his imagination. Possibly the report on Alexine was a mixture of truth and fiction, for Abdullah may have found Alexine's body in his search, and moved it to a fitting place of rest. One day we may know.

In this book I have attempted to record for posterity the story of Alexine and her remarkable travels. She was a perplexing character, and people assess her motives from different viewpoints according, perhaps, to their own ideals. In her short life she experienced the extremes of success and adversity, and though she died tragically young, her life was full. Perhaps this was her wish, for she had once written:

> I always feel as if there must be an end to everything, and often in the middle of a pleasant thing – be what it may: a journey, a friendship, a pleasant stay somewhere. I only ask myself, I wonder how it will end? And I always prefer a thing finishing too soon and leaving a pleasant impression, than trailing on till the disenchantment of the end embitters even the souvenir.[2]

Appendix 1

List on last page of Mrs. Tinne's diary, Volume V.

Persons and Animals who Travelled up the White Nile

STEAMER	DAHABIAH
Mde Tinne	Mlle Alexine
Mlle Addy	Anna
Flora	Tolba
Joseph	Pietro
Kalluk	Rosa
Manam	Officer
Mundy	10 soldats
Amine	1 Reis
Contarini	1 Pilot
Slave	12 Matelots
Ahmad	Osman Aga
Slave	Ahmad Aride
8 chasseurs	Carpenter
1 Reis	2 Women
1 Pilot	*35*
12 Sailors	
2 Women	NUGGER
36	Mustafa
	5 Sailors
	1 Reis
	1 Pilot
	1 horse
	2 donkeys
	4 dogs
	2 gazelles
	15

Outre les dindes et les poules il y avait 86 bouches a remplir tous les jours.

Appendix 2

OSMAN AGA'S GRAVE

Next day they wrapped him in a shroud
Regretting him they could not save;
His comrades all, a mourning crowd
Placed Osman Aga in his grave.

They dug it near a sycamore
Close to the wild and rapid wave
(A weedy but a sandy shore)
Where Osman Aga found his grave.

They called the forest by his name
A short inscription to the 'Brave',
The only tribute to his fame
Was given to Osman Aga's grave.

And other boats in passing by
Hearing the name the ladies gave,
Perhaps may cast a sorrowing eye
On Osman Aga's lonely grave.

Appendix 3

GONDOKORO

We've arrived! And whatever may happen
It never can alter the past.
We have been a long time in arriving,
But we're come to the Mountain at last.
And altho' there are yearly some merchants
Their ivory trade to pursue,
Few have braved all the dangers that we have
And got safely to Gondokoro.

We have passed through the Shilluks and Dinkas,
And done all the kindness we could.
The Nuers, the Kitches, the Bari,
We have burnt their old tuguls for wood.
Passed elephants, buffaloes and lions,
Drunken captains and quarrelsome crew,
Crocodiles, hippopotami,
And got safely to Gondokoro.

We can boast we made friends with the Shilluks,
Rode on horseback with Mohammed Kher,
Bought our mutton for onions and turbans,
An ox for a lance or a spear.
We have ventured where very few ladies,
In fact I have heard but of two,
Who have suffered the hardships that we have
And got safely to Gondokoro.

For weeks we saw only green garches,
Where we'd nothing but pancakes to eat,
Been devoured by gnats in the marshes,
To whom we white men were a treat.
We have suffered from heat in the sunshine.
We have suffered from damp in the dew.
But at least here is earth where a biped
Walks safely at Gondokoro.

We've escaped many dangers of weather,
Wind, thunder and lightning, and rain.
We've escaped all the turnings and windings,
Without having dared to complain.
We've escaped being crashed in the steamer
In a cataract nobody knew,
And though rather the worse for the contact
We got safely to Gondokoro.

And here we've been feasted and shot for.
We've been to a torch ball at night,
Where the Negroes danced, drunk with merissa,
A beautiful curious sight.
We've sat under tamarhinds and citrons
Distributing presents not few,
For you must not be stingy in giving
To live safely at Gondokoro.

We've pitied the Austrian Mission,
Poor devils who die here like mice,
Though they planted a garden quite pretty
And built a brick house very nice.
At St. Croix six still are existing
Though the ague has turned them all blue,
Who declared it was useless attempting
To live safely at Gondokoro.

We've been to the Mountain Bellenia
O'er a plain with fine trees like a park,
With oxen and sheep and bad Negroes
Who would murder you after it's dark.
We took them five cows as a present.
It seems very odd but it's true,
Blue beads, copper bracelets and cattle
Give safety at Gondokoro.

We've been up as high as the Rejaf,
Which is quite at the back of beyond,

But there we could get on no further
For the steamer had stuck on the ground.
Now as we can't go further southward,
There is nothing more for us to do
Than to turn our boats round to the northward
And get safely from Gondokoro.

Principal Sources and References

When specific dates are not given the excerpts are from Harriet Tinne's Journal.

INTRODUCTION

Life of Livingstone by William G. Blackie, 1880, pp. 397–8 (John Murray).

The spelling of names is left as in the Journal and letters.

CHAPTER 1, *pp.* 3–11

Reminiscences d'une vie insignificante, a brief autobiography by P. F. Tinne. Tinne Family Papers.
Notes on the Tinne Family by Carel Gülcher. T. F. P.
1. Letter from E. Hedges to Alexine. T.F.P.
2. Letter from Harriet to Alexine. T.F.P.
3. Fragment of Letter from Harriet to a friend. T.F.P.

CHAPTER 2, *pp.* 12–17

Journal of Harriet Tinne, 27th July 1854–17 November 1854. T.F.P.
1. Journal of Harriet, 15th August 1854.
2. Journal of Harriet, 19th September 1854.
3. Journal of Harriet, 8th October 1854.
4. Journal of Harriet, 30th October 1854.
5. Journal of Harriet, 7th November 1854.

CHAPTER 3, *pp.* 18–27

Journal of Harriet Tinne, 19th September 1855–9th December 1855. T.F.P.
1. Lineage of Adolf Königsmark: *Taschenbuch der Gräflichen Häuser*.
2. 'Regular blond beast' comes from note written by Raymond Tinne Berthon, son of Anna Berthon, *née* Tinne. T.F.P.
3. Valentine. T.F.P.
4. Letter from Harriet to Margaret Tinne. T.F.P.
5. Journal of Harriet, 12th November 1855.
6. Journal of Harriet, 10th December 1855.

CHAPTER 4, *pp.* 31–36

Journal of Harriet Tinne; 10th December 1855–20th January 1856. T.F.P.

1. Journal of Harriet, 13th December 1855.
2. Journal of Harriet, 17th December 1855.

CHAPTER 5, *pp*. 37-48

Journal of Harriet Tinne, 21st January 1856–19th April 1856. T.F.P.
1. Journal of Harriet, 2nd February 1856.
2. Journal of Harriet, 5th February 1856.
3. Journal of Harriet, 16th February 1856.
4. Journal of Harriet, 26th February 1856.
5. Journal of Harriet, 28th February 1856.
6. Journal of Harriet, 8th March 1856.

CHAPTER 6, *pp*. 49-57

Journal of Harriet Tinne, 20th April 1856–31st December 1856. T.F.P.
1. Journal of Harriet, 22nd April 1856.
2. Journal of Harriet, 24th April 1856.
3. Journal of Harriet, 26th April 1856.
4. Journal of Harriet, 1st May 1856.
5. Journal of Harriet, 12th May 1856.
6. Journal of Harriet, 16th May 1856.
7. Journal of Harriet, 24th May 1856.
8. Journal of Harriet, 3rd June 1856.
9. Journal of Harriet, 30th June 1856.
10. Journal of Harriet, 14th July 1856.
11. Journal of Harriet, 13th July 1856.
12. Journal of Harriet, 28th July 1856.

CHAPTER 7, *pp*. 58-63

Journal of Harriet Tinne, 1st January 1857–27th March 1857. T.F.P.
1. Journal of Harriet, 21st January 1857.
2. Journal of Harriet, 15th February 1857.
3. Journal of Harriet, 8th March 1857.
4. Journal of Harriet, 14th March 1857.

CHAPTER 8, *pp*. 64-69

Journal of Harriet Tinne, 28th March 1857–7th November 1857. T.P.F.
1. Journal of Harriet, 22nd May 1857.
2. Journal of Harriet, 26th May 1857.

Principal Sources and References

3. *Footnote. *Taschenbuch der Gräflichen Häuser.*
4. Journal of Harriet, 7th November 1857.

CHAPTER 9, *pp.* 73–80

Journal of Harriet Tinne, 20th July 1861–13th January 1862. T.F.P.
1. Note from Addy to Alexine. Undated. T.F.P.
2. Journal of Harriet, 15th August 1861.
3. Journal of Harriet, 11th September 1861.
4. Journal of Harriet, 11th January 1862.
5. Journal of Harriet, 8th January 1862.

CHAPTER 10, *pp.* 81–91

Journal of Harriet Tinne, 14th January 1862–10th April 1862. T.F.P.
1. Letter from Harriet Tinne to Jules Van Capellen (*Algemeen Rijksarchief*, The Hague).
2. Journal of Harriet, 18th February 1862.
3. Journal of Harriet, 19th February 1862.
4. Journal of Harriet, 19th February 1862.
5. Journal of Harriet, 22nd February 1862.
6. Letter from Alexine to Yetty Siccama (*Algemeen Rijksarchief*, The Hague).

CHAPTER 11, *pp.* 92–100

Journal of Harriet Tinne: 11th April 1862–10th May 1862. T.F.P.
Biographical Dictionary of the Anglo-Egyptian Sudan by Richard Hill, 1951.
1. Journal of Harriet, 14th April 1862.
2. Journal of Harriet, 14th April 1862.
3. Journal of Harriet, 17th April 1862.
4. Journal of Harriet, 18th April 1862.
5. Journal of Harriet, 29th April 1862.

CHAPTER 12, *pp.* 101–110

Journal of Harriet Tinne, 11th May 1862–21st July 1852. T.F.P.
Le Nil Blanc et le Soudan by M. Brun-Rollet, Paris 1855.
1. Journal of Harriet, 18th May 1862.
2. Journal of Harriet, 26th May 1862.
3. Letter of 16th June 1862 in possession of Mrs. S. J. Baker.
4. Journal of Harriet, 13th July 1862.
5. Journal of Harriet, 21st July 1862.

CHAPTER 13, pp. 111–122

Journal of Harriet Tinne, 22nd July 1862–9th September 1862. T.F.P. (Vol. V ends.)
Victoria Nyanza, the source of the Nile, by Sir Samuel Baker, 1863.
Proceedings of the Royal Geographical Society, Vols. VII and VIII.
1. Journal of Harriet, 22nd July 1862.
2. *A few general directions for travellers on the Nile*, notebook written by Harriet Tinne, including recipes for making cakes and soap. T.F.P.
3. Journal of Harriet, 3rd September 1862.
4. 'Osman Aga's Grave', Appendix 2, copy T.F.P.
5. Letter from Harriet Tinne to Margaret Tinne, August 1862 (*Algemeen Rijksarchief*, The Hague).
6. 'Gondokoro', Appendix 3, copy T.F.P.
7. Letter from Harriet Tinne to Queen Sophia, in English, Khartoum, 24th November 1862, copy T.F.P.

CHAPTER 14, pp. 123–131

A Walk across Africa by J. A. Grant, 1864.
Notebook of Theodor von Heuglin, 25th January 1863–24th April 1863. (Linden Museum, Stuttgart.)
Die Tinne'sche Expedition im Westlichen Nil by Theodor von Heuglin, *Peterman's Mittheilungen, Erganzunsheft 15*.
Geographical Notes on Expeditions in Central Africa by Three Dutch Ladies by J. A. Tinne, *Transactions of the Historical Society of Lancashire and Cheshire*, 1864.
1. Letter from Harriet Tinne to Jules van Capellen (*Algemeen Rijksarchief*, The Hague).
2. as above.
3. as above.
4. Notebook of Theodor von Heuglin, 10th March 1863.

CHAPTER 15, pp. 132–142

A walk across Africa by J. A. Grant, 1864.
Notebook of Theodor von Heuglin, 25th April 1863–5th May 1863.
Die Tinne'sche Expedition im Westlichen Nil by Theodor von Heuglin.
Travels in Central Africa, and explorations of the White Nile tributaries by John Petherick, 1869.
Geographical Notes by J. A. Tinne

Principal Sources and References 237

1. Letter from Addy Van Capellen to Jules Van Capellen, 22nd February 1863 (*Algemeen Rijksarchief*, The Hague).
2. as above.
3. Letter from J. H. Speke to Baroness Adriana Van Capellen, 11th April 1863.
4. Letter from Harriet Tinne to J. A. Tinne, 1st July 1863 (*Algemeen Rijksarchief*, The Hague).
5. as above.
6. as above.

CHAPTER 16, *pp.* 143-153

Notebook of Theodor von Heuglin.
Geographical Notes by J. A. Tinne.
The Heart of Africa by George Sweinfurth, 1874.
1. Letter from Harriet Tinne to Margaret Tinne, 1st July 1863 (*Algemeen Rijksarchief*, The Hague).
2. as above.
3. Note from Harriet Tinne to Alexine, undated. T.F.P.
4. Fragment of letter in Alexine's writing. T.F.P.
5. Letter from Alexine to Jemima Van Capellen, Barbar, 5th August 1864. (*Algemeen Rijksarchief*, The Hague), (see also p. 271).
6. Notebook of Theodor von Heuglin, August 1863.

CHAPTER 17, *pp.* 154-160

Notebook of Theodor von Heuglin.
Letter from Addy Van Capellen. T.F.P.
1. Notebook of Theodor von Heuglin, 1st March 1864.
2. See *Travels in Africa during the years 1875-86, 1890-92* by Johann Junker, 1892.

CHAPTER 18, *pp.* 161-171

Notebook of Theodor von Heuglin.
Travels in Central Africa, and explorations of the White Nile tributaries by John Petherick, 1869.
1. Letter from Katie Petherick to her sister. See *Travels in Central Africa* by John Petherick, 1869.
2. Letter from J. A. Tinne to Hora Siccama, 3rd March 1864 (*Algemeen Rijksarchief*, The Hague).

R

3. Letter from Alexine to Jemima Van Capellen, Barbar, 5th August 1864 (*Algemeen Rijksarchief*, The Hague).
4. Letter from Alexine to Jules Van Capellen, Touti, 8th May 1864 (*Algemeen Rijksarchief*, The Hague).
5. as above.
6. Letter from Alexine about Jemima van Capellen, Barbar, 5th August 1864 (*Algemeen Rijksarchief*, The Hague).
7. Letter from J. A. Tinne to Jules Van Capellen, 10th January 1865 (*Algemeen Rijksarchief*. The Hague).

CHAPTER 19, *pp*. 175–183

Biographie van Alexine Tinne by William Gentz, Die Gartenlaube, No. 38, 1869.
Letters between Alexine, J. A. Tinne and Jules Van Capellen.
1. Letter from Jules Van Capellen to Alexine, 17th July 1864 (*Algemeen Rijksarchief*, The Hague).
2. Letter from Alexine to J. A. Tinne, 20th October 1865.

CHAPTER 20, *pp*. 184–197

Letters of Alexine to Jules Van Capellen.
1. Letter from Alexine to Jules Van Capellen, March 1866 (*Algemeen Rijksarchief*, The Hague).
2. as above.
3. as above.
4. Letter from Alexine to Jules Van Capellen, June 1866 (*Algemeen Rijksarchief*, The Hague).
5. as above.
6. as above.
7. as above.
8. as above.
9. Letter from Alexine to Jules Van Capellen, June 1866 (*Algemeen Rijksarchief*, The Hague).
10. as above.

CHAPTER 21, *pp*. 198–204

Letters of Alexine to Jules Van Capellen and J. A. Tinne.
1. Letter from Alexine to J. A. Tinne, Tripoli, 16th November 1868. (*Algemeen Rijksarchief*.)

Principal Sources and References

2. Letter from Alexine to Jules Van Capellen, 21st December 1868.
3. Letter from Alexine to J. A. Tinne, 6th February 1869. T.F.P.
4. as above.

CHAPTER 22, *pp*. 205–211

Letters from Alexine to J. A. Tinne, Hora Siccama, and Jules Van Capellen.
Sahara und Sudan by Gustav Nachtigal, 1889.
1. Letter from Alexine to J. A. Tinne, 20th March 1869, T.F.P.
2. Letter from Alexine to J. A. Tinne, 2nd June 1869, T.F.P.
3. Letter from Alexine to J. A. Tinne, 2nd June 1869 (*Algemeen Rijksarchief*, The Hague).
4. as above.

CHAPTER 23, *pp*. 212–221

Letters from Alexine to J. A. Tinne, T.F.P.
Sahara und Sudan by Gustav Nachtigal, 1889.
1. Letter from Alexine to J. A. Tinne. T.F.P.
2. as above.
3. as above.
4. Sources for Alexine's death:
   (i) *The Times*, 6 September 1869.
   (ii) Letter from Theodore Tinne to J. A. Tinne, Malta, 29th August 1869. T.F.P.
   (iii) Letters from Testa, Dutch Consul in Tripoli, 1869–70. T.F.P.

CHAPTER 24, *pp*. 222–226

Account of trial in French dated January 1870 (*Algemeen Rijksarchief*. The Hague).
Letters from Ernest and Theodore Tinne from Tripoli to J. A. Tinne, 29th August 1869–18th September 1869.
1. Letter from Theodore Tinne to J. A. Tinne, 19th August 1869. T.F.P.
2. Letter from Alexine to Jules Van Capellen, Au Sahara, 1st May 1886 (*Algemeen Rijksarchief*, The Hague).

Bibliography

BAKER, SIR SAMUEL WHITE, *Victoria Nyanza, the Source of the Nile*, Macmillan, 1863

BARTH, HEINRICH, *Travels and Discoveries in North and Central Africa*, 2nd edition, Longman, 1857

BOVILL, EDWARD WILLIAM, *The Golden Trade of the Moors*, Oxford University Press, 1958

BRUCE, JAMES, *Travels to Discover the Source of the Nile*, Longman & Rees, 1804

BURCKHARDT, JOHN LEWIS, *Travels in Nubia*, 2nd edition, Murray, 1822

DAVIDSON, BASIL, *Old Africa Rediscovered*, Longman, 1959

DENTZ, FRED OUDSCHANS, *History of the English Church at the Hague, together with a short account of the Tinne family*, 1929

DU CAMP, MAXIME, *Le Nil* (Égypte et Nubie), Paris, 1854

DUVEYRIER, HENRI, *Les Touaregs du Nord*, Paris, 1864

GESSI, ROMOLO, *Seven Years in the Sudan*, Sampson Low, Marston, London, 1892, (original Italian version, Milano, 1891)

GRANT, JAMES AUGUSTUS, *A Walk across Africa*, Blackwood, 1864

GRAY, RICHARD, *A History of the Southern Sudan*, Oxford University Press, 1961

HEUGLIN, THEODOR VON, *Reise in das Gebiet des weissen Nil und seiner westlichen Zuflüsse in den Jahren 1862–64*, C. Heyn, Leipzig, 1869

HILL, RICHARD, *Bibliography of the Anglo-Egyptian Sudan*, Oxford University Press, 1939; *A Biographical Dictionary of the Sudan*, 2nd edition, Cass, 1967; *Egypt in the Sudan 1820–81*, Oxford University Press, 1959

HURST, FRANCIS, *The Nile*, revised edition, Constable, 1957

JOHNSTON, SIR HARRY HAMILTON, *The Nile Quest*, Lawrence & Bullen, 1903

JUNKER, JOHANN WILHELM, *Travels in Africa during the Years 1875–86 1890–92* Chapman & Hall, 1892

KOTSCHY, CARL GEORG THEODOR, *Plantae Tinneanae*, Vindobonae, Vienna, 1867

LINANT DE BELLEFONDS, LOUIS MAURICE ADOLPHE, *Journey of Navigation of the Bahr-el-Abiad or the White Nile,* African Association, 1828

MELLY, GEORGE, *Khartoum and the Blue and White Niles,* Colburn, 1851

MIDDLETON, DOROTHY, *Baker of the Nile,* Routledge & Kegan Paul, 1959

NACHTIGAL, GUSTAV, *Sahara und Sudan, Ergebnisse sechsjäriger Reisen in Afrika,* Berlin, Weidmann and E. Groddeck, 1879-80

Nederland's Adelsboek, The Hague, 1941

PETHERICK, JOHN, *Egypt, the Soudan and Central Africa,* Tinsley Brothers, 1861; *Travels in Central Africa, and Explorations of the White Nile Tributaries,* Tinsley Brothers, 1869

RICHARDS, C. A., *Krapf, Missionary and Explorer,* Nelson, 1900

RODD, FRANCIS JAMES RENNELL, *People of the Veil,* Macmillan, 1926

SCHWEINFURTH, GEORG AUGUST, *The Heart of Africa,* Sampson Low, 1874

SPEKE, JOHN HANNING, *Journal of the Discovery of the Source of the Nile,* Blackwood, 1863

ST. JOHN, JAMES AUGUSTUS, *Egypt and Nubia,* Chapman & Hall, 1841

SUTHERLAND, WILLIAM, *Alexandrine Tinne,* Amsterdam, Van Soest, 1937

TAYLOR, JAMES BAYARD, *A Journey to Central Africa,* Sampson Low, 1854

VAN DE VELDE, C. W. M., *Narrative of a Journey through Syria and Palestine in 1851 and 1852,* Blackwood, 1854

WERNE, FERDINAND, *Expedition to Discover the Sources of the White Nile,* Translation by C. W. O'Reilly, Richard Bentley, 1849

Index

Ababdeh tribe, 84
Abdullah, 184, 189, 195, 209–10, 218, 219, 222, 223, 226
Abu Hamad, 84, 89, 119, 167
Abu Simbel, 62
Abyssinia (*see* Ethiopia)
Ador, 116
Agati, Pietro, 99
Alexander II, Tsar, 74
Alexandria, 32–35, 58, 59, 76, 178, 179
Algiers and Algeria, 183, 184 ff., 189, 198, 225
Ali Almori, 136, 139, 146
Ali Riza, 199, 200
Amsterdam, 75
Anna, 77, 86, 87, 117, 128, 137, 138, 139, 147, 148, 149, 152, 153, 156
Anna Paulowna, Queen, 22, 74
Arconate, Marquis of, 95
Aswan, 36, 37, 43, 44, 60, 61, 82, 83
Aswan Dam, 44, 83
Asyut, 40, 59, 60
Athens, 67
Atlas Mts, 187, 189
Azande tribe, 124, 151

Baalbek, 56, 65
Bahr-al-Ghazal, 112, 123–31, 133, 134, 135, 142, 156, 157, 158, 159
Bahr-al-Jebel. 112, 114, 115
Bahr Jur, 136, 140, 141, 143
Bahr Wau, 143
Baker, Samuel, xi, 106, 110, 121, 135
Baker, Florence, xi, 106, 121, 135
Barbar, 90, 93, 119, 155, 157, 163, 167, 168
Barth, Heinrich, 125, 188, 191, 195, 217
Barthélemy Family, 94, 98, 106, 107, 108
Bary, Erwin von, 224
Beirut, 55, 56, 57, 64, 66
Bellefonds (*see* Linant de Bellefonds)

Benolid, 204
Beni Suef, 40
Bergen, 13, 14
Berthon, Anna, 224
Beurmann, 125
Biskra, 195
Blue Nile, R., 75, 92
Bondjem, 203
Bornu, 199, 213
Bornu, Sultan of, 199, 200, 207
Bruce, James, 75
Bu Bekker, 216, 219, 220, 223, 224
Buselli, 143, 144–8, 151, 157, 166

Cairo, 35–36, 48, 58, 64, 76 ff., 132, 167, 169, 170, 176, 178, 222
Calais, 3
Cape of Good Hope, 124, 132
Caradja, Prince Jean, 19
Cavour, Count, 95
Chaltin, xi
Claymore, The, 179–81, 183
Congo, R., 124, 134
Constantine, 188, 197
Contarini, Carlo, 105, 108, 111, 114, 138
Copenhagen, 12–13, 15–16

d'Ablaing, Baron, 126, 128, 129, 130, 137, 138, 139, 140, 144, 145, 147, 148, 149, 151, 157, 162
Daily Telegraph, 225
Damascus, 52, 54–55
Darfur, 200
d'Arnaud, 103
Dead Sea, 51, 52
Debono, Andro, 99
de Lesseps, Edmond F., 53, 57, 58, 65
de Lesseps, Ferdinand, 35, 78, 84
Demerara (*see* Surinam)
Dendera, 60
de Tanyon, Mr., 98, 102, 104, 105

de Tuyll, Charlotte, 198
Dimitri, Mr., 93, 95
Dinkas, 105, 106, 127, 131, 229
Djabbour, 216, 220, 223
Djebari, 225
Djelfa, 189, 190
Don Angelo, 116
Don Francesco, 116, 117, 118
Dresden, 21, 24, 68
Duveyrier, Henri, 188, 191, 200, 202, 217

Edfu, 44
Eghmissea, 225
Eisenach, 23
Emin, xi
Esna, 44
Ethiopia, 75, 78, 79, 92, 106, 125

Fashoda, 158
Fernando Po, 124, 132
Fezzan, The, 186, 199, 204
Flatters, Col., 225
Flora, 12, 13, 18, 22, 26, 32, 38, 46, 49, 61, 62, 66, 77, 86, 105, 106, 137, 138, 139, 149, 152-3
Florence, 7
Frederick William IV of Prussia, 17

Genz, Wilhelm, 176-7
Geographical Society, 95, 116, 123, 141, 162
Gessi, Romolo, xi, 145, 159
Ghadames, 188, 203
Ghardaia, 188, 191
Ghat, 188, 206, 216, 219, 220
Ghatta, 146
Gilbert, 78
Gondar, 79
Gondokoro, 102, 103, 116, 118, 119, 120, 121, 123, 134, 135, 136, 149, 160, 229-31
Gordon, Gen., xi, 159
Gossinga Mts, 141, 146, 147
Göteborg, 13, 15
Grant, Capt. J. A., xi, 95, 116, 121, 123, 133, 142
Guerrara, 192
Gülcher, Carel, xii
Gülcher, Christine, 69

Halib, 64, 68, 69, 75, 76, 82, 85, 86, 88, 89, 105, 138
Halim Pasha, 98, 119
Hansal, Martin, 155
Heerengraat, 6
Hendrik, 77, 85, 86, 96, 138
Heuglin, Baron T. von, 125, 126, 127, 128, 129, 130, 131, 137, 139, 140, 143, 144, 145, 147, 148, 149, 151, 152, 155, 156, 157, 158, 162, 164, 167, 168, 169, 170, 176, 208, 213
Hill, Richard, xii
Holy Cross Mission, 115, 116, 117, 118, 136, 230
Holy Land, 49-57
Holy Sepulchre, Church of the, 51
Houdas, Mr., 211, 222

Ibrahim ben Alkia, 205, 206, 212, 216, 224
Ichnuchen, 188, 200, 202, 204, 212, 213, 214, 215, 216, 217, 218, 219, 220
Ismail Pasha, 170, 177, 178
Istanbul, 66, 67

Jacobse, Arij, 203, 220
Jaffa, 49
Jan, 12, 13, 18, 22, 23, 25, 32, 38, 39, 50
Jebel Dinka, 104, 107, 108
Jericho, 51
Jerusalem, 49, 50, 52
Jordan, R., 52
Junker, Johann, 159

Kaka, 108, 110, 160
Kano, 217
Karnak, 42, 43, 62
Keneh, 60
Kenya, Mt., 78, 103
Khartoum, 58, 59, 75, 78, 79, 84, 85, 91, 92-100, 106, 107, 116, 120, 121, 122, 124, 125, 127, 129, 130, 132, 133, 146, 151, 154 ff., 162, 164, 165, 200
Kit, Is. of, 130
Kilimanjaro, 78, 103
Knöblecher, Bishop, xi
Kodok, 158

Index

Kom Ombo, 44
Königsmark, Count Adolf F. J. von, 20, 21, 34, 54, 66, 67, 68
Korosko, 84, 85, 97
Kotschy, Theodor, 171
Krapf, Dr., 78, 79, 103
Kurdufan, 90

Laghouat, 191, 193
Lake Chad, 125, 184, 188, 200, 207, 213
Lake No, 112, 123, 124, 127, 129
Lake Victoria, 133, 142
Lange Voorhout, 8, 18, 19, 69, 181, 198, 224
La Pontie, monks of, 40
Latif Pasha, 90
Lebanon, 56, 58
Lebanon, Cedars of, 56
Lejean, G., 124
Lennox, Lord, 60
Linant de Bellefonds, 35, 59, 78, 79, 85, 102
Liverpool, 4, 6
Liverpool Geographical Society, 162
Livingstone, Dr. David, xi, 142
Louis Bonaparte, 4
Luxor, 41, 42, 45, 60, 62, 82

Malakal, 112
Malta, 76, 197, 222
Marseilles, 75, 76
Mashra ar Riqq, 128, 129, 130, 131, 135, 136, 137, 139, 146, 148, 149, 152, 156, 157, 159
Matruka, 64, 69, 84, 107
Meeuw, 183, 184, 185, 186
Medea, 189
Melly, Andrew, 90
Miyah Signora, 159
Mohammed Ali, xi, 59, 102, 103
Mohammed Effendi, Mudir of Khartoum, 93, 95, 99, 126, 128
Mohammed Kher, 107, 108, 109, 110, 118, 144, 160, 229
Morgan, 37, 38
Mount of Olives, 52
Murzuch, 203, 204, 205, 206, 209, 212, 216, 219, 221, 223, 224
Musa Pasha, 133, 144, 148, 157, 163, 165, 166, 167, 170, 178

Mustafa, 77, 86
Mustapha Alpha, 42
M'zab, The, 186, 188, 189, 191, 192

Nachtigal, Dr. Gustav, 199, 200, 206, 207, 212, 213
Naples, 7, 179-80
Nazareth, 53
Netherlands, King of, 175, 178
Nice, 7
Nielsen, Olans, 13
Nile, R., 35-48 *passim*, 58-63, 81 ff., 92, 95, 99, 103, 106, 120, 123, 129, 133, 178, 200
Nile-Congo Divide, 124, 134, 151
Norway, 12-14
Nyam-Nams, 123, 124, 151

Om il Abid, 203
Oostmans, Cornelius, 220
Osman Aga, 49, 50, 79, 82, 86, 89, 92, 97, 98, 117, 118, 119, 138, 228
Ouadai, 125
Ouadai Aberdjoush, 219
Oudney, 195
Overweg, 125, 195

Palmyra, 64, 65
Paris, 9
Pau, 9, 10
Peney, Dr., 98
Petherick, John, xi, 116, 124, 131, 135, 136, 137, 140, 146, 155, 161, 162, 163, 164, 167, 168, 170
Petherick, Katie, 116, 135, 136, 155, 161, 162, 167, 168, 170
Peyritsch, Dr., 171
Philae, 44, 61, 62, 84
Philippeville, 188, 197
Pietro the Mason, 121
Plantae Tinneanae, 171
Potsdam, 16, 17
Prague, 68
Prussia, King of, 199, 207
Prussian Royal Family, 16-17
Pruyssenaere, Mr., 108

Quseir, 45, 46, 47

Ramadan, 90
Rebecque, Baron C. de, xii, 9

Rebecque, Baroness, xii, 9, 225
Red Sea, 47
Reitz, 125, 130
Rejaf, 102, 230
Richardson, 125, 195
Rome, 7
Rosa, 98
Rosetta, 3
Rothschild, 52
Russenaers, S. W. and Mrs., 34, 59, 79, 169, 170

Sabatier, 103
Sacker, 77, 86, 87, 89, 96, 97, 138
Sahara, 183, 184, 187, 188, 190, 195, 196, 197, 199, 205
Said Pasha, 34, 39, 79
Sainte Roc, Monastery of, 57
Sandbach, Margaret (*see also* Tinne), 7
Sandbach, Sara (*see also* Van Capellen), 181
Sandbach, William, 4
Sandbach, Tinne & Co., 4
Sans Souci, 16, 17
Saxe-Weimar, Grand Duke and Duchess of, 23
Saxony, 24
Sawakin, 167, 168–9
Schubert, 152
Seagull, The, 182–3
Sheikh Ahmad, 86, 87, 88, 89, 97, 103
Sheikh Ahmed, 219
Shilluk tribe, 110, 111, 229
Siccama, Henrietta (*see also* Rebecque, Baroness C. de), xii
Siccama, Harco, 8
Siccama, Hora, 8, 9, 162
Siccama, Petronella, 8, 9
Siccama, Yetty, 8, 9
Sligo, The Marquess of, 60
Smyrna, 66, 67
Sobat, R., 112
Sophia, Princess and Queen, 5, 6, 24, 34, 74, 76, 175, 181, 198
Speke, Capt. J. H., xi, 95, 116, 121, 123, 133, 134–5, 136, 141, 142, 155, 161
Steudner, Hermann, 125, 126, 127, 128, 129, 130, 131, 137, 143

Stockholm, 14, 15
Sudan, 59, 75, 79, 85, 116
Sudd region, 112–13
Suez, 169, 170
Suez Canal, 59, 78, 177
Suquet, Dr., 78
Surinam, 4
Sweden, 13, 14–15

Taharat, 220
Tamachek, 216
Tassili d'Ajjers, 200
Tenmrassan, 216
Testa, Mr., 199, 210, 222, 223, 224
Thebes, 42, 45
The Hague, 3, 5, 6, 9, 22, 69, 151, 198, 222, 224
The Hague, English church at, xi, 10, 224
Theodore of Abyssinia, King, 79
Thibaut, Mr., 93, 94, 98, 99, 101, 103, 154, 155, 157, 163, 164, 165
Thibaut, Sophie, 94
Tibesti, 212
Timbuktu, 125, 184, 188
TINNE, ALEXINE: praised by Livingstone, xi; memorial at Juba, xi; birth, 6, xi; patrimony, 7; childhood, languages and learning, 8; confirmed, 10; education, 10; visit to Scandinavia and Prussia, 12–17; home surroundings, 18–19; first love affair, 20–21; Grand Tour, 22–27; learns Arabic, 35; first camel ride, 46; demands piano in Beirut, 57; self-will of, 55, 58; 'La Reine de Naples', 77; 'La Reine de l'Equateur', 82, 124; her fearlessness, 88, 91; and slave traders, 104–5, 108–10; illness at Gondokoro, 121; prone to exaggerate, 124; comforts on travels, 136; mutiny and illness, 139; troubles with slave merchants, 143 ff.; Harriet's death, 149; self-reproach, 150; death of Flora, 153; death of Anna, 156; dogged by disasters, 151–60; Addy's unselfishness, 163; Addy's death, 164; troubles with Musa Pasha, 165, 166; botanical specimens,

Index

TINNE, ALEXINE—*Continued*
171; financial straits, 177; 'Contessa Ollandese', 178; love for animals, 178; her nationality, 182; and the Wilhelmies, 193 ff.; and slavery, 200, 204; first woman to attempt Sahara crossing, 205; illness at Murzuch, 206; presents for African chiefs, 207–9; on the Tuareg, 217; last letter to John, 219; her death, 220; her memorial at the Hague, 224; reported survival, 225

Tinne, Anna, 4, 5, 9, 10, 19, 20
Tinne, Ernest, 222, 223, 224
Tinne, Fred, 222
Tinne, Family, The, 3
Tinne, Harriet (*see also* Van Capellen), xi; her diaries, xii; marriage, 5; connections at court, 6; widowed, 7–8; as hostess, 19; and travelling, 21; rides donkey to Red Sea, 47; and Alexine, 55; anxiety before third Nile voyage, 75–76; expenses of third Nile voyage, 79; and First Cataract, 83–84; 'the living desert', 88; her correspondence, 93; deserted by Sacker and Hendrik, 96–97; 'General directions for travellers on the Nile', 115; in Alexine's absence, 117; nurses Alexine at Gondokoro, 121; courage, and optimism in adversity, 139; trouble with Buselli, 147–8; illness and death, 149; her memorial, 171

Tinne, J. A., xii, 5, 7, 8, 9, 69, 76, 123, 141, 146, 149, 162, 164, 167, 169, 170, 171, 177, 178, 179, 181–2, 183, 186, 187, 204, 205, 206, 207, 210, 215, 219, 222, 224

Tinne, Margaret (*see also* Sandbach), 7, 9, 21, 76, 169, 170, 171
Tinne, Petronella (*see also* Siccama), 8
Tinne, Philip Frederick, 3–7
Tinne, Theodore, 222, 223, 224
Tinne, William, 5, 7
Tirant, Mr., 93, 98, 101
Touggourt, 192, 195
Toulon, 182, 183
Touti, 163, 164

Trieste, 26
Tripoli, 125, 186, 188, 198, 199, 200, 202, 209, 218, 219, 222, 223, 224
Tuareg, 185, 188, 192, 200, 205, 212, 213, 214, 215, 216, 217, 218, 222, 225
Tulba, 98
Tunis, 186
Tunisia, 186

Uganda, 123

Valley of the Kings, 43, 46
Van Cappellen, Vice-Admiral Jonkheer, 5, 73
Van Capellen, Adriana, xi, 73–74, 85, 86–87, 89, 93, 96, 98, 101, 105, 109, 114, 118, 119, 121, 124, 126, 128, 132, 133, 135, 141, 147, 149, 154 ff., 160, 161, 162, 163, 164
Van Capellen, Harriet (*see* Tinne, Harriet), 5, 6
Van Capellen, Jemima, 34, 164, 165, 170
Van Capellen, Vice-Admiral Jules, 165, 166, 175–6, 182, 183, 185, 186–7, 196, 202
Van Capellen, Sara (*see also* Sandbach), 5, 6, 73
Van de Velde, 31, 35, 36, 37, 38, 39, 41, 42, 43, 45, 46, 49, 50, 52, 69
Van Vheil, 31, 35, 36
Venice, 26
Vienna, 68
Vogel, Edward, 125

Wadi al Gharbi, 212, 213
Wadi Halfa, 60, 61, 62
Wadi Shergui, 219
Wau, 130, 131, 136, 143, 155
Werne, 103
West Ladshal, 202
White Nile, xi, 92, 94, 95, 96, 101–10, 112, 115, 116, 119, 123, 124, 127, 128, 134, 135, 158
Wilhelmie, Capt. and family, 183, 184, 185, 187, 190, 191, 193, 194, 195, 196, 202
William I of the Netherlands, 6
William II of the Netherlands, 5, 6, 74
Württemberg, King and Queen of, 24